AF408404

.DOC

CYBERSECURITY UPSIDE DOWN

Rethink your cybersecurity strategy.

Benny Czarny

This is the first edition and Benny would truly appreciate your
feedback at benny.czarny@opswat.com

Dedicated to
my beloved grandmother,
Neomi Naimi.

I made you a grandmother,
and you made me who I am.

CONTENTS

Preface   viii

Chapter 1   The Awakening   1
Chapter 2   Building the Cybersecurity Language   17
Chapter 3   Building the Firewall of Data   47
Chapter 4   Rethinking Cybersecurity with Data Sanitization   83
Chapter 5   Advanced CDR   133
Chapter 6   The Future of CDR   167

Acknowledgments   188
Glossary   190
About the Author   196

PREFACE

My Mission for This Book

My name is Benny (Benjamin) Czarny. I'm the CEO and founder of OPSWAT, a cybersecurity company committed to protecting the world's critical infrastructure. At OPSWAT, one of our cornerstone technologies is **Data Sanitization,** more commonly known as **Content Disarm and Reconstruction (CDR).** CDR proactively defends against cyberattacks by regenerating the data that flows into companies and other entities through vital networks.

After more than 20 years of building and growing OPSWAT, and after successfully implementing CDR in thousands of organizations, I decided to write this book because **CDR remains under-recognized as a critical solution for data protection.**

The reality is that the market is not adopting this technology or its underlying concept fast enough, even though I firmly believe it has the potential to drastically reduce the number of cyber threats we face today. Despite making a very good living from OPSWAT, I feel a strong sense of responsibility to raise awareness about this transformative approach.

CDR is more than just a technology—it's a mindset that can prevent countless cyberattacks by addressing vulnerabilities in the very files we use every day.

My goal is to provide readers—especially those who shape regulations and compliance mandates—with a clear understanding of how CDR works, why it offers unique protection for productivity files, and how it compares to other cybersecurity solutions like anti-malware and sandboxing. Think of CDR as **the first firewall for the data inside everyday files,** truly safeguarding what conventional firewalls and anti-malware and detection tools often miss.

The principles outlined in each chapter reflect insights gleaned from thousands of conversations with cybersecurity experts and engagements with companies around the world. When you've finished reading, I hope you'll be as enthusiastic about adopting CDR, and a **sanitization mindset,** as I am. More importantly, I want you to come away feeling more confident in navigating the critical cybersecurity decisions you face every day.

This book not only chronicles the technical evolution of CDR, but also the journey of transforming OPSWAT from a modest startup into a global leader in cybersecurity.

Today, OPSWAT is a consistent innovator, with a team of more than 1,000 professionals across 25 countries dedicated to safeguarding critical infrastructure worldwide.

The journey from concept to final draft has been shaped by valuable discussions with my OPSWAT team, occasional collaboration with ChatGPT, numerous insights gleaned during international flights (yes, I can only watch *Iron Man* so many times), and the encouragement of friends back home in New York City. Together, we've distilled complex cybersecurity concepts down to providing accessible knowledge and digital literacy for all. Written in the midst of OPSWAT's continuing expansion, this book is both a resource and a testament to our shared commitment to protecting global critical infrastructures.

Cybersecurity is more than a business—it's a calling. This book represents my attempt to bridge the gap between what the industry needs and how quickly the market is adapting. By introducing the industry to CDR's potential, I hope to accelerate its adoption and contribute to a safer digital future for all.

Talking to Both Business and Tech in a Visual Way

I decided to make this book very visual for multiple reasons: First, people don't like to read lengthy texts, and second, I believe that making it visual will help convey the messages more effectively. This narrative is further augmented by work from several graphic designers, as well as illustrator and character designer Serge Seidlitz, who have provided visually arresting art to complement and enhance the text, mirroring the innovative essence of CDR technology.

This book is not an abbreviated graphic novel, however. It contains extensive content for three different audiences: high-level sections addressed to the general reader, advanced discussions for experts in cybersecurity, and technical information for engineers.

My goal is to strike a balance between providing a clear introduction to CDR for newcomers and diving into the technical intricacies for those already immersed in cybersecurity. This approach ensures that whether you're just starting to explore CDR or you're a seasoned expert looking for a deeper understanding of its mechanisms, there's something valuable here for you.

Additionally, I wanted to share some of my business journey in founding OPSWAT and discovering the need to develop this tech stack. I'll take you through the challenges and triumphs I experienced along the way, and how I turned an innovative idea into a successful business. Through these stories, I hope to offer insights not only into the technology itself but also into the entrepreneurial spirit and perseverance required to bring such a vision to life.

MAYBE WE SHOULD TAKE IT APART AND REBUILD IT INSIDE ?
NO , IT'S GOT WHEELS. LET'S JUST BRING IT IN!

THE AWAKENING

My quest to bring clarity to modern cybersecurity begins.

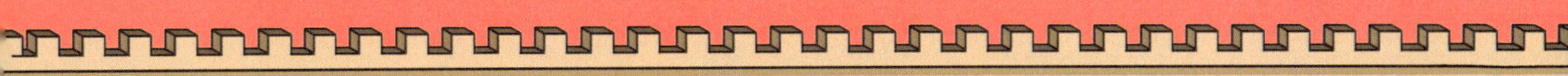

During a cozy evening in 2018, my wife and I were watching *Homeland* (Season 7, Episode 2: "Rebel Rebel"). In that episode, the heroine, Carrie Mathison, was working on her laptop when she downloaded a JPEG image file. As soon as she tried to open it, however, the file unleashed ransomware, a particularly malicious type of computer virus that disabled her computer.

My wife, clearly skeptical, mumbled, "Come on. This can't be real."

Her disbelief highlighted a significant and troubling gap in cybersecurity awareness that even an innocent-seeming image file could harbor malicious code. I've encountered countless cybersecurity experts, legislators, CEOs, and Chief Information Security Officers (CISOs) who similarly overlooked the threats posed by productivity files like images and other seemingly harmless everyday files.

This book aims to address that gap, to demystify those overlooked threats, and explain how CDR technology offers a robust, proactive defense against many cyberattacks. While I'm not claiming that CDR solves every security challenge, I strongly believe it can neutralize a significant share of file-based threats.

In the following chapters, I'll present the CDR approach for sanitizing files and introduce a broader "CDR mindset," which I hope will inspire the development of

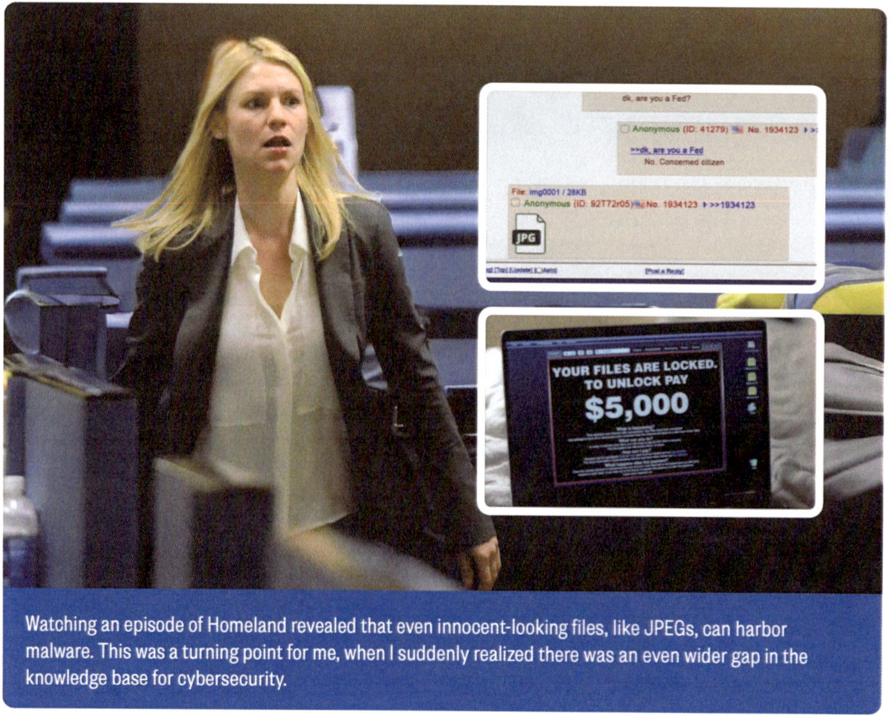

Watching an episode of Homeland revealed that even innocent-looking files, like JPEGs, can harbor malware. This was a turning point for me, when I suddenly realized there was an even wider gap in the knowledge base for cybersecurity.

additional technologies. Together, these advancements can help close critical security gaps across the industry.

Simplifying Content Disarm and Reconstruction

CDR is a cutting-edge cybersecurity method that takes a proactive approach to protecting against malware and cyber threats. Unlike traditional security measures that seek to detect threats within files and block them using technologies such as signatures, heuristics, and machine learning, CDR is not based on detection at all. **It works by assuming a true zero-trust philosophy,** which means it assumes all files are malicious.

CDR disassembles incoming digital content (like word processing documents, spreadsheets, or image files) and safely regenerates a new, clean, and usable version of the file. This is what we mean by "Data Sanitization."

Any part of a file where attacks could reside is identified, and the file is regenerated leaving the dangerous elements behind and/or fixing defects in their structure that may be used for attacks. After sanitization, users receive their files without delay or risk, as both known and unknown threats have been disarmed. It's akin to having a highly skilled digital hygiene team check and reconstruct your documents before you open them to ensure they're safe.

The Journey and Science Behind CDR

For those curious about the nuts and bolts of CDR, it's a story of innovation born out of necessity. The digital world is rife with evolving threats, and traditional security measures often fall short against sophisticated or never-before-seen attacks. Recognizing this gap led to the exploration and development of CDR, which was built on a foundation of research, practical cybersecurity needs, and complex mathematical models.

The science of CDR involves understanding how digital content can carry malicious elements and regenerating files with high fidelity to ensure users can access vital data safely and seamlessly. Implementing CDR requires the capability to handle a vast array of file formats, create effective default regeneration plans to neutralize threats, and enable security administrators to fine-tune policies for their organization's specific needs, all while minimizing delays for end users.

In this book, I will share the journey of trial-and-error that led to the development of CDR, including the setbacks, theories, and iterations that ultimately shaped this solution. I'll also explore why traditional security measures often failed to address certain cyber threats, prompting me to look beyond conventional detection methods and experiment with new approaches.

Bootstrapping and the Business Behind CDR

The journey to bring CDR to life wasn't just a technical challenge—it was also a business endeavor shaped by a bootstrapped approach. Starting OPSWAT without external funding required agility, resourcefulness, and a relentless focus on solving real customer problems. Adopting an agile mindset was critical, not only in developing the technology itself but also in tailoring CDR implementation to meet the diverse needs of our customers.

In this book, I will delve into the entrepreneurial aspects of introducing CDR to the market: How I identified gaps in existing cybersecurity practices, navigated early challenges with limited resources, and worked closely with customers to refine the technology. Building a business around CDR required a deep understanding of not only the threats, but also the operational realities faced by organizations. This meant creating solutions that were practical, adaptable, and aligned with the complexities of enterprise environments.

The business behind CDR is just as important as the technology. By working directly with customers and adopting an iterative approach, we developed a model where feedback from real-world use cases drove continuous improvement. This agility allowed us to fine-tune the application of CDR, ensuring that it delivered measurable value while seamlessly integrating into existing cybersecurity frameworks. These experiences have shaped my belief in the importance of bridging technical innovation with practical business strategies.

Practical Implications and the Broader Impact of CDR

The creation of CDR isn't just a theoretical victory; it has significant real-world implications. By integrating CDR strategies, organizations can protect themselves more effectively against data breaches and cyberattacks, a priority for both business and tech leaders. This book will highlight not only the theoretical foundations of CDR, but also share success stories and case studies where CDR has made a tangible difference in thwarting cyber threats.

In essence, this book takes you through the journey of CDR, from its initial concept to practical application, offering insights into its development and effectiveness. Whether you're new to cybersecurity or have years of experience, understanding CDR is crucial in today's digital age, where new threats emerge with each passing day. Through this dual-layered exploration, the book provides a comprehensive look at CDR, making it an essential read for anyone looking to enhance their knowledge of modern cybersecurity solutions.

My High-Level View of Cybersecurity Challenges

To understand CDR and why it is such a departure from current practice, we must first take a tour of modern cybersecurity, a topic that has always fascinated me because it is such a complex and rapidly changing domain.

Cybersecurity isn't a neat story about good defeating evil. Instead, it's a complex, never-ending battle complicated by a rapidly expanding, ever-shifting "attack surface," which is the sum of all the places where an attacker can get into a system or network to steal data or do damage. As the attack surface grows across its many dimensions, traditional detection methods struggle to keep up, underscoring the importance of CDR technology. The attackers have the swords and they use every trick they can to hide them and penetrate defenses. Cybersecurity vendors provide the shields.

Driven primarily by three forces: The proliferation of computing, the expansion of data and the use of AI/ML, and the changing attack surface complicates defense strategies. Understanding the role of each of these three forces and the interplay between them is critical to grasping the significance of CDR and navigating the evolving cybersecurity landscape. The bottom line is that the number of swords attackers use and the places they can hide them is growing. This makes building shields much harder.

FORCE 1:

The Never-Ending Expansion of Computing, Operating Systems, and Applications

The expansion of computing is driven by three key forces, each of which significantly amplifies the size of the attack surface:

Dimension 1: The explosion of computing devices. From IoT to cloud servers, every new device introduces potential entry points for attackers.

Dimension 2: The diversity of operating systems (OS). Each new OS comes with its own vulnerabilities, making security a continuous challenge.

Dimension 3: The ever-growing number of applications. Each OS includes its own software and as software ecosystems evolve, so do the opportunities for exploitation.

Dimension 1: The Explosion of Computing Devices

I find one of the most visible drivers of the expanding cyberattack surface is the relentless increase in the number and variety of computing devices. These devices now extend far beyond traditional desktops, laptops, and smartphones, reaching deep into industries, homes, vehicles, and even personal wearables.

Every new connected device represents a potential attack vector, especially IoT devices, which often lack robust security protections. The larger and more diverse the device ecosystem grows, the harder it becomes to monitor, secure, and defend against cyber threats.

Estimates suggest that there are now more than 30 billion IoT (Internet of Things) devices connected globally, powered by advances in 5G, edge computing, AI, and cheaper sensors. Many of these devices operate in mission-critical environments, including hospitals, power grids, factories, and transportation networks, making their security essential. Even ordinary household devices, like smart refrigerators and voice assistants, can be exploited and turned into attack vectors if left unprotected.

Dimension 2: The Diversity of Operating Systems

An operating system (OS) is a critical piece of software that serves as an intermediary between computer hardware and the user. It is responsible for

More Devices Mean More Risk

Networking and Telecommunications Devices	
Devices that support internet connectivity and communication	
Routers and Modems	Home, business, and ISP grade network devices
WiFi Mesh Systems	Eero, Google Nest WiFi, Netgear Orbi
Network Switches and Firewalls	Cisco, Juniper, Palo Alto Networks security appliances
Telecom Infrastructure	5G towers, satellite internet systems (Starlink)
Internet Backbone Equipment	Undersea cables, fiber-optic networks, DNS servers

Emerging and Specialized Devices	
Devices that push the boundaries of computing	
Augmented Reality (AR) Devices	Microsoft HoloLens, Magic Leap
Virtual Reality (VR) Headsets	Oculus Quest, HTC Vive, PlayStation VR
Autonomous Delivery Robots	Starship, Nuro AI powered bots
Brain Computer Interfaces (BCI)	Neuralink, NextMind
Smart Clothing and Wearable Textiles	Heated jackets, biometric monitoring clothing
Crypto Mining Machines and Blockchain Devices	ASIC miners, hardware wallets Ledger, Trezor)
Quantum Computers	IBM Quantum, Google Sycamore

Enterprise and Business Devices
Devices used in corporate, industrial, and gov't settings

Enterprise Workstations	High performance computers for business and development
Corporate Laptops and Mobile Devices	Employee issued devices with business applications
Data Center Servers	Cloud hosted or on premises enterprise servers
Mainframes and Supercomputers	Large-scale computing systems used in banking, government, and research
Point of Sale (POS) Systems	Cash registers, payment terminals (Square, Verifone)
ATMs (Automated Teller Machines)	Banking kiosks connected to financial networks
Digital Signage and Smart Displays	Interactive ads, menus, and public information boards
Smart Conference Room Equipment	Video conferencing systems, interactive whiteboards
Cloud Connected Printers and Scanners	Networked office devices with storage and processing capabilities

Personal Computing Devices
Everyday devices used by individuals

Desktop Computers	Windows, macOS, and Linux based PCs
Laptop Computers	Lightweight, portable versions of desktops
Tablets and Hybrid Devices	iPads, Android tablets, Microsoft Surface
Smartphones	iPhones, Android, and other mobile operating systems
Wearables & Fitness Trackers	Apple Watch, Samsung Galaxy Watch, Fitbit, Garmin
E-Readers	E-Readers
Personal Storage Devices	USB flash drives, external hard drives

Internet of Things (IoT) Devices
Consumer and business devices connected to the internet

Smart Home Hubs and Assistants	Amazon Echo, Google Nest Hub, Apple HomePod
Smart Thermostats	Nest, Ecobee
Smart Locks and Security Cameras	Ring, Arlo, August smart locks
Smart Refrigerators and Appliances	Samsung Smart Fridge, LG ThinQ appliances
Smart Doorbells and Motion Sensors	Ring Doorbell, Blink security systems
Voice Controlled Devices and AI Assistants	Alexa, Google Assistant, Siri

Industrial and Critical Infrastructure Devices
Devices in manufacturing, utilities, and public services

Programmable Logic Controllers (PLCs)	Industrial automation controllers for manufacturing
SCADA Systems (Supervisory Control and Data Acquisition)	Used in power grids, water treatment plants, and industrial control systems
Industrial Robots and Cobots	Automated assembly line robots and collaborative robots
Drones (Unmanned Aerial Vehicles UAVs)	Commercial, military, and consumer drones
Smart Agricultural Equipment	Connected tractors, irrigation sensors, AI-driven farming tools
Smart Transportation Systems	Citywide traffic control, AI-driven traffic lights
Autonomous Vehicles and Connected Cars	Tesla, Waymo, self-driving delivery bots
Smart Airplanes and Avionics Systems	Aircraft autopilot, in-flight entertain-ment, and electronic flight bags

managing and coordinating a wide range of tasks, including file organization, memory allocation, and process scheduling. Additionally, the OS handles input/output operations and ensures the seamless functioning of peripheral devices, such as storage drives, printers, and other connected hardware.

While many readers are familiar with operating systems like Windows, macOS, iOS, and Android, there is a vast array of operating systems designed for various purposes. These include widely used platforms for personal computers and mobile devices, specialized operating systems tailored for IoT devices, industrial control systems, and embedded systems in appliances and vehicles.

Each operating system comes with its own architecture, features, and intended use case, but they all share a common challenge: vulnerabilities. These vulnerabilities can be exploited by cyberattackers, posing significant risks to individual users, businesses, and governments. For instance, mobile operating systems, like iOS and Android, often face threats from malicious apps and phishing attacks, while IoT systems are frequently targeted due to weaker security measures and outdated firmware.

CDR is more than just a technology— it's a mindset that can prevent countless cyberattacks.

The diversity in operating systems significantly complicates cybersecurity efforts. Defenders must develop tailored strategies to address the specific vulnerabilities of each OS. This often requires deep expertise because securing an IoT operating system, for example, involves different techniques and tools compared to safeguarding a traditional desktop OS like Windows or macOS. Moreover, attackers continually evolve their tactics, exploiting unique weaknesses in lesser-known systems or leveraging cross-platform vulnerabilities.

To effectively secure systems, cybersecurity professionals need to stay informed about the latest threats and trends across a broad spectrum of operating environments. This dynamic landscape underscores the importance of robust, adaptable security measures and highlights the ongoing need for innovation in cybersecurity tools and practices.

Common OS Platforms and Their Vulnerabilities

I compiled this timeline by combining OS release data from Rutgers CS Department and Preceden OS Timeline.[1,2] I then mapped those milestones against publicly available CVE data from NVD, Microsoft Security Update Guide, and other vendor repositories.[3,4,5,6] The result is a chronological snapshot of major OS platforms, showing their historical release and how vulnerable they became over time.

Year	Operating System Released	Approximate Known Vulnerabilities (Lifetime)
1970	Unix (Bell Labs)	N/A (pre-CVE era)
1971	CP/CMS (IBM System/370)	N/A
1973	Unix v4 (in C)	N/A
1976	CP/M (Digital Research)	N/A
1977	Apple DOS 3.1	N/A
1978	UNIX/32V (Bell Labs)	N/A
1980	Xenix (Microsoft)	N/A
1981	MS DOS 1.0	~100 (across all DOS versions)
1983	Unix System V	~200 (for System V and derivatives)
1984	Macintosh System 1.0	Very limited public data
1985	Windows 1.0	~10
1986	AmigaOS 1.0	Limited
1987	OS/2 1.0	~80
1989	NeXTSTEP 1.0	Merged into macOS CVEs
1990	Windows 3.0	~50 (incl. Windows 3.1x)
1991	Linux Kernel 0.01	~2000+ (aggregated across versions)
1992	Solaris 2.0	~1200+ (SunOS/Solaris combined)
1993	FreeBSD / NetBSD	~1000+
1995	Windows 95	~400
1996	Palm OS	Very limited public data
1997	Mac OS 8	~100

Year	Operating System Released	Approximate Known Vulnerabilities (Lifetime)
1998	Windows 98	~450
1999	Red Hat Linux 6.0	~1000+
2000	Windows 2000	~500
2001	Mac OS X 10.0, Windows XP	~2000+ (each)
2003	Fedora Core 1	~2500+ (all Fedora versions)
2004	Ubuntu 4.10	~6000+ (all Ubuntu versions)
2005	Windows Mobile 5	~50
2006	OpenSolaris	Counted with Solaris
2007	iPhone OS 1.0	~2000+ (iOS cumulative)
2008	Android 1.0	~4000+ (all Android versions)
2009	Windows 7	~1100
2012	Windows 8	~600
2014	Android 5.0	Counted within Android total
2015	Windows 10	~2500+ (ongoing updates)
2016	Ubuntu 16.04 LTS	Included in Ubuntu count
2017	macOS 10.13	Included in macOS count
2019	Windows 10 1903/1909	Counted in Windows 10
2020	macOS 11 "Big Sur"	macOS total: ~2000+
2021	Windows 11	~300+ (growing)
2022	SteamOS 3.0	Counted with Linux kernel CVEs
2023	Android 14	Included in Android total

1 "CS 416 Operating Systems: Class Notes," accessed July 25, 2025, https://people.cs.rutgers.edu/~badri/416f00/notes.html
2 "History of Operating Systems Timeline | Preceden," accessed July 25, 2025, https://www.preceden.com/timeline/history-of-operating-systems
3 "NVD—Home," accessed July 25, 2025, https://nvd.nist.gov
4 "Security Update Guide—Microsoft," accessed July 25, 2025, https://msrc.microsoft.com/update-guide
5 "CVEs," Ubuntu, accessed July 25, 2025, https://ubuntu.com/security/cves
6 "Apple Security Releases," Apple Support, accessed July 25, 2025, https://support.apple.com/en-us/100100

Dimension 3: The Ever-Growing Number of Applications

If there is one layer of the attack surface that is exploding faster than anything else, it is applications. Every time a new operating system, hardware platform, or API is introduced, developers rush in to build apps for it. Sometimes, that means thousands of new apps within months. For example, **Apple's App Store** reported **1.96 million** apps available.[1]

Add to that Microsoft, Google Play, and other operating systems, and the numbers become huge. Now here's the issue: Every one of these apps is a piece of software and every piece of software can become an attack surface.

At the **National Vulnerability Database (NVD),** there were **302,000+ common vulnerabilities and exposures (CVEs)** recorded as of mid-2024 on your phone, laptop, and browser.[2] A user might have 50+ apps installed. Inside a company, that number could be in the hundreds or thousands across teams and cloud services. And that's where things get dangerous.

My HR and Leadership Philosophy

When growing OPSWAT, I have always believed that leadership is about clarity, consistency, and humanity. People need to know what is expected of them, where they stand, and what we stand for as a company. I try to communicate in a way that is simple and memorable.

I often remind my team that there are only three honorable ways to leave OPSWAT: You pass away. This is sad, but it is honorable. Life ends for all of us, and if OPSWAT was part of your story until the end, I am proud of that. You retire. This is natural and respected. I hope you choose to do it at or after the official IRS retirement date, but whenever it comes, it is still honorable. You open your own company. This one excites me the most. Building something of your own, connecting with people, and creating new value in the world, is fulfilling in ways that are hard to describe. If you do this, I will likely cheer you on, and if it makes sense, I might even invest in your firm.

If your departure does not fall into one of these three categories, I take it personally. It means I may have failed to inspire you, to show you a career path that felt fulfilling, or to connect you to the larger mission. When that happens, I want to know. I want to learn from it, because leadership is not about pretending to be perfect, it is about being accountable and growing with your team. For me, OPSWAT is not just a company—it is a community of people who chose to join me on a mission. That trust is sacred, and I will never take it for granted.

1 Apple, 2024-App-Store-Transparency-Report, n.d., chrome-extension://efaidnbmnnnibpcajpcglclefindmkaj/https://www.apple.com/legal/more-resources/docs/2024-App-Store-Transparency-Report.pdf.
2 "NVD—NVD Dashboard," accessed July 25, 2025, https://nvd.nist.gov/general/nvd-dashboard.

FORCE 2

More Data, More Risk

As internet traffic grows, so does the number of breaches. It's not a coincidence; it's cause and effect. Every increase in traffic means more files shared, more apps connected, more APIs called, and more cloud services synced. Each of those provides another pathway into your systems.

More volume means more complexity, and complexity is where attackers thrive. Even if just a tiny fraction of interactions are insecure, at scale, that's still thousands of weak points every single day. And the numbers back it up. Cloudflare, one of the internet's largest infrastructure providers, saw global internet traffic grow by 17.2 percent in 2024 alone.[3]

That traffic doesn't just include web browsing, but also cloud-to-cloud syncs, internal service calls, IoT chatter, mobile apps, edge computing, and shadow IT. It's nonstop.

The bigger the pipe, the more that can leak. And attackers are following the flow. The more your business moves, the more surface area is exposed.

3 "Cloudflare Radar 2024 Year in Review," accessed July 25, 2025, https://radar.cloudflare.com/year-in-review/2024

FORCE 3

AI and ML: An Infinite Cycle That Can Create and Destroy

Artificial Intelligence (AI) and machine learning (ML) are revolutionizing cybersecurity, fueling both progress and peril. These technologies streamline detection, accelerate response, and surface patterns too subtle for human analysts. But they also arm cybercriminals with tools that are faster, smarter, and disturbingly adaptive.

We're now in an arms race. Threat actors are using AI to supercharge phishing, automate reconnaissance, and build polymorphic malware that constantly mutates to evade detection. Deepfake-driven impersonation attacks and AI-generated spear phishing are just the start. Even botnets are evolving with AI-driven logic, adjusting in real time to evade traditional controls.

Defenders aren't standing still, however. AI is transforming threat detection, behavioral analytics, and incident response. ML models can detect anomalies in massive telemetry streams, flagging subtle shifts in user behavior or lateral movement that would go unnoticed in manual reviews. Automated triage, real-time threat scoring, and predictive-threat modeling are no longer theoretical—they're foundational. But let's be clear: AI isn't a silver bullet. The challenges are serious.

AI models are only as good as their training data. Many remain opaque black boxes that can't explain their decisions. Worse yet, adversaries can poison models or exploit weaknesses through adversarial inputs. And as AI becomes more embedded in defense strategies, it's crucial that privacy, governance, and ethical boundaries be deliberately defined and rigorously enforced.

This AI-driven escalation forces a new kind of discipline onto cybersecurity teams. Success requires more than deploying the latest model. It demands robust validation, transparent design, red-teaming, and alignment with evolving global norms.

The bottom line is that AI and ML are reshaping the battlefield. Every innovation that benefits defenders can and likely will be mirrored by threat actors.

As the number of devices, apps, and data sources grow, so too are the attack surfaces that bad actors can exploit to launch cyberattacks. This is why data sanitization is so important to keeping networks safe—now and in the future.

When one app is compromised, especially in a cloud-connected or API-rich environment, it rarely stays contained. That small, overlooked app in marketing or HR might be the attacker's path to your core systems, data lake, or financial platforms. We've seen this movie before. In many breaches, it's not the fancy zero-day exploit that opens the door to a cyberattack—it's a poorly secured app.

Forces That Are Shaping Cybersecurity

In addition to the expanding attack surface, explosion of data, and the rise of AI and ML, several other forces are making it more difficult than ever to sustain strong cybersecurity defenses.

Detection is becoming more elusive.
Threat actors are no longer relying on brute force or obvious malware. Instead, they're using advanced tactics like social engineering, fileless malware, and adaptive ransomware to slip past traditional defenses. What used to be detectable is now subtle, blended, and hard to trace.

The cybersecurity talent gap is growing.
Skilled defenders are in short supply. The demand far exceeds supply, leaving many organizations under-resourced and vulnerable. Even well-funded teams struggle to hire and retain the right people to keep pace with evolving threats.

Compliance often misses the point.
While regulatory frameworks aim to improve security posture, they can backfire when treated as checklists. Rigid mandates may lead to inflexible processes, false assurance, and blind spots. Meeting compliance doesn't always mean being secure.

Cybercrime has no borders.
Attackers can strike from anywhere, and legal jurisdiction rarely aligns with threat origin. The globalization of threats makes attribution and enforcement nearly impossible, forcing defenders to assume a borderless threat model and prepare for everything.

Detect or Sanitize? A Crossroads for Cybersecurity

To break free from the exhausting, asymmetric battle in which attackers always seem to hold the upper hand, we need a fundamental shift in how we think about cybersecurity.

This book shares the story of how I arrived at that shift, one that changed how I build and approach cybersecurity solutions. After years of research and product development aimed at stopping malware, I reached a sobering realization: The cybersecurity industry is stuck in what I call a "detection mindset," which is the belief that to stop threats, we must first detect them.

This mindset dominates how we deal with malware and vulnerabilities—ironically, the areas where the most damage occurs. But this approach is inherently reactive. It's like building a dam after the flood has begun. Detection-based defenses, no matter how well-intentioned, often trail behind fast-moving threats.

Chapters 2 and 3 detail some of the hard lessons I learned trying to fight malware using detection alone. Eventually, I asked a different question: *What if we simply assumed every file is malicious?*

That shift led me to a new way of thinking which I now call the **sanitization mindset.** Here's how I distinguish between detection and sanitization:

- **Detection-based security** scans for malware using signatures, behavioral indicators, or AI models, and then attempts to remove the threat once it's identified.

- **Sanitization-based security** assumes all files are untrusted and proactively regenerates safe versions of those files, neutralizing threats without needing to detect them. This is the foundation of **Content Disarm and Reconstruction (CDR).**

CDR doesn't guess, it acts. And as the chapters that follow will show, it consistently outperforms traditional detection in defending against zero days, targeted attacks, and evasive malware.

!
++
GRR!
RRR!
!!!
!@*?
WOOF!
MEOW!
ER!
!
?!?
?
!
?
?
!
△⊙ℏ
LA DI DA!
!
YO!
!
?
!
!?!
!!!
GRRRR!!
?
△∩ℙ∏
!
//1,0,0^!
*!
c = A V^?
末凡万
!
书๗ぬ争
VII
?
?
?!?
WHA!?
?!
BLAH...
!?
TWEET TWOO!

CHAPTER TWO

BUILDING THE CYBERSECURITY LANGUAGE

Why cybersecurity tools must speak the same language
to build a smarter, unified defense strategy.

The cybersecurity landscape is vast and intricate, which can be intimidating. However, I believe everyone can grasp the essential principles and technology needed to not only safeguard themselves, but enhance the security of their communities and organizations. In writing this book, my aim is not only to expound upon the fundamental concept of data sanitization—also known as Content Disarm and Reconstruction (CDR)—but to shed light on the methodology I have adopted in thinking about cybersecurity. My objective is to share my experiences and provide insights into a critical form of cyber protection, while equipping you with a variety of pragmatic principles to build better defenses against cyber threats.

Growing up, I had a distinct vision for my life. By the seventh grade, I could tell you without hesitation that I would be a pilot and work in technology—likely in cybersecurity. Those dreams may have seemed ambitious for a kid, but I set a goal for myself to achieve them before I turned 30.

Flying turned out to be the easier goal—log the hours, pass the exams, and earn my license. But somewhere between countless takeoffs, hours in the cockpit, and completing a stack of certifications, it became more than a skill—it became a hobby, something I loved purely for the thrill of it. Starting my own tech venture, however, was a completely different kind of challenge—one driven by three major influences.

The Three Things That Influenced Me Most

Looking back, I can pinpoint three key influences that shaped my decision to build a cybersecurity company:

1. **My mother's success in running her architecture business.** My mom was deeply committed to her work, and watching her navigate challenges with dedication, honesty, and sharp negotiation skills left a lasting impression on me. She taught me the value of perseverance, mission-driven work, and transparency—qualities that would later become the foundation of my own leadership style.

2. **My father's service
   with the government.**
   Though much of my father's work
   was classified, his unwavering
   sense of duty inspired my own
   desire to contribute to public
   safety and work on something
   that truly mattered.

3. **My early
   exposure to programming.**
   In the fourth grade, I discovered my
   passion for computing—tinkering
   with my Sinclair ZX81 and pushing
   its limits. That early fascination
   with technology gradually evolved
   into a deeper understanding of
   cybersecurity's role in shaping the
   future. The more I explored, the
   clearer it became that protecting
   digital infrastructure wasn't
   just a technical challenge—it
   was a critical mission.

My first computer, a Sinclair ZX81, was a tiny playground that opened up a vast universe of programming for me.

These influences, combined with an insatiable curiosity about cybersecurity, set me on a path that would ultimately lead me to build my own company. The road wasn't easy—but looking back, every challenge, every lesson, and every moment of inspiration played a part in shaping my journey.

My Journey Begins

After graduating from high school, I served more than four years in the Israel Defense Forces (IDF). I began as a soldier and ultimately became an officer. After finishing active duty, I enrolled at the Technion–Israel Institute of Technology in Haifa to study computer science, fueling my passion for the field. A course at Technion ignited the idea of starting my own business, but I knew I had a lot to learn.

I didn't want to be just another young entrepreneur who jumped into the deep end, relying on investor money to stay afloat. I wanted to earn my success, so understanding the business inside and out was crucial for me. My goal was to bring a solid idea to market, backed by a clear operational plan. Acknowledging my lack of fundamental experience in starting and running a business, I was determined to be fully prepared as an executive before stepping into entrepreneurship.

I prioritized the valuable experience I would need to gain in preparation for launching my own company. My journey began in 1995, while still at Technion, when I landed my first technology job at NetManage, a well-established, international software firm headquartered in Cupertino, California, with an office in Haifa. This opportunity marked a significant milestone by eventually allowing me to lead an R&D group. The experience at NetManage was invaluable, offering me a deep dive into the workings of a large-scale, international company and bolstering my passion for computing, while also providing the practical insight I needed to venture into entrepreneurship.

Three years after graduating from Technion, I moved from NetManage to Netect, an Israel-based startup focused on detecting, prioritizing, and remediating network-based vulnerabilities.

At Netect, I led the research and development of software designed to map networks and identify exploitable vulnerabilities in applications. Our mission was clear: to detect all software-based vulnerabilities. To achieve this, we developed code that mapped networks and scanned devices for a wide range of weaknesses. Each time a new vulnerability was discovered, we quickly developed code to detect it—and in some cases, even patch it. My time at Netect taught me a couple of fundamental lessons: First, accurately detecting and classifying vulnerabilities was immensely complex. Second, the vulnerability life cycle—particularly the growing difficulty of detection and the near impossibility of predicting zero-day threats—was a huge challenge. While this realization was humbling, it also fueled my determination to push the boundaries of cybersecurity innovation.

Having worked at both a large, established company and an agile startup, I gained a unique perspective on how businesses operate, what drives success, and, more importantly, what leads to failure. I learned the value of patience and continuous learning, recognizing that achieving ambitious goals wasn't just about reaching the destination but about embracing the entire journey. It was about laying a strong foundation, setting clear and achievable milestones, and always preparing for the next step forward.

Beyond the technical work, I also gained insights into other parts of the business—sales, marketing, finance, global operations, and legal. I enjoyed networking across departments, learning how each function contributed to the company's growth. That experience broadened my understanding of how an organization truly works, and many of the colleagues I connected with back then remain close friends today.

My First Big Idea

I had put in the work, sharpened my skills, and was just waiting for that spark—the idea that would push me to build something game-changing.

When I founded OPSWAT in 2002, I had a few ideas about products I wanted to develop, but nothing that truly clicked. So, I dug in. I spent my time dissecting cybersecurity breaches, analyzing attack patterns, and searching for that eureka moment.

And then it hit me: a vision for something different—a cybersecurity framework in which security products didn't operate in isolation, but worked together, seamlessly communicating to create a stronger defense. That was the moment everything changed.

The cybersecurity landscape I stepped into at the start of my journey was fragmented. Companies relied on a patchwork of security tools: antivirus software, VPNs, Software-Defined Perimeters (SDP), encryption, vulnerability, patch management, Security Information and Event Management (SIEMs), Intrusion Prevention System (IPS), Intrusion Detection System (IDS), and Identity Provider (IdP) services. But these systems operated in silos. They didn't talk to each other, leaving security teams battling blind spots and inefficiencies, and in a constant struggle to keep everything in sync.

OPSWAT: What We Do Is In Our Name

The name "OPSWAT" was coined by merging "OPS" (Operations) and "SWAT" (Special Weapons and Tactics). In the IT world, OPS encompasses a broad range of responsibilities associated with managing and maintaining computer systems, networks, and infrastructure. This includes monitoring systems, managing servers, deploying software, and ensuring overall reliability, security, and performance. Additionally, OPS can denote specific teams or roles, such as "DevOps" or "NetOps."

SWAT typically refers to a specialized division in law enforcement that is deployed for complex and high-risk situations. However, when applied to my interests, SWAT takes on a new meaning that emphasizes speed and promptness.

I envisioned a company that embodied all of these principles. We would apply the efficiency and rapid deployment of a SWAT team to cybersecurity by focusing on the swift implementation and management of cybersecurity solutions. My aim was to ensure quick and effective responses to cyber threats, including expedited installation of security measures, to provide clients with a nimble and proactive defense against cyber incidents.

The Communications Gap

Most companies use complex networks for a variety of cybersecurity technologies and products. The problem is that many solutions are not designed to work seamlessly together. This can result in breaches because the tools don't communicate effectively.

Anti-Malware

Network Access Control

Compliance

SDP
CISCO
FORTINET
zscaler
perimeter 81
paloalto NETWORKS
NordLayer
CHECK POINT
Twingate
PRISMA
BY PALO ALTO NETWORKS
SIEM
LogRhythm
FORTINET
McAfee
solarwinds
RAPID7
AT&T Cybersecurity
MICRO FOCUS
ArcSight
splunk>
exabeam
QRadar

VPN
citrix
FORTINET
Google Cloud
paloalto NETWORKS
CHECK POINT
Endpoint Backup
inSync
Barracuda Cloud-to-Cloud Backup
CARBONITE
CrashPlan
CODE42
Backblaze
Acronis Cyber Protect
SOPHOS
COMMVAULT
veeAM
Endpoint Firewalls
Symantec
SOPHOS
McAfee
paloalto NETWORKS
kaspersky
TREND MICRO
CISCO
eset
CORTEX
BY PALO ALTO NETWORKS
FORTINET

Data Loss Prevention
Symantec
SOPHOS
DIGITAL GUARDIAN
ENDPOINT PROTECTOR
CISCO
McAfee
TREND MICRO
CHECK POINT
Forcepoint
GTB Technologies
Data Protection that Works
Endpoint Encryption
CHECK POINT
CISCO
TREND MICRO
McAfee
SOPHOS
IBM Security
Windows 11 BitLocker
eset
DELL Technologies
Symantec

IDP
Ping Identity
CYBERARK
Workforce Identity Cloud
salesforce
Auth0 by Okta
onelogin
Google Cloud
ORACLE IDENTITY MANAGEMENT
Microsoft Azure
IBM Security

This lack of interoperability was a serious flaw. Without seamless integration, organizations couldn't build a truly resilient defense. I saw a better way—a cybersecurity ecosystem where security products didn't just coexist but actively communicated, sharing meaningful data and working as a unified force. By enabling cross-product collaboration, security solutions could become exponentially more effective, allowing organizations to enforce policies, ensure compliance, and stop threats in real time—before they had a chance to spread.

Before I could focus on revolutionizing cybersecurity, however, I had to figure out how to fund the initiative. Quitting my job to build OPSWAT meant I needed a way to sustain my journey. I had two options: start looking for investors or take on a consulting gig. I chose the latter.

OPSWAT's initial offering wasn't a cutting-edge security platform, but rather a consulting and professional service for companies seeking operations security (OPSEC) certification. This became our foundation—a way to establish credibility, gain industry experience, and build the resources needed to turn a vision into reality.

The more I engaged in operational security consulting, the more it became clear that most companies using complex networks had installed a variety of cybersecurity technologies and products. As the graphic on pages 22 and 23 shows, the vendor landscape is vast. There is no shortage of products.

Despite the constant introduction of new cybersecurity products, many still have critical gaps. Even today, many solutions just aren't designed to work seamlessly together. I've seen—and continue to see—security breaches happen simply because these tools don't communicate effectively.

Without seamless integration, organizations couldn't build a truly resilient defense.

Fragmented communication between cybersecurity solutions creates critical vulnerabilities, leaving organizations exposed to exploitation. Security tools—such as Virtual Private Networks (VPNs), Software-Defined Perimeters (SDPs), and anti-malware solutions—must work in unison to detect, mitigate, and respond to threats in real time.

Without seamless interoperability, security gaps emerge, regulatory compliance becomes more challenging, and incident response slows—demonstrating that even the most advanced security tools are ineffective in isolation. A striking example of these risks is the Conficker malware outbreak of 2008, which exploited the MS08-067 vulnerability in Windows to spread across networks worldwide.

It became increasingly clear to me that many of these cybersecurity breaches could have been avoided if different security products from various vendors had the capability to communicate and collaborate dynamically. Instead of operating in isolated silos, these tools needed a way to share intelligence and coordinate their defenses in real time.

Taking this a step further, if cybersecurity products could effectively interact, they could enhance each other's detection, analysis, and response capabilities—creating a more robust and adaptive defense against cyber threats.

Take VPN or SDP access. Enterprises rely on VPNs and SDPs to connect users to cloud applications and internal systems. However, granting access to a corporate network should depend on multiple security checks that answer key questions:

- Can the device be trusted?
- Is it protected by an anti-malware engine? If so, is that anti-malware solution trusted by the organization?
- Is it properly configured, up-to-date, and actively defending against threats?

If VPNs and anti-malware solutions communicate effectively, they can determine whether a device meets security standards before granting access. Allowing a user to log in without verifying their device's security posture makes no sense.

- Can the device be trusted?
- If the device is infected or noncompliant, access should be restricted to prevent potential cyber risks.
- If the device lacks encryption, should the VPN or SDP allow data access to it?

The challenge was to create a secure communication framework that would allow a VPN or SDP to query an endpoint's third-party cybersecurity product's anti-malware status and receive real-time updates. Ideally, the VPN would be able to determine:

- If an untrusted or unauthorized anti-malware solution is installed, then access to the network should be blocked until compliance is achieved.
- If the anti-malware solution is outdated, then an automatic update should be triggered before lab-gate access is granted.

If real-time protection is disabled, then the anti-malware solution should turn it back on automatically.

Right now, these checks often happen in isolation. Each security tool does its own assessment, unaware of what other defenses are in place. As a result, cybersecurity vendors frequently create custom, one-off integrations to make their solutions compatible with others. This patchwork approach increases complexity, requires constant maintenance, and ultimately weakens security posture.

Smooth integration between cybersecurity products has two major benefits: First, it enhances overall security by enabling different layers of protection to work together seamlessly, preventing cyber threats before they can cause damage. Second, it simplifies regulatory compliance by ensuring that security policies are consistently enforced across all connected devices and applications.

My experience with numerous cybersecurity products also made another thing clear: Getting them to communicate would not be easy. Every company had its own proprietary interfaces, protocols, and standards. There was no universal framework for interoperability, making partnerships and integrations cumbersome. While some vendors managed to link their own products together, they weren't solving the broader issue: to create a standardized way for security solutions to interact, regardless of the provider.

The need for this kind of orchestration was obvious. A shared language for cybersecurity products could improve coordination and effectiveness. Yet, no one was actively working on a solution of that kind. That realization planted the seed for what would later become OPSWAT—a platform designed to unify cybersecurity, streamline communication, and build a stronger, more resilient defense against modern threats. Here's a more detailed example of how this works.

How Cross-Product Communication Can Secure Remote Access

Although a standardized cyber language can serve many purposes—compliance checks, network access control (NAC), and automated patch management—remote access provides a clear illustration of how cross-product communication could work in practice.

When an endpoint attempts to connect from a remote location to an enterprise or cloud network, tools such as a VPN, Software-Defined Perimeter (SDP), or Identity Provider (IdP) should ensure that this endpoint is truly secure. Otherwise, even a well-encrypted tunnel can pose a serious threat if the device itself is compromised.

Consider a laptop that is infected or has a severe, unpatched vulnerability. If the VPN or SDP grants access without verifying its security status, that vulnerability could spread inside the organization's network—negating any benefits of remote-access solutions. The challenge here is twofold: First, identifying the security posture of the endpoint; and second, automating the appropriate responses to any risks discovered.

Key Security and Compliance Questions

Before granting full network access, a remote-access solution would ideally query the endpoint (and its installed security products) about a number of key categories:

1. **Connection Validity**

   - Is the VPN/SDP actually talking to the correct security solution on the endpoint, rather than an imposter?

2. **Anti-Malware Presence and Status**

   - Is an antivirus (AV) or other anti-malware protection installed?
   - Which product, vendor, version, and language is it running? Is it approved by the organization?
   - Is it a high-quality solution?

3. **Definition Updates**

   - When was the AV definition last updated, and is it current with the latest threat patterns?

4. **Configuration and Real-Time Protection**

   - Is the endpoint's anti-malware configured correctly and scanning critical folders in real time?

5. **Encryption Compliance**

   - Does the endpoint have an encryption solution, and are essential drives or folders secured?

6. **Recent Threat Activity**

   - When did the endpoint last complete a full scan?
   - Is the anti-malware solution struggling to remove any threats?

7. **Unwanted Applications**

   - Are there unauthorized tools (such as public file-sharing apps) that could increase the risk of data leakage?

Coordinating Multiple Solutions

To gather these details, each network access mechanism—be it VPN, SDP, or IdP—should communicate with relevant endpoint security products, including local anti-malware engines, firewalls, and encryption agents. As shown in the diagram on page 29, seamless, secure collaboration allows these solutions to exchange information about the device's security-and-compliance posture in real time.

A Broader Vision of Interoperability

Remote access is just one example of how a standardized cyber language could transform security. The same principles—rapidly querying device posture, sharing threat intelligence, and enforcing consistent policies—apply to a range of use cases:

- **Compliance Audits:** Automatically validating that systems adhere to regulations such as HIPAA, GDPR, NIS2, CRA, or PCI-DSS.

- **Network Access Control (NAC):** Dynamically blocking devices that fail posture checks from moving laterally.

- **Patch Management:** Identifying and installing critical updates across diverse environments.

The Big Question: Could Cybersecurity Products Cross-Communicate?

The next question was challenging: Do cybersecurity products have the technical capabilities to support this question-and-answer process?

Going further, if cybersecurity products grant access to the network to ask endpoints about the state of their security, could there be a way to improve network security, improve compliance, and maybe even create a new class of product?

As I started looking into how network and endpoint products worked, I was pleased to find that many of those products exposed application programming interfaces (APIs) and command line interfaces (CLIs) that delivered the functionality needed to support cross-product communication. When products didn't have these mechanisms, other means—such as configuration files, registry keys, operating systems, network pipes, configurations, or dot directories—could be used to communicate.

My research revealed how each of those methods enabled communication, which is shown on page 29.

In theory, this research demonstrated that achieving the desired level of coordination was possible. However, developing a functional communication system would

The Cybersecurity Communication Challenge

Network Access Control systems have a variety of methods to choose from when communicating with endpoints—each with its own weaknesses and strengths.

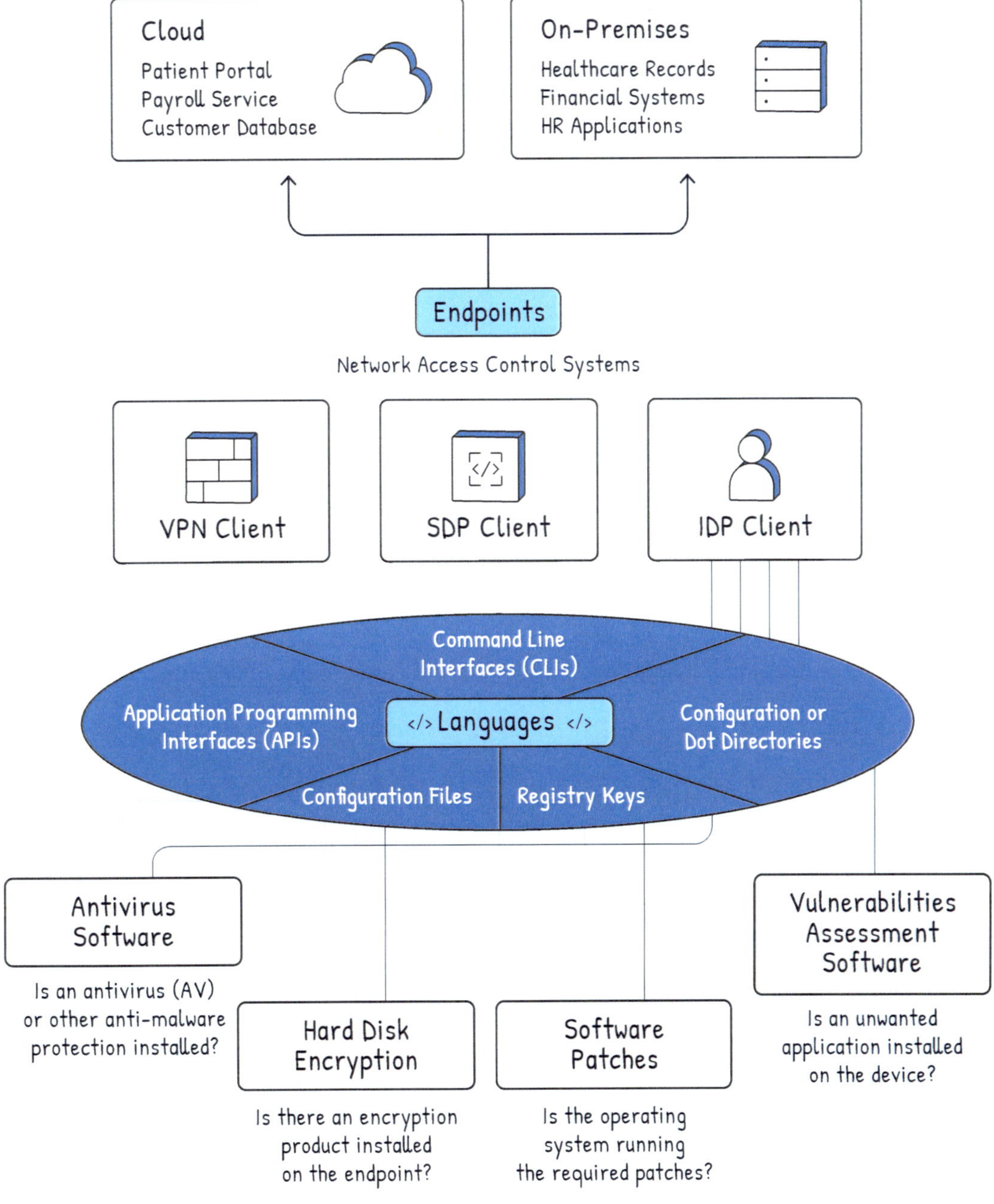

require extensive effort—acquiring, integrating, standardizing, and rigorously testing compatibility with every cybersecurity product. This process could only begin after securing partnership agreements with each vendor, which would be a complex and time-consuming endeavor.

Yet, if I could successfully enable cross-product communication, it would solve a critical cybersecurity challenge and have the potential to reshape the industry entirely.

Defining the Opportunity

I was confident there was a strong market for a solution that enabled seamless communication between cybersecurity products, and I believed the economics would work in my favor. The sheer complexity of building a system that could integrate with all endpoint security products—anti-malware, encryption, firewalls, and privacy tools—posed a formidable challenge for any single vendor. Even if one company managed to develop such a solution, would every other vendor invest the time and resources to create and sustain an equivalent capability? That would be highly unlikely in my view, as the effort would be too resource-intensive and impractical to sustain at scale.

One of the strongest indicators of a viable market is when a capability is highly desirable but too complex or resource-intensive for individual buyers to develop on their own. I was convinced that network security and compliance vendors, along with many others in the cybersecurity and networking space, would see immense value in a solution that enabled seamless cross-product communication.

To validate my idea, I presented it to CTOs of various cybersecurity companies. Their reactions were immediate and enthusiastic—some even said they would buy it on the spot if it were available. They acknowledged they had previously dedicated engineering resources to solving this problem, but admitted they had never managed to do so effectively.

As mentioned earlier, the cybersecurity landscape was expanding at an unprecedented pace, making this challenge more urgent and the need for a solution even greater.

I found the real opportunity, however, lay in the complexity and inefficiency of existing integration methods—APIs, CLIs, and other interfaces. These technologies were constantly evolving, requiring continuous updates, testing, and optimization. Even when integrations worked, they demanded ongoing maintenance. Additionally, since many vendors maintained multiple concurrent versions of their products, they often had to support several API versions simultaneously, which compounded the challenge even further. This escalating complexity, combined with the industry's growing demand for seamless interoperability, made one thing clear: The market was ready for a breakthrough solution.

OESIS

OPSWAT Endpoint Security Integration SDK

The OESIS SDK created a common language, which allowed OESIS to come to life.

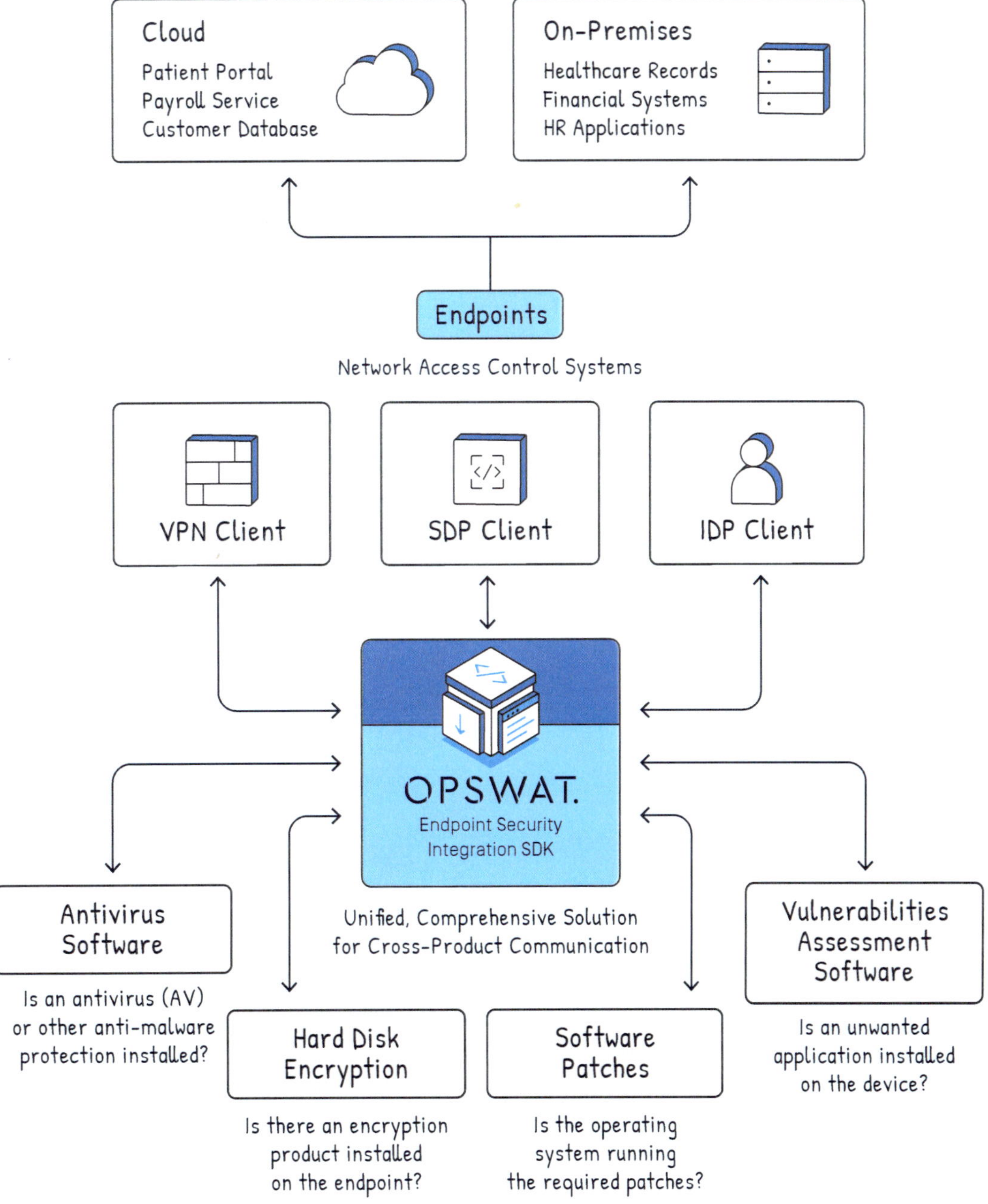

The Idea That Changed Everything

Driven by a desire to create something revolutionary, in 2004, I embarked on developing a solution that would enable seamless communication between cybersecurity products to significantly decrease global risk. I can still remember the rush I felt before going to sleep that first night, convinced that this innovation would be a game-changer. I believed that every cybersecurity company would want to license this technology.

The first step was to design initial prototypes of a standardized cybersecurity communication language and determine which security products would serve as the foundation for implementation. I started with the anti-malware sector, given its widespread use and critical role in endpoint protection. From there, I rapidly expanded the scope to include VPNs, browsers, and endpoint encryption solutions, ensuring the language could accommodate a broad range of security tools.

For the language itself, I chose C++ to leverage its robust object-oriented architecture. This approach provided a solid foundation of methods and properties, allowing the language to function as a translator—capable of detecting, assessing, and managing the state of any endpoint security product. The prototypes were designed to evaluate responses to all the critical questions posed earlier about cross-product communication, ensuring secure and seamless interoperability between different security solutions.

To make adoption straightforward, we developed the language in the form of software development kits (SDKs), which we intended to license to customers. Each SDK was designed to act as an intermediary, enabling communication between cybersecurity solutions:

- One SDK for antivirus and anti-malware products
- Another for firewalls
- Additional SDKs for encryption solutions, VPNs, browsers, and SDPs

Given the increasing number of modules, we eventually merged all SDKs into a single, unified solution.

These efforts culminated in the development of OPSWAT Endpoint Security Integration SDK (OESIS)—a comprehensive solution that integrated all these capabilities into a single, cohesive framework. Built upon our SDK foundation, OESIS became the first cybersecurity language designed to eliminate the fragmentation that had long plagued the industry.

The goal for the OESIS framework was to go beyond product integration to set a new industry standard by introducing a certification process open to any cybersecurity product capable of adopting a unified communication protocol. This initiative promised to not only facilitate easier licensing of products, but to democratize access to our platform.

Bootstrapping OEM Distribution Model Funding

Even in the wake of the dot-com bust, in the early 2000s, aggressive venture capital funding was all the rage in the San Francisco Bay Area. Investors prioritized rapid growth and scaling over the gradual development of a sustainable business model. Many startups were compelled to seek large-scale investments early in their life cycle, a practice that seemed too much like gambling to me.

To be fair, many entrepreneurs in this region successfully navigated startup funding by meticulously preparing investor decks, developing proofs of concept, and conducting in-depth market analyses. Their approaches often entailed creating detailed operational plans, projecting financial outcomes, showcasing their strong team, and actively engaging with investors to build trust and secure the funding they needed to get started.

While I always knew I wanted to establish my own company, I was skeptical of the typical route of attracting investor funding before I clearly understood my business model's profit potential.

Though I initially considered following the traditional funding checklist, the overwhelming success of our proof of concept and the unexpectedly positive response from our early-customer engagements prompted a critical reevaluation.

It was at this point that I decided to use the OEM model, which would require less capital. I would also bootstrap OPSWAT instead of seeking external funding at such an early stage. I harbored significant concerns that the total addressable market (TAM) for OESIS wasn't large enough to deliver the high returns that most external investors would expect. After all, OESIS is a cybersecurity language we marketed primarily to engineering or R&D teams, rather than the larger market of IT or cybersecurity buyers.

Bootstrapping would allow us to reinvest all of our returns directly into R&D, talent acquisition, and targeted marketing. It would also enable me to preserve equity and maintain autonomy in steering the company. While bootstrapping using the OEM model isn't suitable for every idea or entrepreneur, it was the right choice for OPSWAT when it came to OESIS.

My Principle: Startups Undervalue the Benefits of the OEM Model

Initially associated with the hardware business, "OEM" refers to developing products meant to be embedded into other products. As I thought through the implications of

OESIS Support Charts

This partial chart represents some of the breadth and depth of OESIS's impact on the cyber community (there is far more) while underscoring the difficulty in building a product that supports so many different companies and software versions.

Legend: ✔ Implemented   ◑ Implemented, Requires Admin   ✘ Not Implemented

Product Name	Tested Points	Test Covered Major Version	Test Covered Minor Version	Supported Languages	Get Version	Get Running State	Run	Terminate Processes	Get Installation Directories	Get Components	Get Uninstall String	Manage Labels	Is Authentic	Get Product Info	Get Real Time Protection State	Get Definition State	Get Threats	Update Definitions	Get Last Scan Time	Get Scan State	Enable RTP	Scan	Uninstall
avast! Endpoint Protection Suite	8.0.1603.399	8	8.0.X	EN	✔	✔	✔	✔	✔	✔	✔	✔	✔	✔	✔	✔	✔	✔	✔	✘	✔	✔	✔
avast! Endpoint Protection Suite Plus	8.0.1603.399	8	8.0.X	EN	✔	✔	✔	✔	✔	✔	✔	✔	✔	✔	✔	✔	✔	✔	✔	✘	✔	✔	✔
AVG File Server Edition	13.0.0.3552	13	8.0.X	EN	✔	✔	✔	✔	✔	✔	✔	✔	✔	✔	✔	✔	✔	✔	✔	✘	✔	✔	✘
Avira Antivirus Pro	15.0.13.193	15	8.0.X	EN, FR, DE, JA, IT, ZH, RU, TR, PT, NL	✔	✔	✔	✔	✔	✔	✔	✔	✔	✔	✔	✔	✔	✔	✔	✘	✔	✔	✔
	15.0.8.644	15	8.0.X	EN, FR, DE, JA, IT, ZH, RU, TR, PT, NL	✔	✔	✔	✔	✔	✔	✔	✔	✔	✔	✔	✔	✔	✔	✔	✘	✔	✔	✔
	7.0	7	8.0.X	EN, FR, DE, JA, IT, ZH, RU, TR, PT, NL	✔	✔	✔	✔	✔	✔	✔	✔	✔	✔	✔	✔	✔	✔	✔	✘	✔	✔	✔
	8.0	8	8.0.X	EN, FR, DE, JA, IT, ZH, RU, TR, PT, NL	✔	✔	✔	✔	✔	✔	✔	✔	✔	✔	✔	✔	✔	✔	✔	✘	✔	✔	✔
	9.0	9	8.0.X	EN, FR, DE, JA, IT, ZH, RU, TR, PT, NL	✔	✔	✔	✔	✔	✔	✔	✔	✔	✔	✔	✔	✔	✔	✔	✘	✔	✔	✔
	10.0	10	8.0.X	EN, FR, DE, JA, IT, ZH, RU, TR, PT, NL	✔	✔	✔	✔	✔	✔	✔	✔	✔	✔	✔	✔	✔	✔	✔	✘	✔	✔	✔
	11.0	11	8.0.X	EN, FR, DE, JA, IT, ZH, RU, TR, PT, NL	✔	✔	✔	✔	✔	✔	✔	✔	✔	✔	✔	✔	✔	✔	✔	✘	✔	✔	✔
	12.0	12	8.0.X	EN, FR, DE, JA, IT, ZH, RU, TR, PT, NL	✔	✔	✔	✔	✔	✔	✔	✔	✔	✔	✔	✔	✔	✔	✔	✘	✔	✔	✔
	13.0	13	8.0.X	EN, FR, DE, JA, IT, ZH, RU, TR, PT, NL	✔	✔	✔	✔	✔	✔	✔	✔	✔	✔	✔	✔	✔	✔	✔	✘	✔	✔	✔
	14.0	14	8.0.X	EN, FR, DE, JA, IT, ZH, RU, TR, PT, NL	✔	✔	✔	✔	✔	✔	✔	✔	✔	✔	✔	✔	✔	✔	✔	✘	✔	✔	✔
	15.0.30.25	15	8.0.X	EN, FR, DE, JA, IT, ZH, RU, TR, PT, NL	✔	✔	✔	✔	✔	✔	✔	✔	✔	✔	✔	✔	✔	✔	✔	✘	✔	✔	✔
Avira Professional Security	13.0	13	8.0.X	EN, FR, DE, JA, IT, ZH, RU, TR, PT, NL	✔	✔	✔	✔	✔	✔	✔	✔	✔	✔	✔	✔	✔	✔	✔	✘	✔	✔	✔
	14.0	14	8.0.X	EN, FR, DE, JA, IT, ZH, RU, TR, PT, NL	✔	✔	✔	✔	✔	✔	✔	✔	✔	✔	✔	✔	✔	✔	✔	✘	✔	✔	✔
Avira Server Security	14.0.0.411	14	8.0.X	EN, FR, DE, JA, IT, ZH, RU, TR, PT, NL	✔	✔	✔	✔	✔	✔	✔	✔	✔	✔	✔	✔	✔	✔	✔	✘	✔	✔	✔
	13.0	13	8.0.X	EN, FR, DE, JA, IT, ZH, RU, TR, PT, NL	✔	✔	✔	✔	✔	✔	✔	✔	✔	✔	✔	✔	✔	✔	✔	✘	✔	✔	✔
Bitdefender Business Client	3.5.1.0	3	3.5.X	EN	✔	✔	✔	✔	✔	✔	✔	✔	✔	✔	✔	◑	✔	✔	✔	✘	◑	✔	✔

Product Name	Tested Points	Test Covered Major Version	Test Covered Minor Version	Supported Languages	Get Version	Get Running State	Run	Terminate Processes	Get Installation Directories	Get Components	Get Uninstall String	Manage Labels	Is Authentic	Get Product Info	Get Real Time Protection State	Get Definition State	Get Threats	Update Definitions	Get Last Scan Time	Get Scan State	Enable RTP	Scan	Uninstall
Bitdefender Endpoint Security Tools	6.2.20.87	6	6.2.X	EN	○	✓	○	○	✓	✓	✓	✓	✓	✓	✓	○	○	○	○	○	○	○	✗
	6.2.21.42	6	6.2.X	EN	○	✓	○	○	✓	✓	✓	✓	✓	✓	✓	○	○	○	○	○	○	○	✗
	7.0.3-2004	7	7.0.X	EN	○	✓	○	○	✓	✓	✓	✓	✓	✓	✓	○	○	○	○	○	○	○	✗
	7.0.5-200049	7	7.0.X	EN	○	✓	○	○	✓	✓	✓	✓	✓	✓	✓	○	○	○	○	○	○	○	✗
	6.2.4.575149290	6	6.2.X	EN	✓	✓	✓	✓	✓	✓	✓	✓	✓	✓	✓	○	✓	✓	○	✗	✓	✓	✓
	6.2.4.599150708	6	6.2.X	EN	✓	✓	✓	✓	✓	✓	✓	✓	✓	✓	✓	○	✓	✓	○	✗	✓	✓	✓
	6.6.8.111	6	6.6.X	EN	✓	✓	✓	✓	✓	✓	✓	✓	✓	✓	✓	○	✓	✓	○	✗	✓	✓	✓
	7.1.2.33	7	7.1.X	EN	✓	✓	✓	✓	✓	✓	✓	✓	✓	✓	✓	○	✓	✓	○	✗	✓	✓	✓
	7.2.1.70	7	7.2.X	EN	✓	✓	✓	✓	✓	✓	✓	✓	✓	✓	✓	○	✓	✓	○	✗	✓	✓	✓
	7.2.1.65	7	7.2.X	EN	✓	✓	✓	✓	✓	✓	✓	✓	✓	✓	✓	○	✓	✓	○	✗	✓	✓	✓
	7.2.1.73	7	7.2.X	EN	✓	✓	✓	✓	✓	✓	✓	✓	✓	✓	✓	○	✓	✓	○	✗	✓	✓	✓
	7.2.2.90	6	7.2.X	EN	✓	✓	✓	✓	✓	✓	✓	✓	✓	✓	✓	○	✓	✓	○	✗	✓	✓	✓
	7.3.0.22	6	7.3.X	EN	✓	✓	✓	✓	✓	✓	✓	✓	✓	✓	✓	○	✓	✓	○	✗	✓	✓	✓
	7.4.3.146	7	7.4.X	EN	✓	✓	✓	✓	✓	✓	✓	✓	✓	✓	✓	○	✓	✓	○	✗	✓	✓	✓
	7.4.4.159	7	7.4.X	EN	✓	✓	✓	✓	✓	✓	✓	✓	✓	✓	✓	○	✓	✓	○	✗	✓	✓	✓
	7.5.2.186	6	7.5.X	EN	✓	✓	✓	✓	✓	✓	✓	✓	✓	✓	✓	○	✓	✓	○	✗	✓	✓	✓
	7.7.1.216	6	7.7.X	EN	✓	✓	✓	✓	✓	✓	✓	✓	✓	✓	✓	○	✓	✓	○	✗	✓	✓	✓
Bitdefender Endpoint Security Tools	7.6.2.207	6	7.6.X	EN	✓	✓	✓	✓	✓	✓	✓	✓	✓	✓	✓	○	✓	✓	○	✗	✓	✓	✓
	7.7.2.228	7	7.7.X	EN	✓	✓	✓	✓	✓	✓	✓	✓	✓	✓	✓	○	✓	✓	○	✗	✓	✓	✓
	7.8.2.254	7	7.2.X	EN	✓	✓	✓	✓	✓	✓	✓	✓	✓	✓	✓	○	✓	✓	○	✗	✓	✓	✓
	7.8.3.265	7	7.8.X	EN	✓	✓	✓	✓	✓	✓	✓	✓	✓	✓	✓	○	✓	✓	○	✗	✓	✓	✓
	7.8.4.270	7	7.8.X	EN	✓	✓	✓	✓	✓	✓	✓	✓	✓	✓	✓	○	✓	✓	○	✗	✓	✓	✓
	7.9.1.285	7	7.9.X	EN	✓	✓	✓	✓	✓	✓	✓	✓	✓	✓	✓	○	✓	✓	○	✗	✓	✓	✓
	7.9.2.290	7	7.9.X	EN	✓	✓	✓	✓	✓	✓	✓	✓	✓	✓	✓	○	✓	✓	○	✗	✓	✓	✓
	7.9.3.298	7	7.9.X	EN	✓	✓	✓	✓	✓	✓	✓	✓	✓	✓	✓	○	✓	✓	○	✗	✓	✓	✓
	7.9.4.313	7	7.9.X	EN	✓	✓	✓	✓	✓	✓	✓	✓	✓	✓	✓	○	✓	✓	○	✗	✓	✓	✓
	7.9.8.346	7	7.9.X	EN	✓	✓	✓	✓	✓	✓	✓	✓	✓	✓	✓	○	✓	✓	○	✗	✓	✓	✓
	7.9.8.350	7	7.9.X	EN	✓	✓	✓	✓	✓	✓	✓	✓	✓	✓	✓	○	✓	✓	○	✗	✓	✓	✓
	7.9.9.370	7	7.9.X	EN	✓	✓	✓	✓	✓	✓	✓	✓	✓	✓	✓	○	✓	✓	○	✗	✓	✓	✓
Bitdefender Windows 8 Security	16.34.0.1913	16	16.34.X	EN	✓	✓	✓	✓	✓	✓	✓	✓	✓	✓	✓	○	✓	✓	○	✗	✓	✓	✓
Emsisoft Internet Security	10.0.0.5532	10	10.0.X	EN	✓	✓	✓	✓	✓	✓	✓	✓	✓	✓	✓	✓	✓	✓	✓	✗	✓	✓	✓
	11.9.0.6513	11	11.9.X	EN	✓	✓	✓	✓	✓	✓	✓	✓	✓	✓	✓	✓	✓	✓	✓	✗	✓	✓	✓
	12.2.0.7060	12	12.2.X	EN	✓	✓	✓	✓	✓	✓	✓	✓	✓	✓	✓	✓	✓	✓	✓	✗	✓	✓	✓
	2017.6.0.7681	2017	2017.6.X	EN	✓	✓	✓	✓	✓	✓	✓	✓	✓	✓	✓	✓	✓	✓	✓	✗	✓	✓	✓
ESET Mail Security for Microsoft Exchange Server	4.0	4	4.X	EN, FR, DE	✓	✓	✓	✓	✓	✓	✓	✓	✓	✓	○	✓	✓	✓	✓	✗	✓	✓	✓
	6.3.10005.0	6	6.3.X	EN, FR, DE	✓	✓	✓	✓	✓	✓	✓	✓	✓	✓	○	✓	✓	✓	✓	✗	✓	✓	✓
	7.1.10011.0	7	7.1.X	EN, FR, DE	✓	✓	✓	✓	✓	✓	✓	✓	✓	✓	○	✓	✓	✓	✓	✗	✓	✓	✓
	10.0.10016.0	10	10.0.X	EN, FR, DE	✓	✓	✓	✓	✓	✓	✓	✓	✓	✓	○	✓	✓	✓	✓	✗	✓	✓	✓
F-Secure Client Security	10.18.224.9999	10	10.18.X	EN, DE	✓	✓	○	○	✓	✓	✓	✓	✓	✓	○	✓	✓	✓	✓	✓	✓	✓	✓
	14.01	14	14.X	EN, DE	✓	✓	○	○	✓	✓	✓	✓	✓	✓	○	✓	✓	✓	✓	✓	✓	✓	✓
	14.10	14	14.X	EN, DE	✓	✓	○	○	✓	✓	✓	✓	✓	✓	○	✓	✓	✓	✓	✓	✓	✓	✓
	14.22	14	14.X	EN, DE	✓	✓	○	○	✓	✓	✓	✓	✓	✓	○	✓	✓	✓	✓	✓	✓	✓	✓
	15.11	15	15.X	EN, DE	✓	✓	○	○	✓	✓	✓	✓	✓	✓	○	✓	✓	✓	✓	✓	✓	✓	✓

this model, it seemed quite attractive because I could avoid a number of expenses and focus our attention and resources on building a better product.

Under the OEM model:

- I wouldn't need a direct sales team or a marketing team to support them. The partners would bring our product to market for us, embedded inside their products.

- I could avoid building a Level 1 and Level 2 support organization, as the partners would handle these. We only needed to supply Level 3 support when the partners couldn't solve a problem.

- Sales and marketing would be much easier because we would focus exclusively on reaching the partners' senior product management executives and engineers. Only a few dozen companies could use our product, and given my seniority and reputation, I could easily reach out to them and get a meeting.

Choosing the OEM model didn't exclude the possibility of going directly to market later, which is exactly what we did. But when we eventually went directly to market, we had a steady cash flow, a mature product, and massive validation, because the partners had deployed our product to millions of their customers.

Refining Through Customer Feedback

My decision to self-fund OESIS made it vital to minimize our burn rate and total investment by finding the quickest route to profitability. My goal was to adopt principles of agility and lean startup methodologies, while also implementing strategies to reduce customer acquisition costs. I believed it was important to be involved in many of the details—everything from software development to daily logistics, such as providing morning bagels, managing Google keyword campaigns, and conducting sales outreach.

This hands-on approach, combined with our sophisticated, multifaceted product strategy, quickly attracted the attention of key industry players, including cybersecurity firms, system integrators, and large enterprises. They recognized the potential of the OESIS language to enhance their cybersecurity measures.

Our first major breakthrough came in 2004, when F5 (now valued at more than $10 billion) became one of our early adopters and beta customers.

This encouraging initial response motivated the formation and investment in a dedicated development team. In 2004, hiring engineers in the San Francisco Bay Area was relatively easy, and I was fortunate to have worked with an amazing group of individuals—including Tom Mullen and others—who still work with me today. They not only helped shape the product, but each played a key role in defining the culture

Locking down Linux

Security, regulatory compliance and intellectual property law were all hot topics at last week's LinuxWorld in Boston. **PAGE 8.**

Clear Choice Test: Wireless multimedia

Ruckus Wireless offers a MIMO-like multimedia access point. **PAGE 52.**

Share and SharePoint alike

Microsoft is making its SharePoint server the foundation for sharing all the document types produced by Office desktop applications. **PAGE 29.**

NETWORKWORLD

Volume 23, Number 14

60 • www.networkworld.com • 4.10.06

OPSWAT

continued from page 1

security software brands out there.

Vendors such as Cisco, F5 Networks, Symantec and Juniper Networks license the OPSWAT code that checks for more than 400 versions of security software from more than 35 vendors. They embed the code, a software development kit (SDK), into their network-access control products (see list, below).

This has made OPSWAT (which informally stands for Omni-Platform Security with Access Technologies), a security vendor to security vendors, supporting methods of network-access control ranging from Microsoft's Network Access Protection to Cisco's Network Admission Control.

The anti-virus answer

"What is anti-virus, is the question," says Czarny, a 34-year-old computer science graduate of

OPSWAT inside

Products that include OPSWAT technology.

- Cisco's Clean Access NAC Appliance
- Endforce - Endforce Enterprise
- F5 Networks FirePass SSL VPN
- IPDiva SSL VPN
- iPass GoRemote
- Impulse SafeConnect Security Assistant
- Juniper Networks SSL VPN security appliances
- Lockdown Networks Network Access Control
- Looking Glass Systems LG Vision
- Senforce Smart Home Networking service
- Symantec Whole Security Confident Online

Note: 40 other undisclosed vendors use the Oasis or VPNGuard software development kits in their products.

Multitasking

What OPSWAT SDKs can do:

- Identify 400 versions of anti-virus, anti-spyware, VPN, anti-spam and anti-phishing software from 35 security vendors.
- Enforce patch updates.
- Monitor programs running on endpoints before granting network access.

Israel's Technion, Israeli Institute of Technology, who confesses to being a "bit nerdy" in his fascination with software code, which he started programming when he was 11 years old. "Anti-virus is configuring a system to scan and update."

Every anti-virus vendor, Czarny says, accomplishes this a different way — sometimes even differently in separate versions of the same product.

The API is supposed to be the direct path into how products work, so OPSWAT licenses every virus package it can find and seeks business relationships with as many vendors as it can to obtain the APIs.

But that approach doesn't always work.

"Sometimes vendors are open, sometimes they hide things," Czarny says. And he adds about the much-desired APIs: "Sometimes they just don't have them."

When OPSWAT meets those kinds of barriers, its software engineers in the United States and Israel have to dive into the security code using their own methods to be able to add the anti-virus software to the OPSWAT framework, which is basically an API for all other APIs.

Part of OPSWAT's mission is to uncover new anti-virus and anti-spyware companies. While McAfee, Symantec and Trend Micro have practically become household names in the United States, there are younger firms — such as Beijing Rising Technology, KingSoft and Jiangmin in China, and MicroWorld in India — that OPSWAT also works with.

"The reason we're contacting them is we have prospective customers based in East Asia that says these companies are important to our market, and we expect you to support them," says Tom Mullen, OPSWAT's vice president of business development.

Getting through the language barrier is a struggle, because the OPSWAT engineers don't speak Mandarin or other Asian languages, but sometimes OPSWAT's large global customers help with translation, Mullen says.

Several of OPSWAT's vendor clients, including Cisco, Lockdown Networks and Juniper, demur at discussing the developer's role in their products. But F5 gave credit where it is due.

A year ago F5 embedded

Benny Czarny: The man behind the company behind the security companies.

OPSWAT software in its FirePass SSL VPN gateway and client software to quickly add a security-check function that customers wanted.

"In an access scenario, a user would log on and perhaps provide credentials, perhaps just a simple password," for authentication, says Hari Krisnan, product manager at F5. "Now, before allowing access, FirePass can check the integrity of the client device for use of anti-virus software, for the latest signature files or just make sure patches are installed."

If FirePass determines a client machine doesn't meet security policy, that machine can be quarantined on a network for remediation purposes. (OPSWAT notes that its code is limited to the health check, and doesn't play a role in quarantine or actual remediation).

F5 turned to OPSWAT for help on the health-check portion of network-access control because "there are so many versions and vendors of anti-virus products to be supported, and a wide range of firewalls," Krisnan says.

Without OPSWAT, the software development process would have been long and tedious. By licensing the code, which can check a desktop using a Java or ActiveX applet, F5 was able to comprehensively add health-check functionality, he says.

OPSWAT licenses its code directly to only two customers: California State University, Fullerton, and Microsoft.

While Microsoft wouldn't discuss what it's doing with OPSWAT, Sean Atkinson, California State Fullerton's network analyst, says the college two years ago licensed OPSWAT's software and mandated that staff and faculty

working at home to use the VPN and to update anti-virus software.

"We use a Microsoft server for the quarantine," he says. "We're saying, 'we're not allowing you access to the campus network anymore without this [OPSWAT software]'."

The software works by informing users whether they meet security requirements. Atkinson says he knows OPSWAT is small, but its tech support has been good, and he has volunteered the college for beta tests of new versions.

Czarny says having Fullerton as a customer has helped gain attention from some larger vendors as the idea of policy-based access control gained sway in the industry a few years ago. But OPSWAT's focus will remain on development work for vendors, not users, he says.

For vendors embedding the code into their products, there is risk that a competitor with deep pockets could swoop in and buy OPSWAT, some analysts warn.

"OPSWAT is in the right place at the right time," says Gartner analyst John Pescatore. "But there is the risk that some player could grab it, and there would be a period of time the licenses are valid; that might end."

Others, including Joel Snyder, senior partner at consulting firm Opus One, says such fears are overblown. If OPSWAT gets gobbled up, he notes, another firm will come along to take on the task of pouring over endless numbers of security software products to support them in an API-based framework, if the need remains.

Perhaps so, F5's Krisnan says, but he hasn't seen one yet.

As for Czarny — whose hobbies include running the New York marathon — he says he's in OPSWAT for the long run and has no plans to sell out. ■

nww.com

Security event

Application and content security means more than a password and a firewall. It requires layered protection, perpetual scanning of all Web, SMTP, IM and FTP traffic, total defense in depth — the topics of Application & Content Security: Building a Defensible Network, the new Network World LIVE Technology Tour event for May. Register now and qualify to attend free. **www.nwdocFinder.com/3421**

■ **Network World** 118 Turnpike Road, Southborough, MA 01772-9108, (508) 460-3333.

Periodicals postage paid at Southborough, Mass. and additional mailing offices. Posted under Canadian International Publication agreement #40063800. Network World (ISSN 0887-7661) is published weekly, except for a single combined issue for the last week in December and the first week in January by Network World, Inc., 118 Turnpike Road, Southborough, MA 01772-9108.

Network World is distributed free of charge in the U.S. to qualified management or professionals.

To apply for a free subscription, go to www.subscribenw.com or write Network World at the address below. No subscriptions accepted without complete identification of subscriber's name, job function, company or organization. Based on the information supplied, the publisher reserves the right to reject non-qualified requests. Subscriptions: 1-508-490-6444.

Nonqualified subscribers: $5.00 a copy, U.S. $129 a year, Canada $160.50 (including 7% G.S.T. G.S.T. #126684662), Central & South America $150 a year (surface mail); all other countries $300 a year (airmail service). Four weeks notice is required for change of address. Allow six weeks for new subscription service to begin. Please include mailing label from front cover of the publication.

Network World can be purchased on 35mm microfilm through University Microfilms Inc, Periodicals Entry Dept, 300 Zeeb Road, Ann Arbor, Mich. 48106.

PHOTOCOPYRIGHTS: Permission to photocopy for internal or personal use or the internal or personal use of specific clients is granted by Network World, Inc. for libraries and other users registered with the Copyright Clearance Center (CCC), provided that the base fee of $3.00 per copy of the article, plus 50 cents per page is paid to Copyright Clearance Center, 27 Congress Street, Salem, Mass. 01970.

POSTMASTER: Send Change of Address to **Network World**, PO Box 3090, Northbrook, IL 60065. Canadian Postmaster: Please return undeliverable copy to PO Box 1632, Windsor Ontario N9A 7C9.

Copyright 2006 by Network World, Inc. All rights reserved. Reproduction of material appearing in Network World is forbidden without written permission.

Reprints (minimum 500 copies) and permission to reprint may be purchased from Reprint Management Services at (717) 399-1900 x128 or networkworld@reprintbuyer.com.

USPS735-730

MICROSOFT
CISCO
JUNIPER

of our company. We worked hard and played hard. It wasn't just about building a business—it truly felt like we were shaping the industry.

We used revenue from my consulting work to fund OESIS development, engaging closely with users for feedback and suggestions. This collaborative effort proved instrumental in refining our product while also enhancing network access and endpoint security solutions across the industry.

Our partnership with early adopters such as F5 was mutually beneficial. These early engagements provided valuable input into the product's development and helped shape a pricing model that rewarded these initial contributors. By working together, we did more than improve OESIS; we helped drive advancements in the broader cybersecurity industry and accelerated the improvement of early-adopters' products.

By 2008, it became clear that scaling OESIS to support multiple modules and applications would require a much larger R&D operation. To achieve this, I decided to establish a presence in Ho Chi Minh City, Vietnam, building a large engineering team, which allowed us to scale rapidly.

This strategic move enabled us to grow our technology from supporting thousands of applications to tens of thousands. The expansion not only strengthened our development capabilities, it also laid the foundation for continuous innovation at an unprecedented pace.

Competing With the Major Players

In the early days of OESIS, the warning signs were flashing, but not for the usual reasons most startups face. Often, if no one has attempted something similar, it might indicate there's no real market for the idea. But our dilemma was the opposite: We weren't the only ones working on this—we were up against the biggest names in cybersecurity.

From Microsoft to Cisco to Juniper Networks, everyone was racing to define the standards for NAC, VPNs, and SDPs—directly competing with our vision for a universal cybersecurity communication language. Like us, these companies recognized that the ability for security products to communicate seamlessly would determine who set the rules for the industry.

The Industry Giants Take Notice

It wasn't long before I started getting calls from the biggest tech companies.

First, Microsoft invited me to Redmond, Washington, where they pitched their vision for Network Access Control—a framework they wanted the entire cybersecurity industry to adopt.

I was then called to Cisco's headquarters in San Jose, California, to listen to their CTO outline a proprietary NAC system, which they fully expected to become the industry standard. Meanwhile, Juniper introduced its Trusted Network Connect (TNC) initiative, aiming to define the future of NAC through open standards.

The message was clear: If one of these giants succeeded in setting the standard, OESIS could become obsolete overnight.

The Race to Control Network Security Standards

Each company pushed its own framework, convinced it would dominate the market.

1. Juniper's Trusted Network Connect (TNC)

- Enforced Network Access Control, verified if devices had up-to-date antivirus software and system patches before allowing them onto the network.

- Built on standards from the Trusted Computing Group, offering enterprises a structured way to validate devices before granting access.

2. Cisco's Network Access Control (NAC)

- The centerpiece of Cisco's security strategy was enforcing strict compliance checks before letting devices into corporate networks.

- Cisco's massive reach meant enterprises had little choice: Align with their ecosystem or be left behind.

3. Microsoft's Network Access Protection (NAP)

- Designed for Windows Server environments, ensuring only health-patched systems could connect.

- For a time, NAP seemed unstoppable—until Microsoft eventually abandoned it in favor of newer security models.

How OESIS Beat the Competition

For OESIS, the release of these solutions by the three titans presented an existential threat. If cybersecurity vendors started implementing only these standards, our nimble solution would be rendered irrelevant. We had but one path forward: Deliver a platform so compelling, so flexible, and so inclusive that it transcended the giants' walled gardens.

Despite the intense competition, I was never willing to give up. From the outset, I saw fundamental flaws in each of the competing approaches and was dismissive of their narrow, vendor-locked vision. While companies like Microsoft, Cisco, and Juniper sought to dictate how cybersecurity products communicated, OESIS was built to do the opposite.

We envisioned a universal translator—a superset of interoperability—that could seamlessly bridge the gaps between security products, regardless of who the vendor was. This wasn't just about integration; it was about breaking down silos and creating a common language for cybersecurity.

Bringing the Common Cybersecurity Language to Life

To bring this vision to life—and to survive in a market dominated by industry giants— we built OESIS on three strategic pillars.

1. Simple to Join, Simple to Integrate

Where the big players created complex, expensive integration processes, OESIS prioritized accessibility and ease of adoption. For example, integrating with Cisco required expensive, six-figure networking hardware, weeks of setup time, and a cumbersome API integration process.

We chose a completely different path. Instead of forcing vendors to jump through technical and financial hoops, we simply requested a software license and handled the entire integration ourselves.

While Juniper, Microsoft, and Cisco held exclusive, invitation-only meetings at their corporate headquarters, we went directly to the cybersecurity community. At every event, we pitched partnership over dominance. While the tech giants dictated proprietary standards, we emphasized:

- **Compatibility:** Seamless integration with any security tool, from antivirus to NAC, VPNs, and SDPs.
- **Flexibility:** No rigid frameworks, just easy adoption and seamless security orchestration.
- **Ease of Integration:** No major development overhead—just plug-and-play interoperability.

By meeting vendors where they were, we bypassed corporate bureaucracy, built trust, and rapidly expanded OESIS's adoption. Instead of locking vendors into a walled garden, we gave them an open door to security collaboration.

UG!
SALOM
HI
SALUT
SVEIKI
HALLO
HI!
HOLA
HELLO
HEJ
BOK
AHOJ
CIAO
SAWATDEE
BİTAЮ
TERE
MOA OTI
BONJOU
SAWUBONA
BONJOUR
MERHABA
GEIA SAS
TALOFA
KAMUSTA
ALOHA!
XIN CHÀO
SALAM
MOLO
NǏ HǍO
KONNICHIWA
SZIA
SABAIDEE
HAI
OLA
CZEŚĆ
안녕하세요
AHOJ
ODI
HEI
MURAHO
MOHORO
WABULA
NÉIH HŌU!
SHALOM

2. A Business Model That Puts Partners First

The big players made it costly for cybersecurity vendors to join their ecosystems—charging program fees, requiring heavy integration investments, and favoring their own technologies. We did the opposite by making OESIS free for any cybersecurity technology partner. A licensing fee would be applied only to vendors actively using OESIS in their products.

This model made perfect sense. If a company was saving R&D costs or unlocking new security features using OESIS, it was fair for us to share in that success. Unlike restrictive vendor lock-in models, our open framework encouraged widespread adoption across cybersecurity vendors.

By eliminating up-front costs while linking monetization to real-world usage, OESIS became the industry-standard integration layer—a sustainable, mutually beneficial ecosystem where vendors could innovate freely while leveraging our security interoperability framework.

3. An Aggressive Go-to-Market Strategy

While Juniper, Microsoft, and Cisco relied on exclusive, invite-only partnerships, we took the opposite approach by actively participating in cybersecurity events. We also marketed OESIS's partnership program directly to vendors. And we demonstrated live integrations instead of just pitching theoretical ideas.

This aggressive marketing approach made OESIS impossible to ignore. By positioning ourselves as the practical, scalable alternative to the big players' closed ecosystems, we gained rapid visibility and industry trust.

As I write this, we are working on the fifth generation of OESIS, and I'm actively involved in planning the sixth. While we are no longer the only option for establishing communication between cybersecurity products, our journey has shown that even small and emerging companies can outthink initiatives from industry giants. Instead of imposing rigid frameworks, we focused on listening to real-world security challenges—and that made all the difference.

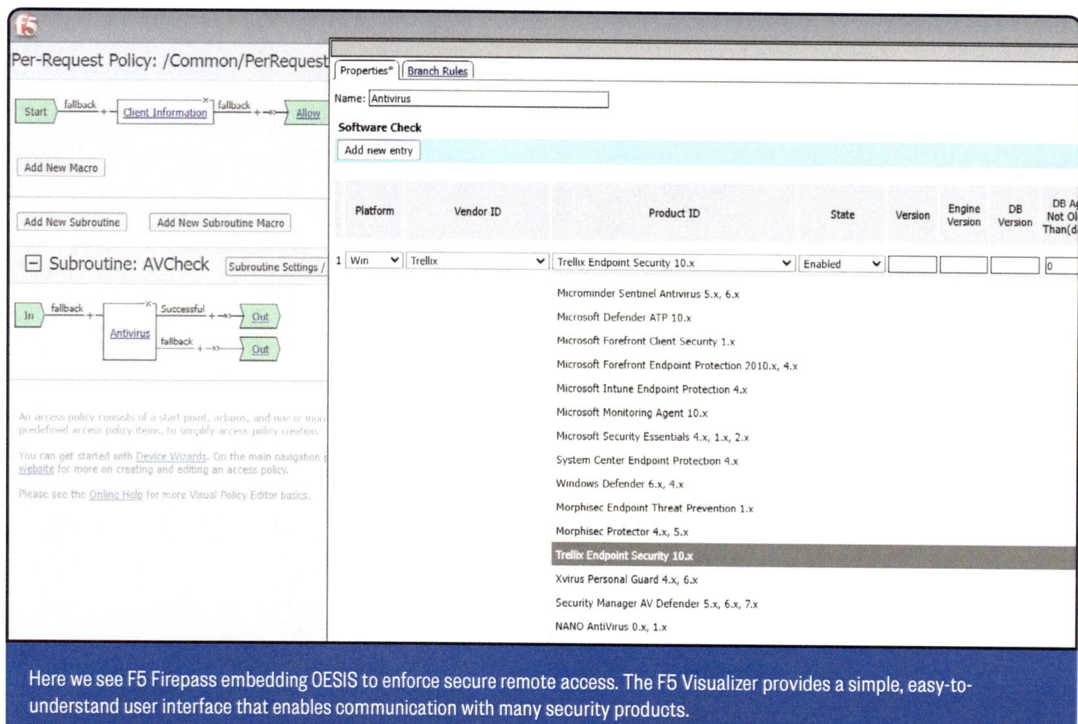

Here we see F5 Firepass embedding OESIS to enforce secure remote access. The F5 Visualizer provides a simple, easy-to-understand user interface that enables communication with many security products.

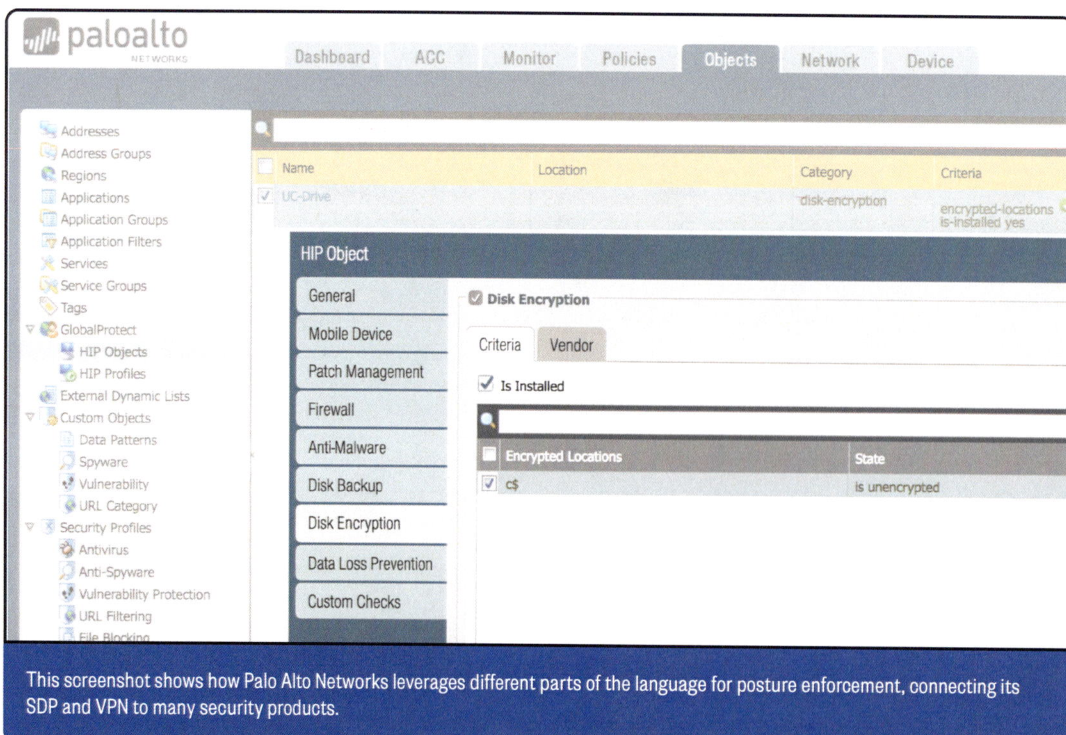

This screenshot shows how Palo Alto Networks leverages different parts of the language for posture enforcement, connecting its SDP and VPN to many security products.

Market Acceptance and Product Expansion

After our 2005 launch of general availability (GA), OESIS rapidly gained traction, with such industry leaders as Cisco, Hewlett-Packard, Palo Alto Networks, and many of their competitors adopting it. The OESIS language, acting as a universal translator, enabled detection, assessment, and management of many endpoint security products. Within three years, it was deployed on more than 100 million endpoints—which set the entire company on fire. Today, more than 150 million business devices across dozens of OEMs are benefitting from OESIS.

We were excited and felt a deep sense that we weren't just building a great business— we were making a real impact on the cybersecurity landscape.

This remarkable success stemmed from a collective decision among OESIS customers to integrate its capabilities by default. Companies such as Cisco and Palo Alto Networks embedded it directly into their VPN and NAC clients and other security products, making OESIS an essential component of modern endpoint security architecture. This broad adoption not only reinforced its value, but also positioned it as an industry standard.

Success in cybersecurity, however, isn't just about widespread adoption—it's about rigorous testing and continuous refinement. As we moved forward, a new challenge emerged: How could we ensure that OESIS maintained its reliability across an ever-evolving security landscape?

The accompanying screenshots on page 44 provide a detailed look at OESIS's integration, deployment scale, and functionality within endpoint security environments. They illustrate how it operates across different systems, manages security policies, and interacts with various endpoint security products.

Today, more than 150 million business devices across dozens of OEMs are benefitting from OESIS.

In Chapter 3, I will dive deeper into the testing methodologies that allowed us to push OESIS to its limits...and in the process, uncover a critical flaw in antivirus detection that reshaped our approach.

CHAPTER THREE

BUILDING THE FIREWALL OF DATA

Evolving threat defense with a data-first approach.

R eleasing a product is never the finish line—it's just the starting point. Once OESIS was deployed, our real work began: refining its capabilities, expanding integrations, and keeping up with an evolving cybersecurity landscape.

The launch wasn't a peak but a pivot—one that deepened our engagement with endpoint security. As OESIS gained traction, it provided us with a broad view of the cybersecurity ecosystem. We weren't just integrating with security products—we were mapping their features, identifying gaps, evaluating their effectiveness, and exposing their limitations. This insight allowed us to push the industry forward in a revolutionary new way.

Ensuring OESIS could seamlessly work with encryption products, anti-malware solutions, VPNs, identity and device posture systems, software-defined perimeter (SDP) technologies, compliance solutions, and network access control (NAC) required more than just compatibility—it demanded real security.

This required our team to focus relentlessly on quality. To accomplish this, we took four significant steps:

- **Build an extensive testing lab** to evaluate VPNs, antivirus solutions, NAC systems, and endpoint security products.

- **Enhance our core security functions,** diving deep into encryption, patch management, data loss prevention (DLP), and vulnerability assessments.

- **Scale our automated testing,** moving beyond manual quality assurance (QA) to catch and resolve issues faster.

- **Engage with cybersecurity vendors** to ensure OESIS was applied effectively in real-world scenarios.

As OESIS adoption skyrocketed, however (we were securing multiple original equipment manufacturers [OEM] deals each month), it became clear that traditional, manual testing methods couldn't keep up.

Accelerating Testing With Nexperior

With OESIS deployed on more than 100 million endpoints, I felt the weight of responsibility. Any defect could ripple across a significant portion of the cybersecurity ecosystem. Ensuring compatibility and reliability across a constantly shifting landscape of vendors, products, and operating systems quickly became a daunting task.

Security vendors pushed updates on unpredictable timelines, and those updates needed to work flawlessly across everything from Windows XP to Windows 11, macOS, Android, Chromebooks, and more. We needed an innovative solution that was faster, smarter, and truly scalable.

To meet this challenge, we created Nexperior, a next-generation automated testing system that became the backbone of our quality-assurance process.

Instead of manually validating each operating system, product, and command, Nexperior leveraged thousands of virtual machines to test every new version of OESIS against a vast array of security applications, operating systems, and configurations.

To make it work we:

- **Deployed thousands of virtual machines**, each configured with different operating systems, security applications, and settings.

- **Preloaded each machine** with a unique combination of OS versions and security software to mirror real-world environments.

- **Ran automated tests** across these environments, executing various commands and security scenarios while comparing results to expected benchmarks.

- **Generated detailed reports,** allowing us to make go/no-go decisions on releases and pinpoint areas of the code that needed improvement.

Nexperior didn't just speed up testing—it transformed how we ensured security, stability, and compatibility at scale. With every iteration, it allowed us to adapt, refine, and deploy OESIS with greater confidence, ensuring that each release met increasingly higher quality standards.

Developing Nexperior took months, but the effort paid off. More than just a tool, Nexperior completely revolutionized our testing methodology—expanding our testing capacity, validating our hypotheses, and uncovering unforeseen issues.

This led to faster, more informed release decisions and higher customer satisfaction. Some of our customers were so impressed they developed their own similar testing systems, inspired by Nexperior's success.

Nexperior Leads to a Startling Discovery

Our commitment to testing the quality of anti-malware systems led to a significant breakthrough, which was the concept of a "firewall for data" powered by multiscanning. Interestingly, part of this discovery was made purely by chance—an insight that surfaced while analyzing Nexperior's testing reports. Had I not taken a deep dive into these reports, I might have never uncovered it.

Nexperior evaluated dozens of product types and hundreds of detection methods per product. However, two key anti-malware techniques stood out as particularly crucial:

1. **Real-Time Protection**: This is a fundamental feature of modern anti-malware software. It continuously monitors the system, scanning files, applications, and processes the moment they are accessed or executed. Unlike scheduled scans, real-time protection instantly blocks, quarantines, or removes threats before they can cause harm.

2. **File Scanning**: This allows users to manually check specific files, folders, or an entire system for malware. Unlike real-time protection, which operates automatically in the background, file scanning is user-initiated or scheduled at set intervals. The system inspects files for known threats and suspicious behavior, alerting users when malware is detected. This is especially useful for external drives, newly downloaded files, or suspected infections that might have bypassed real-time protection.

Why Integration Is Critical

The OESIS framework has long supported these two functions across almost every anti-malware vendor and product. Nexperior was specifically designed to test these capabilities, proving that integrating real-time protection and file scanning was crucial for various security solutions.

This is particularly important for browsers, VPNs, SDPs, identity and device posture, and NAC solutions. Many organizations do not allow devices with real-time protection disabled to access their networks. Additionally, some organizations require a file scan or full-system scan as part of their compliance policies to ensure security before granting access.

Live Malware Testing in Nexperior

To thoroughly assess our interaction with anti-malware, we used live malware, including trojans and test viruses. Some of these threats were stored in Nexperior's virtual machines, while others were executed directly. We automated actions across all virtual machines to introduce malware under real-world conditions, ensuring a rigorous evaluation of endpoint security solutions.

Our mission was to **detect whether the OESIS language call for real-time protection and file scans was functioning properly.**

Once we automated our testing, we accidentally uncovered a significant anomaly: While moving sample malware into a folder, file scanning often failed to detect it as a threat. However, executing the same malware almost always triggered real-time

Nexperior Test Results

● Pass   ○ Fail

Virtual Machine	Operating System	Vendor	Product	Version	OESIS Version	Vendor Detected	Product Detected	Version Detected	Product Identity Test	Scan File	Get Threat Log	Update Definition File	Definition Version Detected	Detect Real Time Status
1	Windows XP	NortonLifeLock	Norton 360	22.5.4	3.5.34	●	●	●	●	●	●	●	●	●
2	Windows XP	McAfee	McAfee Total Protection	2023.1	3.5.34	●	●	●	●	●	●	●	●	●
3	Windows XP	Trend Micro	Trend Micro Maximum Security	19	3.5.34	●	●	●	●	●	●	●	●	●
4	Windows XP	Bitdefender	Bitdefender Total Security	25.0.10.52	3.5.34	●	●	●	●	○	●	●	●	●
5	Windows 7	Kaspersky Lab	Kaspersky Total Security	21.3.10.391	3.5.34	●	●	●	●	●	●	○	●	●
6	Windows 7	Avast	Avast Premium Security	21.4.2464	3.5.34	●	●	●	●	●	●	●	●	●
7	Windows 7	AVG Technologies	AVG Internet Security	22.2.3221	3.5.34	●	●	●	●	●	●	●	●	●
8	Windows 7	ESET	ESET Smart Security Premium	14.0.22.0	3.5.34	●	●	●	●	●	●	●	●	●
9	Windows 7	Sophos	Sophos Home Premium	3.1.2	3.5.34	●	●	●	●	●	●	●	●	●
10	Windows 7	Malwarebytes	Malwarebytes Premium	4.3.0	3.5.34	●	●	●	●	●	●	●	●	●
11	Windows 7	F-Secure	F-Secure SAFE	18.2	3.5.34	●	●	●	●	●	●	●	●	●
12	Windows 7	Panda Security	F-Secure SAFE	20.00.00	3.5.34	●	●	●	●	●	●	●	●	●
13	Windows 7	Webroot	Webroot SecureAnywhere AntiVirus	9.0.28.48	3.5.34	●	●	●	●	●	●	●	●	●
14	Windows 7	Comodo	Comodo Antivirus	12.2.2.7036	3.5.34	●	●	○	●	●	●	●	●	●
15	Windows 7	G Data Software	G Data Total Security	25.5.7.26	3.5.34	●	●	●	○	●	●	○	●	●
16	Windows 7	BullGuard	BullGuard Premium Protection	21.0.385.9	3.5.34	●	●	●	●	○	●	●	●	●
17	Windows 7	ZoneAlarm (by Check Point)	ZoneAlarm Extreme Security	15.8.139.18543	3.5.34	●	●	●	●	●	●	●	●	●
18	Windows 7	VIPRE	VIPRE Advanced Security	11.0.5.203	3.5.34	●	●	●	●	●	●	●	●	●

Virtual Machine	Operating System	Vendor	Product	Version	OESIS Version	Vendor Detected	Product Detected	Version Detected	Product Identity Test	Scan File	Get Threat Log	Update Definition File	Definition Version Detected	Detect Real Time Status
19	Windows 7	AhnLab	V3 Internet Security	9.0.9.1	3.5.34	✓	✓	✓	✓	✓	✓	✓	✓	✓
20	Windows 7	Avira	Antivirus Pro	15.0.2101.2070	3.5.34	✓	✓	✓	✓	✓	✓	✓	✓	✓
21	Windows 10	Quick Heal	Total Security	22	3.5.34	✓	✓	✓	✓	✓	✓	✓	✓	✓
22	Windows 10	Dr.Web	Security Space	12.0.2.9280	3.5.34	✓	✓	✓	✓	✓	✓	✓	✓	✓
23	Windows 10	Emsisoft	Anti-Malware	2021.10.0.11201	3.5.34	✓	✓	✓	✓	✓	✓	✓	✓	✓
24	Windows 10	ClamAV	ClamAV	0.103.2	3.5.34	✓		✓	✓	✓		✓	✓	✓
25	Windows 10	Microsoft	Defender Antivirus	2004	3.5.34	✓	✓	✓	✓	✓	✓	✓	✓	✓
26	Windows 10	Intego	Mac Internet Security X9	10.9.5	3.5.34	✓	✓	✓	✓	✓	✓	✓	✓	✓
27	Windows 10	Carbon Black (VMware)	Cloud Endpoint Standard	3.5.1	3.5.34	✓	✓	✓	✓	✓	✓	✓	✓	✓
28	Windows 10	CrowdStrike	Falcon	6.28.105	3.5.34	✓	✓	✓	✓	✓	✓	✓	✓	✓
29	Windows 10	Cylance	PROTECT	2.0.1570	3.5.34	✓	✓	✓	✓	✓	✓	✓	✓	✓
30	Windows 10	K7 Computing	K7 Total Security	16.0.0415	3.5.34	✓	✓	✓	✓	✓	✓	✓	✓	✓
31	Windows 10	Norman Safeground	Security Suite	22.5.4	3.5.34	✓	✓	✓	✓	✓	✓	✓	✓	✓
32	Windows 10	Total Defense	Essential Anti-Virus	2023.1	3.5.34	✓	✓	✓	✓	✓	✓	✓	✓	✓
33	Windows 10	TrustPort	Total Protection	19	3.5.34	✓	✓	✓	✓	✓	✓	✓	✓	✓
34	Windows 10	Fortinet	FortiClient	25.0.10.52	3.5.34	✓	✓	✓	✓	✓	✓	✓		✓
35	Windows 10	WatchGuard	Endpoint Security	21.3.10.391	3.5.34	✓	✓	✓	✓	✓	✓	✓	✓	✓
36	Windows 10	Sophos	Endpoint Security and Control	21.4.2464	3.5.34	✓	✓	✓	✓	✓	✓	✓	✓	✓
37	Windows 10	Norton	Norton 360	22.2.3221	3.5.34	✓	✓	✓	✓	✓	✓	✓	✓	✓
38	Windows 10	McAfee	Total Protection	14.0.22.0	3.5.34	✓	✓	✓	✓	✓	✓	✓	✓	✓
39	Windows 10	Trend Micro	Maximum Security	3.1.2	3.5.34	✓	✓	✓	✓	✓	✓	✓	✓	✓
40	Windows 10	Bitdefender	Total Security	4.3.0	3.5.34	✓	✓	✓	✓	✓	✓	✓	✓	✓
41	Windows 10	Kaspersky Lab	Total Security	18.2	3.5.34	✓	✓	✓	✓	✓	✓	✓	✓	✓
42	Windows 10	Avast	Premium Security	20.00.00	3.5.34	✓	✓	✓	✓	✓	✓	✓	✓	✓
43	Windows 11	AVG Technologies	Internet Security	9.0.28.48	3.5.34	✓	✓	✓	✓	✓	✓	✓	✓	✓
44	Windows 11	ESET	Smart Security Premium	12.2.2.7036	3.5.34	✓	✓	✓	✓	✓	✓	✓	✓	✓

Virtual Machine	Operating System	Vendor	Product	Version	OESIS Version	Vendor Detected	Product Detected	Version Detected	Product Identity Test	Scan File	Get Threat Log	Update Defenition File	Defenition Version Detected	Detect Real Time Status
45	Windows 11	Sophos	Home Premium	25.5.7.26	3.5.34	✓	✓	✓	✓	✓	✓	✓	✓	✓
46	Windows 11	Malwarebytes	Premium	21.0.385.9	3.5.34		✓	✓	✓	✓	✓	✓	✓	✓
47	Windows 11	F-Secure	SAFE	15.8.139.18543	3.5.34	✓	✓	✓	✓	✓	✓	✓	✓	✓
48	Windows 11	Panda Security	Panda Dome Premium	11.0.5.203	3.5.34	✓	✓	✓	✓	✓	✓	✓	✓	✓
49	Windows 11	Webroot	SecureAnywhere AntiVirus	9.0.9.1	3.5.34	✓	✓		✓	✓	✓	✓	✓	
50	Windows 11	Comodo	Antivirus	15.0.2101.2070	3.5.34	✓	✓	✓	✓	✓	✓	✓	✓	✓
51	Windows 11	G Data Software	Total Security	22	3.5.34	✓	✓	✓	✓	✓	✓	✓	✓	✓
52	Windows 11	BullGuard	Premium Protection	12.0.2.9280	3.5.34	✓	✓	✓	✓	✓	✓	✓	✓	✓
53	Windows 11	ZoneAlarm (by Check Point)	Extreme Security	2021.10.0.11201	3.5.34	✓	✓	✓	✓	✓	✓	✓	✓	✓
54	Windows 11	VIPRE	Advanced Security	0.103.2	3.5.34	✓	✓	✓	✓	✓	✓	✓	✓	✓
55	Windows 11	AhnLab	V3 Internet Security	2004	3.5.34	✓	✓	✓	✓	✓	✓	✓	✓	✓
56	Windows 11	Avira	Antivirus Pro	10.9.5	3.5.34	✓	✓	✓	✓	✓	✓	✓	✓	✓
57	MAC OS	Quick Heal	Total Security	3.5.1	3.5.34	✓	✓	✓	✓	✓	✓	✓	✓	✓
58	MAC OS	Dr.Web	Security Space	6.28.105	3.5.34	✓	✓	✓	✓	✓	✓	✓	✓	✓
59	MAC OS	Emsisoft	Anti-Malware	2.0.1570	3.5.34	✓	✓	✓	✓	✓	✓	✓	✓	✓
60	MAC OS	ClamAV	ClamAV	16.0.0415	3.5.34	✓	✓	✓	✓	✓	✓	✓	✓	✓
61	MAC OS	Microsoft	Defender Antivirus	22.5.4	3.5.34	✓	✓	✓	✓	✓	✓	✓		✓
62	MAC OS	Intego	Mac Internet Security X9	2023.1	3.5.34	✓	✓	✓	✓	✓	✓	✓	✓	✓
63	MAC OS	Carbon Black (VMware)	Cloud Endpoint Standard	19	3.5.34	✓	✓	✓	✓	✓	✓	✓	✓	✓
64	MAC OS	CrowdStrike	Falcon	25.0.10.52	3.5.34	✓	✓	✓	✓	✓	✓	✓	✓	✓
65	MAC OS	Cylance	PROTECT	21.3.10.391	3.5.34	✓		✓	✓	✓	✓	✓	✓	✓
66	MAC OS	K7 Computing	K7 Total Security	21.4.2464	3.5.34	✓	✓	✓	✓	✓	✓	✓	✓	✓
67	MAC OS	Norman Safeground	Norman Security Suite	22.2.3221	3.5.34	✓	✓	✓	✓	✓	✓	✓	✓	✓
68	MAC OS	Total Defense	Essential Anti-Virus	14.0.22.0	3.5.34	✓	✓	✓	✓	✓	✓	✓	✓	✓
69	MAC OS	TrustPort	Total Protection	3.1.2	3.5.34	✓	✓	✓	✓	✓	✓	✓	✓	✓

protection, effectively blocking the infection and preventing the virtual machine from being compromised.

After analyzing thousands of virtual machines with Nexperior, we found that:

- Real-time protection was highly effective—detecting threats around 80 percent to 95 percent of the time when connected to the internet, and around 60 percent to 90 percent when offline.

- In contrast, file scanning had a roughly 50-percent detection rate.

This stark difference was unexpected. Why was real-time protection so much more effective than file scanning? After all, both are designed to detect malware, yet one was failing far more often. More importantly, this issue wasn't unique to a single vendor—it was a widespread problem, affecting both reputable and disreputable antivirus engines.

My brain was spinning: Was it a fluke? If not, this could be huge. The entire industry relies on anti-malware file scanning, and if it's this ineffective, we have a serious problem. I needed to validate the whole thing.

Validating Our Findings

To me, the weakness of file scanning was big news. Could I be the only one who had noticed this? The intriguing results prompted me to validate our findings. I turned to external anti-malware testing companies and spoke with numerous anti-malware researchers and engineers.

How to Measure and Compare Anti-Malware Performance

It is important to note that the 95-percent success rate of real-time protection we achieved is not merely twice as effective as the 50-percent rate of file scanning.

Think of real-time protection and file scanning like the windshield of a car. Real-time protection is like near-bulletproof glass that stops 95 out of every 100 projectiles, while regular file scanning is like low-grade glass that stops only 50 out of 100 projectiles.

As many as 50 dangerous missiles can get through regular file scanning, while only five get through when using real-time protection. This means real-time protection is as much as 10 times more effective than regular file scanning. Just like a car's windshield, when it comes to security, the critical factor is how many threats manage to get through.

I began with AV-TEST and AV-Comparatives, independent organizations based in Germany and Austria, respectively. These firms are known for their rigorous testing of antivirus software and security solutions. My research confirmed (see diagram below) that their evaluations focused primarily on real-time protection, assessing how effectively anti-malware protects endpoints.

Vendor	Offline Detection Rate	Online Detection Rate	Online Protection Rate	False Alarms
Avast	95.6%	98.8%	99.95%	10
AVG	95.6%	98.8%	99.95%	10
Avira	94.3%	98.9%	99.95%	12
Bitdefender	96.1%	96.1%	99.92%	8
ESET	93.5%	96.3%	99.93%	10
F-Secure	95.7%	98.5%	99.97%	33
G DATA	96.7%	96.7%	99.93%	10
Kaspersky	71.1%	91.8%	99.90%	3
McAfee	58.7%	98.7%	99.91%	19
Microsoft	63.1%	97.5%	99.94%	18
Norton	81.8%	98.9%	99.97%	26
Panda	49.1%	89.5%	99.57%	39
Quick Heal	44.6%	67.4%	99.24%	157
TotalAV	95.7%	97.8%	99.94%	12
Total Defense	96.0%	96.0%	99.94%	15
Trend Micro	45.1%	84.5%	97.10%	3

While industry vendors do a good job of offering real-time, endpoint protection for devices, their solutions lack the depth, context, and accuracy needed to analyze individual files to detect malware before an actual attack occurs.

Attending the Virus Bulletin and AVAR conferences, where anti-malware experts shared their latest research, gave me a chance to dig deeper. Conversations with specialists from different security companies confirmed what I had suspected—real-time protection was far more effective than file scanning.

The more I learned, however, the more questions I had. Why was real-time protection more effective? And if the benefits were so obvious, why wasn't anyone talking about it?

These questions led me to take a deeper look at modern anti-malware architecture to understand why real-time protection outperforms file scanning.

Why File Scanning Falls Short

To break this down, let's first look at the key components of a typical anti-malware system. While the list on the accompanying diagram isn't exhaustive (apologies to my fellow anti-malware architects), it provides enough context to explain how these systems work. More importantly, it sheds light on why real-time protection consistently outperforms traditional file scanning.

The illustration on page 57 shows the layered architecture of a modern, anti-malware solution, highlighting how detection and protection mechanisms work together with a focus on real-time protection and scanning capabilities.

Real-time protection excels over file scanning in detecting and responding to threats because it has access to immediate, comprehensive information. The sensors described above that monitor processes, memory, registry, file systems, network traffic, and peripheral media allow real-time protection to identify suspicious activities quickly. For example, real-time protection can detect unusual network traffic or repetitive, abnormal behavior patterns as they happen. It can then immediately block potential threats through drivers and control mechanisms while alerting the user. This immediacy enhances security and provides a steady stream of real-world data that helps further train machine-learning models to reinforce security.

While file-scanning methods catch a lot of malware under certain conditions, they fall short when compared to real-time protection. File scanning relies on foreknowledge to make pre-execution predictions about a file's behavior before execution. This can be difficult or sometimes impossible, especially when dealing with encrypted, executable payloads and other complex, obfuscated, or delayed execution malware.

File scanners look for evidence within a file to detect viruses using the following methods:

- **Signature-Based Detection** compares files against a database of known malware signatures (a unique string of bytes or a pattern that is characteristic of a specific piece of malware). It is effective against recognized threats, but highly dependent on frequent updates.

- **Heuristic Analysis** looks at a file's characteristics and how it behaves to detect suspicious patterns. It uses algorithms to predict if a file might be harmful based on its structure, how it interacts with the system, and whether it tries to hide itself. For example, if a binary was compiled just an hour ago, that could be suspicious—especially if it comes from an unknown source—because most legitimate software is compiled well before it is widely distributed.

The Layered Architecture of a Modern Anti-Malware Solution

The numbers here correspond to the definitions on the following pages.

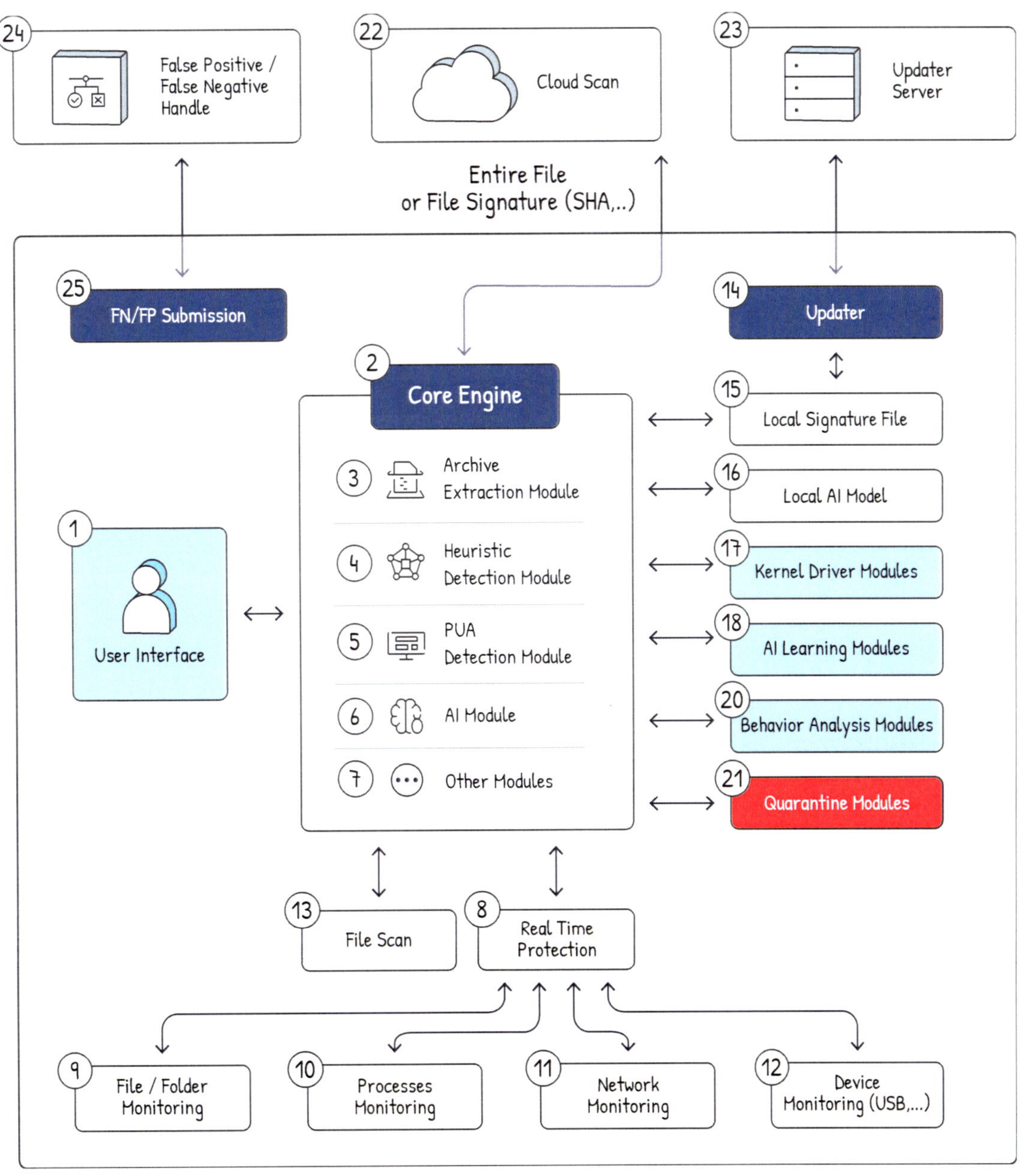

(1) **User Interface**: The front end of the anti-malware software, where users can interact with the program. This interface allows users to initiate file scans, check the security status, configure settings, and view alerts.

(2) **Core Engine**: Where most of the essential security operations occur. Multiple modules are orchestrated here.

(3) **Archive Extraction Module**: Handles the extraction and scanning of files contained within archive formats, including purely archival ZIP and ARJ files, and other archive types, such as Word, PPT, Docs, and many other productivity tools that are archived.

(4) **Heuristic Detection Module**: Employs heuristic analysis to detect new or unknown malware based on behavior and characteristic patterns rather than known signatures. For example, it can check when files were constructed and compare them to the original date.

(5) **PUA Detection Module**: Identifies potentially unwanted applications, such as torrents (a method of sharing and distributing files using the BitTorrent protocol) or specific browser extensions, which, while not always harmful, can affect system performance and compromise privacy.

(6) **AI Module**: Uses artificial intelligence technologies to enhance the detection of complex threats and improve response strategies. It typically uses other modules and sensors (below) to arrive at this conclusion.

(7) **Other Modules**: Various additional security functions tailored to specific needs.

(8) **Real-Time Protection**: A continuous monitoring system that detects and stops threats in real time. It includes sensors (usually installed as drivers to the operating system) to detect and prevent threat propagation at the operating system level.

(9) **File/Folder Monitoring Sensor**: Monitors changes in files or folders that might indicate a security threat (e.g., for file replication or file creation in specific parts of the operating system). The sensor driver can block files from being created or replicated to prevent malware propagation.

(10) **Processes/Memory Monitoring Sensor**: Watches active processes for signs of malicious behavior, such as process interaction with other parts of the operating systems, the replication of the process, threat creation, and memory consumption. The sensor can also prevent a process from being created, terminate processes or applications, and restrict process forking.

(11) **Network Monitoring Sensor:** Checks network traffic for unauthorized or malicious communications, such as suspicious IPs or URLs. It can also block network traffic in case of suspicious activity.

(12) **Peripheral Device Monitoring Sensor**: Monitors external devices such as USB drives to detect and block threats.

(13) **File Scan**: A system that enables users to manually or automatically initiate scans of specific files, directories, or entire systems to detect and eliminate malware using signature databases, heuristics, and pattern matching, with notifications and quarantine actions for identified threats.

(14) **Updater**: Regularly updates the anti-malware software with the latest virus definitions and AI models to ensure protection against new threats. It also updates the anti-malware components.

(15) **Local Signature Files**: Maintain a database of known malware signatures that the software uses to recognize and block known threats. It is key to speeding up malware detection for common or known malware.

(16) **Local AI Model**: Houses the AI learning model that is trained to predict and detect potential threats based on learned patterns.

(17) **Kernel Driver Modules**: Operate at a low level within the system to monitor and protect against threats that are deeply integrated into the operating system.

(18) **AI Learning Modules**: Where the AI system continually learns from new data updating its model to recognize new threats. AI learning tends to connect with the anti-malware vendor's cloud and helps train other anti-malware components from the same vendor about common threats detected on this specific endpoint.

(19) **Behavior Analysis Modules**: Analyze software or file behaviors to identify actions that may indicate the presence of malware.

(20) **Quarantine Modules**: Safely isolate suspicious files to prevent them from causing damage while further analysis or remediation takes place.

(21) **Cloud Scan**: Leverages cloud-based resources to perform additional layers of scanning and analysis on threats.

(22) **Updater Server**: A remote server from which the local updater fetches updates to keep the anti-malware solution current.

(23) **False Positive/False Negative Handler**: Manages the instances where files are incorrectly flagged (false positives) or threats are missed (false negatives), including mechanisms for users to submit feedback on these errors. It typically connects to the AI module to train for known good, known bad, and the quarantined module.

While heuristic analysis is great for spotting new malware, it can sometimes flag harmless files as threats if the detection rules are too broad.

- **File Reputation** evaluates the reputation of files against a cloud-based database, which is based on factors such as the file's age, its prevalence among users, and whether it has been previously identified as malicious by other users. It requires a cloud connection and big-data analysis.

- **Machine Learning-Based Detection** analyzes large datasets of known malware and legitimate files to train predictive models. These models detect subtle patterns and anomalies that traditional methods might miss, allowing them to identify zero-day threats and polymorphic malware. Machine learning improves accuracy over time, but it requires significant computational resources and ongoing model refinement to minimize false positives and adversarial manipulation.

My conclusion was that file scanning had a fundamental weakness—it had to guess whether a file was malicious before execution by relying on predefined rules and limited detection capabilities. Conversely, real-time protection continuously monitors system activity and identifies threats based on behavioral anomalies that indicate an attack is in progress. This makes it far more effective, especially against unknown threats.

This is also where machine learning thrives in real-time environments by cross-referencing massive datasets and correlating alerts with live attack patterns to improve detection and response accuracy.

Ultimately, it all clicked when I realized that anti-malware solutions were never truly designed for file scanning. Their core function had always been endpoint protection—built to detect and neutralize threats at runtime as they attempted execution. File scanning wasn't a primary feature. It was tacked on later to support scheduled scans or improve system performance by preemptively checking files.

Over time, security vendors and enterprises misused anti-malware engines as file scanners, integrating them into email security, web-application firewalls, and secure-web gateways, even though they were never built for that purpose. These tools lacked the necessary depth, context, and accuracy to analyze files in isolation. Even the vendors blurred the lines between real-time protection and file scanning, in part because testing organizations weren't distinguishing between the two. This made it even harder to see the gap.

At the end of the day, even technical audiences and CTOs at anti-malware companies could check the box without delving into the details of what the test was actually measuring when presented with 99.9 percent detection rates by AV-Comparatives.

The industry had placed blind trust in a security model that was fundamentally broken. The failures were obvious, and I didn't need theoretical models to prove it. I had real-world cases in which malware had completely bypassed traditional file-scanning, antivirus solutions.

I started to ask myself: *Am I onto something bigger? Can I solve a deeper problem in cybersecurity?*

File Scanning in Modern Cybersecurity

File scanning is a foundational component of modern cybersecurity defenses, acting as a proactive measure to detect and eliminate malware before execution. It provides a pre-execution security layer, ensuring that malicious files are identified and neutralized before they reach an endpoint, network, or cloud environment.

Rather than developing proprietary malware detection capabilities, however, the cybersecurity industry has increasingly relied on OEM anti-malware engines. Security vendors integrate third-party file-scanning solutions into their products instead of building their own detection systems. This is very similar to how I described OEMing OESIS in Chapter 2. Instead of reinventing a security framework, companies embed proven technologies into their offerings.

Nearly every major anti-malware company OEMs its scanning engine to other vendors, allowing them to perform file scanning across different security layers. The widespread OEM integration highlights how file scanning extends beyond endpoint security by powering critical security products across multiple data channels.

Here are some key cybersecurity solutions that rely on OEM file scanning. The reason I've listed them is to underscore the many ways that data can flow into your organization and how file scanning is so tightly woven into so many cybersecurity products that are used today. What's critical to understand here, however, is that while file scanning is great, without prior file sanitization, you're simply opening the door for bad actors to access your data.

Email Security Gateways (SEG)

- **Role:** Scans emails, attachments, and embedded links to detect malware, phishing, and other malicious payloads before they reach end users.

- **Use of OEM File Scanning:** Email security solutions integrate OEM anti-malware engines to inspect malicious attachments, hidden scripts, and phishing links.

- **Examples:** Proofpoint, Mimecast, Barracuda, and Microsoft Defender for Office 365.

Web Application Firewalls (WAFs)

- **Role:** Protects web applications by filtering and monitoring Hypertext Transfer Protocol (HTTP) traffic, blocking malicious payloads, web exploits, and injected scripts.

- **Use of OEM File Scanning:** WAFs leverage file-scanning engines to detect malware embedded in file uploads, HTTP/HTTPS traffic, and API requests.

- **Examples:** Imperva, Akamai, Cloudflare, and Fortinet.

Secure Web Gateways (SWGs)

- **Role:** Monitors and filters internet traffic to enforce security policies, block malicious sites, and prevent malware downloads.

- **Use of OEM File Scanning:** SWGs integrate anti-malware scanning to inspect downloaded files, website scripts, and encrypted HTTPS traffic for threats.

- **Examples:** Zscaler, Forcepoint, Netskope, and Cisco Umbrella.

Cloud Access Security Brokers (CASBs)

- **Role:** Provides visibility and control over cloud applications while enforcing security policies for cloud data protection.

- **Use of OEM File Scanning:** CASBs scan cloud-stored files for malware, data leaks, and compliance risks before allowing access or transfer.

- **Examples:** McAfee MVISION Cloud, Microsoft Defender for Cloud Apps, and Palo Alto Networks Prisma Cloud.

Managed File Transfers (MFTs)

- **Role:** Secures and automates file transfers between enterprise systems, ensuring compliance with data-protection regulations.

- **Use of OEM File Scanning:** MFT solutions integrate malware scanning to prevent infected files from being sent, received, or stored in corporate environments.

- **Examples:** GoAnywhere MFT, MOVEit, and IBM Sterling Secure File Transfer.

Cross-Domain Security Solutions

- **Role:** Ensures secure data exchange between isolated security domains by enforcing content inspection and malware scanning.

- **Use of OEM File Scanning:** Cross-domain gateways integrate file scanning to prevent malicious file infiltration across different security zones.

- **Examples:** Forcepoint High-Speed Guard, Owl Cyber Defense, and OPSWAT NetWall.

System Integration and Embedded Security

- **Role:** Embeds file-scanning technology directly into enterprise workflows to ensure continuous security across all IT environments.

- **Use of OEM File Scanning:** Anti-malware scanning is integrated into SIEMs, SOAR platforms, DLP (Data Loss Prevention) systems, and enterprise security frameworks.

- **Examples:** Splunk (Cisco), IBM QRadar (Palo Alto Networks), Symantec DLP (Broadcom), and Microsoft Defender XDR.

Secure Browsers and Remote Browser Isolation (RBI)

- **Role:** Prevents malware infections by isolating web content and executing it in a remote, sandboxed environment.

- **Use of OEM File Scanning:** Secure browsers scan file downloads, web scripts, and plug-ins before execution to prevent drive-by attacks.

- **Examples:** Menlo Security, Cloudflare Browser Isolation, and Citrix Secure Browser.

Such dependence on traditional file-scanning, anti-malware engines within so many of the security apparatus's cornerstones created substantial gaps in threat detection and prevention, through which all manner of nastiness could slip through.

My Second Big Idea: Use Multiscanning to Build a Firewall for Data

The question facing OPSWAT now became: How to build a file scanner that could be a "firewall for data" that worked just as well as real-time protection? It was clear to me that the file scanners on the market were all weak, but that was likely because the problem they were attempting to solve was extremely difficult.

Rather than trying to reinvent the wheel, I envisioned a "firewall for data" based on "multiscanning"—a solution that used multiple file scanners at once. Each file-scanning engine would capture a distinct set of malware, which would boost detection rates significantly. My thinking was that if one engine had a 50-percent chance of catching malware, combining two independent engines could improve detection by 75 percent (assuming there was no overlap in their capabilities).

Adding a third engine could potentially increase effectiveness to around 87.5 percent, and adding a fourth would up the detection rate to more than 93 percent. This integrated approach could dramatically enhance cybersecurity defenses, and it quickly became OPSWAT's second big idea for a product—multiscanning.

If we could make file scanning work better using multiscanning, we could build a system that was purpose-built to intercept and analyze data across all vectors, including file uploads, downloads, emails, USB transfers, and storage systems.

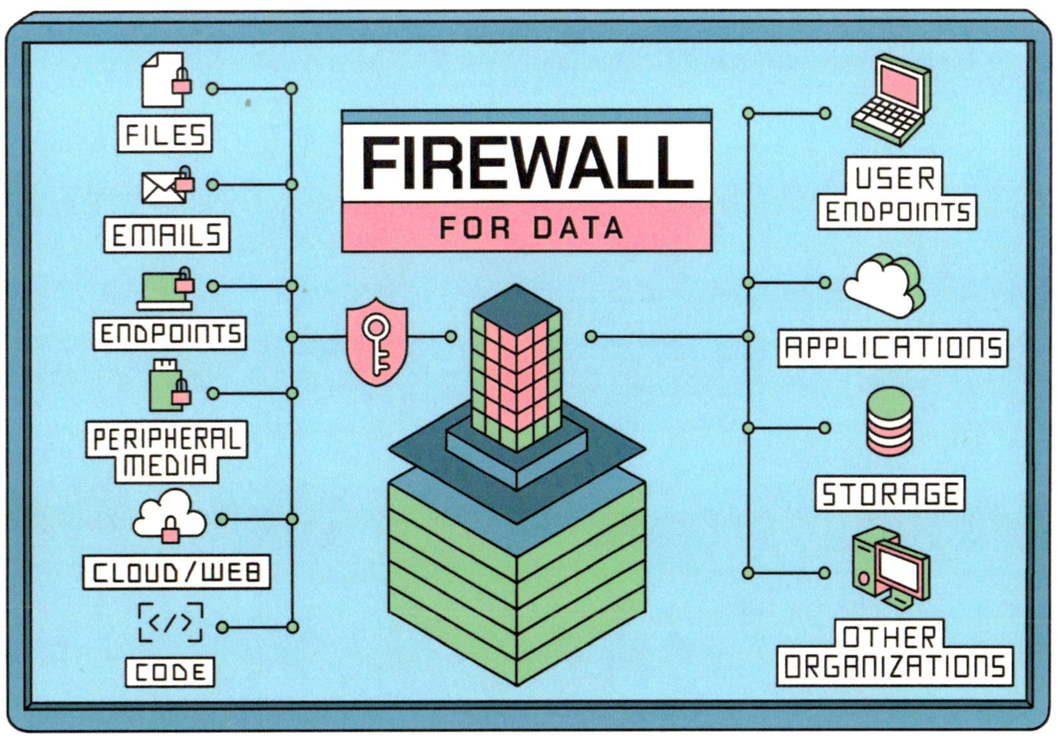

The Mathematical Foundations of Multiscanning

I wondered how many engines I would need to include in my firewall for data to protect an organization fully. Here is the statistical analysis I undertook to evaluate the potential of combining multiple anti-malware systems.

Let's consider two independent antivirus solutions: Antivirus A and Antivirus B.

- $P(A)$ is the probability that Antivirus A detects a specific malware.
- $P(B)$ is the probability that Antivirus B detects the same malware.

To determine the likelihood that at least one of these antivirus solutions detects the malware, we can follow this mathematical progression:

- Miss A: The probability that Antivirus A fails to identify the malware = $1 - P(A)$.
- Miss B: The probability that Antivirus B similarly misses = $1 - P(B)$.
- Both Miss: The combined probability that both A and B fail to identify the malware = Miss A × Miss B.
- At Least One Detects: The probability that one (or both) antivirus engines spot the malware = 1 − Both Miss.

This can be encapsulated in this formula:

$$At\ Least\ One\ Detects = 1 - [(1 - P(A)) \times (1 - P(B))]$$

Building the Firewall for Data Based on Multiscanning

I considered forming a separate company to address the unique challenges of enterprise- and OEM-focused businesses. Unlike the partner-driven OEM model used by OESIS, the multiscanning-based firewall for data required a direct-sales approach that included marketing, customer support, and a scalable sales team. This was not a decision I took lightly, as very few companies have successfully pivoted from an OEM business to an enterprise security company.

Ultimately, I decided to keep the project within OPSWAT while ensuring the R&D, support, and sales teams remained separate. This structure allowed us to retain the agility of an enterprise product without disrupting the OEM side of the business.

Keeping our firewall for data in-house also allowed us to leverage OPSWAT's engineering, financial, and legal infrastructure, while still meeting the unique needs of an enterprise customer base.

One of the most important factors in this decision was my long-standing relationships with antivirus (AV) vendors. At OPSWAT, I had direct access to key AV providers, many of whom I had worked with for years.

These relationships were critical to our success, giving us an edge in securing malware-scanning engines for integration. Keeping the project within OPSWAT also maximized our strengths and set us up for long-term success.

Overcoming the Biggest Hurdle: Gaining Access and Building Trust

As we launched the firewall for data project (we later officially named it "Metascan"), I knew that the biggest challenge would be gaining access to multiple anti-malware engines. Security vendors were hesitant to license their engines, out of fear that we might compete with their primary endpoint protection businesses.

However, thanks to our strong industry relationships—facilitated by OPSWAT's SVP of Business Development, Tom Mullen—we were able to directly engage with key decision-makers at leading AV companies. Still, getting them to trust us with their intellectual property required careful positioning.

I made it clear that Metascan was not designed to compete with traditional antivirus solutions but to enhance enterprise security workflows, where endpoint protection alone was insufficient. We demonstrated that Metascan could drive broader adoption of their scanning engines by integrating them into multiscanning solutions.

In addition, we always aimed to exceed forecasts—even if our initial projections were modest, we consistently pushed to outperform them. And, more often than not, we succeeded.

Overcoming the Complexities of Multiscanning

Scaling Metascan to support 30 different anti-malware engines demanded a deep dive into the heart of each vendor's technology. We found ourselves in near-constant contact with OEM teams—frequently tracking feature updates, release cycles, bug reports, and sometimes even negotiating directly with CEOs. The toughest hurdle was persuading these companies to trust us with their intellectual property.

To address this, we built a transparent and detailed accounting system that tracked every usage instance and ensured payments reached them on time. That level of financial clarity convinced many AV vendors that OPSWAT was both safe to work with and uniquely poised to deliver real innovations in multiscanning. As our relationships grew stronger, some vendors even offered to publicly endorse Metascan themselves, which added further credibility to our approach.

A key turning point came when I received a phone call from the Department of Homeland Security, in which they recognized Metascan's potential. This validated our vision to protect some core systems and helped tip the scales for several additional antivirus vendors who had been on the fence about licensing their engines to us.

With those partnerships in place, Metascan began to evolve into a truly comprehensive product capable of leveraging a wide range of detection methods, heuristics, and machine learning.

Building a Robust Multiscanner

Persuading vendors to adopt Metascan, however, was only half the story. Actually integrating these engines into a single system took an intense engineering push. We needed to handle simultaneous scans on massive file batches, master the complexities of multiple-archive formats, and wrangle the idiosyncrasies of more than two dozen scanning engines into one comprehensive solution.

Adding to the complexity was that each antivirus engine vendor had its own architecture, performance quirks, API, and upgrade path. This created countless potential points of failure if our solution was not carefully orchestrated. Overcoming this technical challenge would be difficult, but the payoff would be worth it. Ultimately, our Metascan solution was able to provide a number of significant benefits:

1. **Higher Detection Coverage:** The more engines we used, the broader the detection coverage would become. By leveraging multiple AV engines, we could identify which ones detected the outbreak first, allowing for quicker response and mitigation.

2. **Hedging Against Vulnerabilities:** Relying on multiple engines safeguarded against the risk of any single scanner having a critical flaw or being affected by compliance mandates. For example, if an engine had a security vulnerability, it could be temporarily disabled without significantly impacting overall protection. Additionally, if an engine was restricted due to government regulations in certain countries, the system could continue to function without major disruption by relying on the remaining engines.

Eliminating False Positives and Other Challenges

Along with these key benefits, multiscanning also raised several key challenges. One of the biggest issues was false positives. By using multiple AV engines to analyze the same file, detection logic discrepancies often led to conflicting verdicts. If one engine had an $X\%$ false-positive rate and another had $Y\%$, a simple expectation would be that the total false positive rate would be $X+Y$. In reality, however, the increase was less than expected, as AV engines tended to make similar classification mistakes.

Despite this, the increase in false positives was still significant, which created unnecessary noise for security teams. To address this, we developed our own allow-list engine to filter out known clean files. This reduced unnecessary quarantines and improved overall scan efficiency.

Another major challenge was cost management. As we scaled Metascan to 30 AV engines, the costs of licensing additional AV engines quickly added up. Each AV vendor had its own pricing structure and API usage fees, which made large-scale licensing complex and expensive. To mitigate this, we introduced AV engine "packages," which allowed customers to select only the engines relevant to their needs. This reduced costs without sacrificing security. In addition, we negotiated bulk licensing deals with AV vendors, offering higher-volume commitments in exchange for cost reductions. This proved beneficial for both OPSWAT and our vendors.

Performance optimization also became a growing concern. Running 30 AV engines in parallel significantly increased CPU, memory, and disk I/O usage, which could potentially lead to slowdowns. To counter this, we built a custom archive-handling engine that extracted files once and distributed the extracted contents to all AV engines in memory, rather than having each AV engine perform redundant extractions. This drastically reduced disk I/O bottlenecks and improved efficiency. We also leveraged multi-core processor architectures, assigning different AV engines to different CPU cores. This ensured optimal resource distribution.

Our biggest challenge, however, was that Metascan needed to operate seamlessly across radically different environments, each with unique deployment challenges. Some clients required cloud-based deployments with elastic scaling, while others needed on-premises systems capable of receiving real-time updates from the internet. Meanwhile, highly secure organizations operated air-gapped facilities that were entirely disconnected from external networks.

To meet these challenges, we had to build specialized engineering teams—each with different skill sets tailored to specific deployment models. Supporting air-gapped environments required us to develop a manual update packaging system, which ensured that AV engines and signatures could be securely transferred and updated without internet access.

For cloud customers, we engineered native cloud deployments, which optimized resource allocation, automated scaling, and seamless API integrations. By tailoring our approach to each environment, we ensured Metascan could provide consistent, high-performance threat detection, regardless of the deployment mode.

More Engines. Better Detection.

Running through a series of 30 iterations, where each antivirus engine starts with a 50-percent detection rate, we observed a fascinating trend: The more antivirus engines you use, the likelihood of malware evading detection diminishes rapidly, eventually becoming infinitesimal. Based on my calculation I would need about 30 different anti-malware engines to achieve greater than 99-percent "effectiveness," meaning that the system would miss no more than one out of 1 billion malware instances. Here's how I expected the detection rates to improve as we incorporated more antivirus engines into our model.

Number of Engines	Probability of Detecting Malware
1	50%
2	75%
3	87.5%
4	93.75%
5	96.875%
6	98.4375%
7	99.21875%
8	99.609375%
9	99.8046875%
10	99.9023438%
11	99.9511719%
12	99.9755859%
13	99.987793%
14	99.9938965%
15	99.9969482%
16	99.9984741%
17	99.9992371%
18	99.9996185%
19	99.9998093%
20	99.9999046%
21	99.9999523%
22	99.9999762%
23	99.9999881%
24	99.999994%
25	99.999997%
26	99.9999985%
27	99.9999993%
28	99.9999996%
29	99.9999998%
30	99.9999999%

Building Metascan was an engineering triumph, but turning it into a market-ready product was a completely new challenge. The concept of a firewall for data was revolutionary by focusing on files rather than just networks or endpoints. This also meant we had to persuade a skeptical market to adopt an entirely new security approach.

My experience with OESIS had been within a narrow, OEM-driven model, with a small number of customers and a lean sales approach. However, Metascan required a broader go-to-market strategy that spanned marketing, direct sales, support, and product packaging.

Even though file scanning wasn't as proactive as real-time protection, I knew that a data firewall could still block a massive number of cyber threats, provided we did an exceptional job explaining its value. Without clear messaging and strong marketing, however, even the best security innovations risked being overlooked.

A Strategic Focus on System Integrators and API-Driven Growth

I decided to target system integrators first, addressing specific parts of the firewall for data vision before expanding into other areas. I took this approach because, while bootstrapping the business, I remained pragmatic and disciplined. Even though we were generating cash, I didn't want to overextend or become overconfident. I wanted to take an agile and calculated approach that focused on system integrators, who typically understand enterprise security architectures. These specialists often step in after a breach has occurred and, I hoped, were technically savvy enough to see the value in Metascan's approach.

I also realized that the fastest go-to-market strategy for an API-based product was to prioritize building a stable engine with a well-structured API, rather than focusing too much on user interface (UI) development upfront. This style suited how I liked to operate.

Of course, our initial attempts at pitching Metascan didn't gain traction, so we quickly revamped our messaging, simplified our website content, and replaced all the technical jargon with real-world examples to illustrate how a single, unscanned file could lead to a security breach. This shift helped system integrator prospects visualize how Metascan might fit into their existing security infrastructure and how it could catch advanced malware that traditional scanners missed.

Growing Metascan's Capabilities

The next data channel we tackled was **removable media security.** This included USB drives and SD cards, which were still a blind spot for many organizations. To address this, we built "Metascan for Secure Media," a kiosk-based scanning station that worked like an ATM and provided an automated, self-service security checkpoint for guests and employees to scan removable media.

This system allowed users to insert their USB drives or SD cards, scan them against multiple AV engines, and receive a security report before connecting the device to the network. Many organizations—particularly those in government, defense, and critical infrastructure—quickly realized that securing removable media this way significantly reduced their exposure to malware.

Building on this success, the next logical step was endpoint enforcement, so we developed an endpoint agent that applied Metascan's removable-media security directly on devices. Now, instead of relying only on self-service kiosks, companies could scan and enforce security policies in real time whenever a USB drive was plugged into a machine in their network.

From there, we turned our focus to email, web, and network security channels—the most common avenues for malware delivery. This led us to integrate ICAP (Internet Content Adaptation Protocol), a technology used by web proxies, secure web gateways, and network firewalls to offload content scanning and filtering to external security engines. By integrating Metascan with ICAP, we made it possible for organizations to scan web traffic, email attachments, and network-transferred files at scale to block malicious payloads before they reached users or critical infrastructure.

As Metascan's capabilities grew, so did our go-to-market strategy. Selling a single file-scanning product was one thing, but selling a full security platform meant expanding our sales capabilities. To meet this challenge, we onboarded traditional channel partners and distributors, which gave more organizations access to our technology while ensuring stronger regional support for enterprise customers.

By this point, the Firewall for Data vision was truly taking shape. No longer just a concept, OPSWAT was becoming a real enterprise security company, protecting hundreds of organizations from threats hidden inside data. We had gone from a niche file-scanning tool to a comprehensive security solution, embedding deep, multilay-ered scanning into enterprise workflows—whether on endpoints, networks, email, or removable media.

Questions Arise About Metascan's Detection Acumen

By 2008, hundreds of customers were utilizing Metascan features, including API integrations, USB scanning, and email protection. Metascan-Online, our public-facing offering that allowed people to upload and test files, was seeing increased traffic and integration requests.

Our support team, led by Dan Lanir, also began worrying about encountering malware that might bypass Metascan even though we were using more than 30 anti-malware engines. We faced incidents where the transferred data did not achieve the industry-standard reliability, commonly referred to as "nine nines," or 99.9999999-percent effectiveness. These discrepancies were troubling: Were my calculations incorrect? Could we genuinely deliver the firewall for data? How could I confidently assure our customers? And what, if anything, could be done to improve our multiscanning approach?

Our first step in answering these questions was to gather malware samples from customers. This offered us direct insight into the threats that were bypassing our security measures. However, it quickly became clear that simply analyzing these samples wouldn't be enough to resolve the underlying issues. We needed a lot more data to be confident about our conclusions.

By 2006, several companies, most notably FireEye, introduced sandbox technology as a potential solution for advanced malware detection. The idea was to execute suspicious files in an isolated environment and observe their behavior to determine if they were malicious. The expectation was that this approach could detect zero-day threats, polymorphic malware, and evasive techniques that traditional file scanning might miss.

We explored whether sandboxing could complement Metascan's multiscanning technology. While the concept seemed promising, practical implementation revealed significant limitations that made sandboxes less effective than we anticipated. Three primary drawbacks stood out:

1. Performance Issues: Malware Evasion Techniques

By the time sandboxes were widely adopted, malware authors had already developed techniques to evade them. Modern threats can detect when they're being executed in sandbox environments, prompting them to either halt activity or stay dormant until they reach a real user's machine. Some threats assume they'll be tested in a sandbox and apply evasion tactics, such as delaying execution or encrypting parts of their payload to avoid inspection.

"Sleep delays" are a common evasion method, whereby the code pauses execution for several minutes or even hours—knowing most sandboxes monitor for only a brief window (typically one to five minutes). Another evasion technique is "environment fingerprinting," scanning for signs of virtualization, low CPU usage, or the presence of analysis tools, such as Wireshark or Process Monitor. When such signs are detected, the code may shut down or mimic benign behavior to bypass detection.

The Carbanak malware, famously used by the FIN7 cybercrime group, checked for these sandbox indicators before launching. If it found unusual registry keys, low system uptime, or no signs of user interaction, it stayed inactive. This approach helped FIN7 remain undetected for years while successfully targeting financial institutions.

2. Specificity Limitations: The Golden Image Constraint

Sandboxing operates on the principle of a "golden image"—a predefined system configuration used to analyze file behavior. This approach relies on static baselines, making it too narrow and file-focused to adapt to the wide variety of malware tactics and execution environments.

For example, if an organization wanted to protect itself, it would create a golden image of its employee environment, including Windows, Office, Adobe, and other business-critical applications. The sandbox would then monitor for potential file-borne threats that could impact these systems. However, this approach is almost impossible to govern due to the growth of bring-your-own-device (BYOD) policies. Organizations often do not control or even know the exact configurations being used on employee devices, which makes it impossible to maintain a single golden image that reflects all potential execution environments. In addition, larger enterprises may require multiple golden images to support different departments, regions, or job roles, further complicating sandbox implementation. As a result, sandboxing technology became less effective, and impractical for large-scale organizations that were struggling to keep pace with the complexity and diversity of modern IT environments. Here's a prime example.

Many banking trojans, such as TrickBot and Emotet, use region-specific execution techniques. If the malware detects that it is running in an unexpected system locale (e.g., a U.S.-configured sandbox instead of a European user system), it stays inactive or deletes itself. Sandboxes that only relied on standardized, U.S.-based golden images were blind to these geolocation-based evasions. One notorious example was the Russian APT group Cozy Bear (APT29), which used malware that only executed properly in enterprise environments with specific domain configurations. If the malware didn't detect a corporate active directory setup, it would terminate. Since many sandboxes don't replicate fully functional enterprise networks, this type of malware escaped detection in sandbox environments but was highly effective in real-world attacks.

3. Operational Inefficiency: Slow, Resource-Intensive, and Costly

Organizations processing large volumes of files daily face other challenges that can impact production and the bottom line. For example, a typical appliance is designed to handle up to 1,000,000 objects per day. And the hardware costs roughly $10,000.

This capacity translates to approximately 116 objects per second. While this through-put may suffice for some organizations, those dealing with millions of files per day would require multiple appliances operating in parallel to meet their demands. The need for numerous high-capacity appliances not only escalates hardware and operational costs, but it also introduces complexities in managing and maintaining infrastructure. Consequently, for large-scale operations, traditional sandboxing solutions may prove impractical and inefficient, prompting the exploration of more scalable and cost-effective security measures.

Revisiting Sandbox Technology: The Filescan.io Acquisition

While we initially moved away from sandboxing due to its well-documented limitations, the technology continued to evolve. What once seemed like an impractical approach was starting to show potential—but only after significant advancements were made.

By 2020, a new model emerged: "adaptive emulation." Unlike traditional sandboxes, which relied on a fixed-system image, adaptive emulation dynamically adjusted to

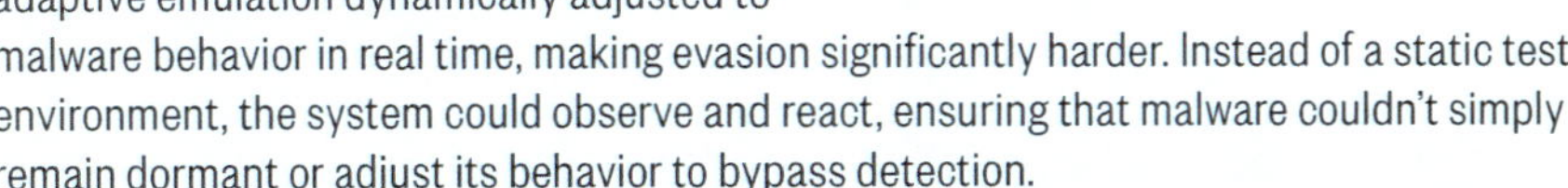

malware behavior in real time, making evasion significantly harder. Instead of a static test environment, the system could observe and react, ensuring that malware couldn't simply remain dormant or adjust its behavior to bypass detection.

Recognizing the potential of this evolved model, we acquired Filescan.io in 2022. This was a modern malware analysis platform developed by Jan Miller, which used adaptive emulation instead of legacy sandboxing. Its key advantages are speed, scalability, and better detection. Unlike traditional sandboxes, Filescan.io didn't require full virtualization for every single file, making it far more efficient while still providing deep behavioral insights.

That said, let's be clear—Filescan.io was not a silver bullet. It did not replace multiscanning, heuristic analysis, or behavioral monitoring. It added another layer of detection, but it didn't eliminate the need for other security measures. Sandboxing—no matter how advanced—is still just one detection technology, not a complete security solution.

Digging Deep Into the Numbers

To test the real effectiveness rate of multiscanning, I needed to go far deeper into the numbers, but how could we do this? I needed data and a study to determine the exact effective rate of multiscanning. After all, I had a growing number of customers using Metascan, more and more deployments, and I had in mind a conceptual 99.9999999-percent protection level that went far beyond what my marketing pitch could yet capture.

Once we recognized that sandboxes weren't the answer, we launched a thorough investigation into the effectiveness of static file scanning. In order to do this, I needed to create a central repository where users, the community, and our customers could upload files (mainly malware) so we could investigate malware efficacy for static scanning using all of our anti-malware solutions. I couldn't get this data from the industry organizations or other testing groups, so we did it ourselves.

To achieve this, we built a site called "Metadefender.com," which was formerly known as Metascan-Online and also Filterbit. The multiscanning feature was originally part of Metascan. Later, however, when Content Disarm and Reconstruction (CDR) was added, Metascan was renamed MetaDefender, as it encompassed more than just multiscanning.

This platform would scan files using all anti-malware engines and serve as a testing ground for all file-scanning capabilities. It also became a great demonstration tool. Users could upload a file and quickly see how our product scanned it.

Through Metadefender.com, we collected invaluable data on the effectiveness of anti-malware engines. However, we wanted to gain even more malware samples and insights, so we enhanced the platform with API-submission capabilities for our customers. We also partnered with anti-malware vendors and asked them to submit malware to the site. Finally, we added a web crawler that constantly fed the site with malware samples.

At one point, we were receiving millions of malware submissions and scanning hundreds of thousands of malware samples daily. Each malware sample was analyzed across all anti-malware engines, and we developed algorithms around classifying malware and measuring anti-malware efficacy.

To get concrete answers, we decided to create a study focused on the 10,000 most common threats (see chart on page 77), since we found them to be more relevant for enterprises when making qualitative decisions about anti-malware solutions. These threats were identified by being recognized by at least four of the anti-malware engines within Metadefender.com. This study provided a comprehensive snapshot of the cybersecurity challenges facing our system and, by extension, our clients and daily users.

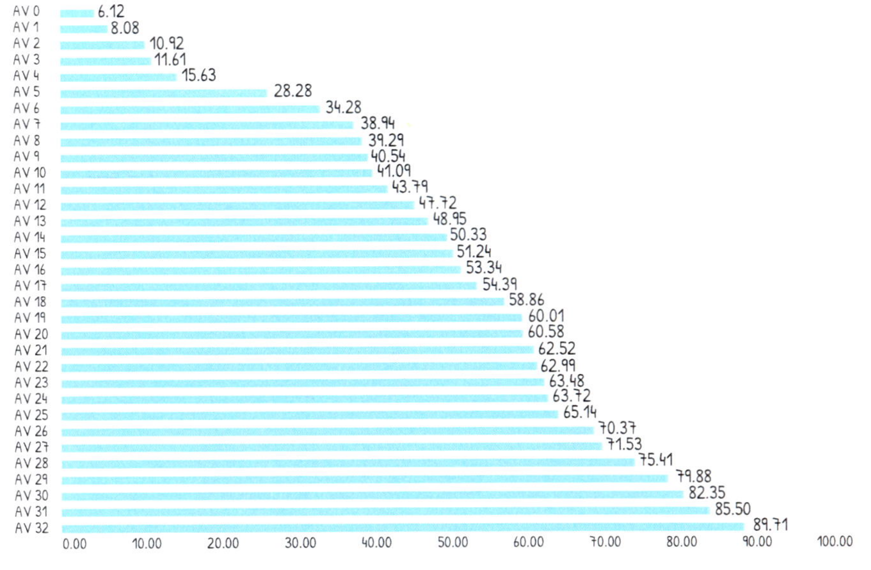

Looking at this graphic, you might be wondering why we kept the names of anti-malware engines private, especially if you're interested in choosing the most effective one. One reason is that this information is very sensitive for our anti-malware partners. In addition, the rankings of these engines fluctuate frequently—an engine rated #1 today might drop to #20 tomorrow, and vice versa. These fluctuations are influenced by a number of factors, including the changing threat landscape, quality controls of anti-malware engines, and even simple things like the fact that R&D members might be on vacation or signature updates might not be available during holidays because some key anti-malware engines don't update during certain holidays.

It's a constantly moving target as vendors race to stay ahead of the latest threats. So, while an engine might rank #1 today, that same engine could drop tomorrow as others catch up or leap ahead.

We then compared the effectiveness of our static-file-scanning capabilities across 32 different anti-malware solutions to deepen our understanding of malware detection dynamics and occasional failures.

The graph on page 78 provides a visual representation of our findings and methodology.

This exercise also pointed out the need for ongoing updates and enhancements to our algorithms and scanning techniques to keep pace with evolving digital threats. It also led us to our next research focus: determining the value of multiscanning.

The insights from our analysis of Metadefender.com data proved invaluable in optimizing our Metascan solution. It helped us enhance our malware detection strategies, select the right engine packages, optimize our archive engine, and identify areas for improvement in anti-malware technologies, which ultimately improved our performance.

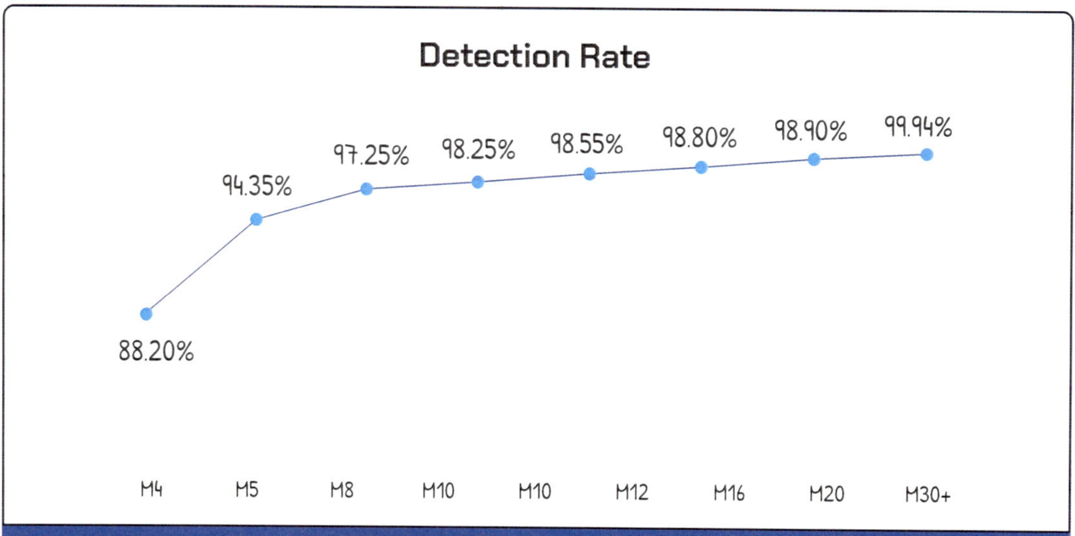

While adding 30 different anti-malware engines boosted the efficacy of malware detection to 99.94%, I was still disappointed; this fell far short of the 99.9999999% detection rate I was after. This setback, however, led me to abandon a "detection-first" mindset and begin thinking about how to eliminate malware in a new way through Content Disarm and Reconstruction (CDR).

Facing an Uncomfortable Reality

Metadefender.com told a story that challenged our assumptions about how well multiscanning could work. We had to come to grips with a key finding from our tests. As we expected, the average effectiveness of individual anti-malware engines, based on Metadefender.com data, was about 48.5 percent. This was consistent with the previously observed 50-percent effectiveness.

However, repeated testing also revealed that while using 30 different anti-malware engines enhanced protection, it only boosted our detection rate to between 99.92 percent and 99.94 percent for the top 10,000 malware threats. While this is significantly above the average, it still fell short of the near-perfect score of 99.9999999 percent we were after.

Repeated tests confirmed that detection rates hit a natural limit, which plateaued at 99.94 percent (see Figure 3). This raised the question of why we weren't reaching a 99.9999999 percent detection rate while multiscanning with 30 anti-malware engines.

Why Perfection Was So Elusive

The question of why we couldn't achieve a higher rate of efficacy became a major topic of discussion between myself and numerous anti-malware CEOs and technology leaders.

Despite the sophistication of modern anti-malware solutions, several factors restrict their effectiveness.

1. **Inherent Limitations of File-Based Detection**

    Anti-malware solutions face an extremely difficult challenge: They need to predict whether a file is malicious or not in a very short time. They usually rely on signatures, heuristics, and machine learning, but each has inherent limitations.

    Signature-based detection is highly effective for known threats, but it fails against zero-day malware and polymorphic attacks, which constantly modify their code to evade detection.

    Heuristic analysis improves detection by identifying behavioral patterns rather than exact signatures. This allows it to spot unknown threats. However, heuristics operate on predefined rules, meaning that if malware behaves just outside those parameters, it can bypass detection. In addition, heuristic detection often triggers false positives, flagging legitimate applications that perform low-level system operations, such as registry modifications, script execution, or encryption, as suspicious. The challenge is balancing aggressive detection without overwhelming users with false alerts that degrade operational efficiency.

    Machine learning and AI-driven detection technologies bring adaptability by learning from large datasets to help identify new and evolving threats without relying on specific patterns or signatures. However, AI models are only as good as the data they are trained on, which means new attack methods can still bypass them.

    Adversarial techniques used by bad actors, such as small code modifications or obfuscation, can fool AI classifiers. This can allow malware to masquerade as benign software. AI is also prone to generating both false positives and false negatives, as attackers can train models to exploit detection weaknesses. This makes such exploits highly effective at evading machine-learning-based security solutions.

2. **Malware File Sharing**

    A common practice among anti-malware engines is the sharing of malware signatures. When one engine detects a new threat, it shares this information with the others. This collaborative approach significantly boosts the capacity to handle outbreaks and provides a competitive edge to the first detector.

However, this method also means that the detection capabilities of different products can quickly become homogenized, leading to similar performance and shared vulnerabilities.

3. **Sharing Algorithms**

   The cybersecurity industry often sees a high turnover of professionals moving between companies. This mobility leads to the sharing of ideas and strategies, including the algorithms used to detect malware. While this can foster innovation and improvement, it also results in the development of many anti-malware products that have similar underlying detection methodologies. Consequently, if malware is crafted to bypass one product, it may also bypass others.

My discussions with industry leaders made it clear that achieving perfect security might be theoretically impossible. It was like we were trying to travel at the speed of light—one might get closer and closer, but the ultimate boundary seemed theoretically unreachable. This was a big deal, because it suggested that my initial assumption about the power of multiscanning might be wrong. I needed to look even deeper.

For years, we struggled to understand why multiscanning didn't perform as well in practice as our mathematical models predicted. We were using 30 anti-malware engines, each with a high individual detection rate, yet the real-world effectiveness fell short of expectations. The breakthrough moment came when I realized that our original probability model was fundamentally flawed because we had overestimated the independence of detection events.

The Aha Moment: Applying Conditional Probability

When I first developed the probability formula for multiscanning detection—

$$At\ Least\ One\ Detects = 1 - [(1 - P(A)) \times (1 - P(B))]$$

—the idea was straightforward: If two antivirus engines are completely independent, combining them should significantly improve your chances of detecting malware.

We quickly realized, however, that anti-malware engines don't work in silos. In fact, they often share signatures, heuristics, and even threat intelligence feeds. So, while the classic probability formula for independent events is $P(A\ or\ B) = P(A) + P(B) - P(A\ and\ B)$, this doesn't quite reflect reality.

If Engine A detects a threat, there's a strong chance that Engine B already knows about it. This overlap means the engines aren't truly independent—their detection capabilities are often correlated. So, the actual boost in detection you get from combining engines may not be as dramatic as the formula suggests. This led me to revise our model using conditional probability, which accounts for overlapping detection capabilities. The new model is represented by the formula:

$$P(A \mid B) = P(A \text{ and } B) / P(B)$$

In this formula:

- $P(A \mid B)$ represents the probability of Engine A detecting malware given that Engine B has already detected it.
- $P(A \text{ and } B)$ is the joint probability of both engines detecting the malware.
- $P(B)$ represents the probability of Engine B detecting the malware.

This discovery now led to a complete change in my original nonconditional probability assumption.

Turning the Page on the Multiscanning Story

Exploring the data this way marked the beginning of a critical new chapter in my pursuit to perfect the firewall for data concept. It was a humbling realization that even with 30 anti-malware engines, I was not able to achieve the level of security I had envisioned. That said, Metascan's failure to perform as expected was more than just a disappointment—it quickly turned into a major frustration and, at times, even anger.

I was disheartened by the industry's overreliance on detection-based security and the realization that, despite all our efforts, traditional multiscanning wasn't enough to achieve true data security. Rather than accepting these shortcomings, I came to an unsettling conclusion that perhaps the issue wasn't just in the technology but in the way the entire industry thought about security. If detection alone wasn't enough, what else was needed?

For years, the cybersecurity industry had built its defenses around detection—scanning for known threats, applying heuristics, and leveraging AI models to predict malicious intent. But even with the most advanced detection techniques, vulnerabilities—especially zero-days—could still slip through undetected. The more I studied, the more I realized that no amount of detection could fully solve the problem. A different approach was needed—one that didn't rely on identifying threats at all.

This realization led me to a new strategy, one that would redefine file security altogether by turning cybersecurity upside down.

CHAPTER FOUR

RETHINKING CYBERSECURITY WITH DATA SANITIZATION

Breaking the cycle of detect-and-respond with a new model: prevention through file regeneration.

OPSWAT's journey so far felt both exciting and frustrating. At each stage I felt like I was able to turn a big idea into a successful product, which was great. However, each successful product launch led to more questions, and the recognition that even bigger problems needed solving. So it was with OESIS, the product that was born out of our first big idea for building a cybersecurity language (cross-product communication), and with the Metascan product that came out of our second big idea about creating a multiscanning-based Firewall for Data.

As our development of Metascan advanced, the strategies we used broadened from partnerships with system integrators to implementing additional products like file upload/download kiosks, Managed File Transfer (MFT), and email solutions. These initiatives proved successful and helped Metascan's business surpass our growing OESIS OEM operations. The OPSWAT Metascan kiosk, equipped with multiscanner technology, even became the standard in nuclear facilities nationwide and a testament to the crucial role of our stakeholders in our success.

Despite our multiscanning technology's market traction and malware prevention capabilities, however, I remained concerned. Part of my role as CEO is to not merely lead our organization forward to build better solutions, but also to be the chief dissatisfaction officer. Most days I wake up happy with what we have built at OPSWAT. But I also have days when I say, "I suck! I need to do better."

I realized I had moved beyond the need for detection altogether.

In 2008, with respect to achieving our ultimate goal of a truly effective Firewall for Data, I felt we'd missed the mark, but everyone else in the industry had missed it as well. As I explained in Chapter 3, detection, in general, even when enhanced with multiscanning, remained problematic. We expected to catch 99.9999999-percent of all malware, but instead we only caught 99.92 to 99.94 percent using our multiscanning technology. Traditional methods, like sandboxes, while helpful, ultimately fell short because they were slow, costly, and still let a lot of malware through. For me, such performance was clearly not good enough.

I felt a profound sense of responsibility—not only to our internal team and customers, but also to myself in my quest to make a substantial impact on the cybersecurity industry. There had to be a better way to achieve the 99.9999999 goal. And it needed to be innovative, practical, and efficient.

Finding a new way forward to safeguard OPSWAT's customers might require a departure from conventional malware detection strategies.

The Third Big Idea: Prevention Through Regeneration

Whether it's malware or vulnerabilities, the cybersecurity industry always seems to be one step behind the bad actors, reacting rather than preventing cyberattacks. I started by asking several fundamental questions:

1. Why is the entire cybersecurity industry constantly playing catch-up?

2. Is this just the nature of cybersecurity, or is it a habit we need to break out of?

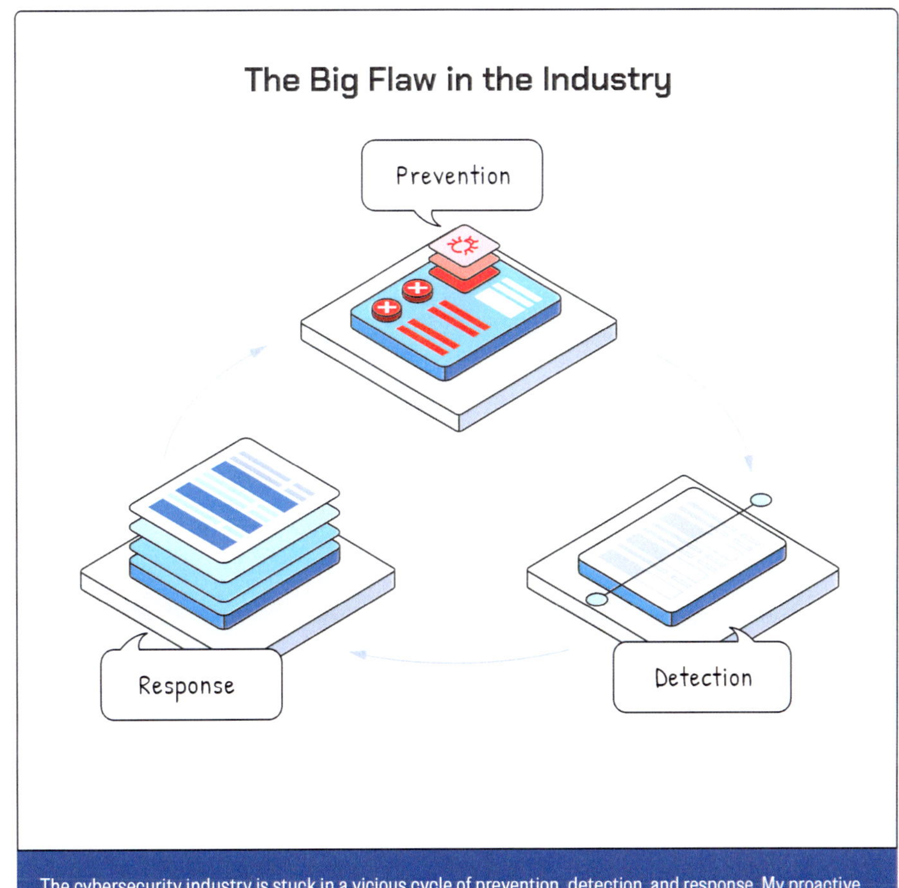

The cybersecurity industry is stuck in a vicious cycle of prevention, detection, and response. My proactive approach to preventing cyberattacks eliminates malware before files enter your network.

At its core, cybersecurity has always been a battle of good versus evil: attackers innovating while defenders scramble to adapt. It's a never-ending cat-and-mouse game, and an AI-versus-AI arms race between detection and evasion.

Signatures, heuristics, and machine learning are all designed to identify threats. Yet, attackers continually succeed in breaching networks by using deception, exploiting new vulnerabilities, and staying ahead of defensive technologies. So the real question is: **Are we stuck in a flawed security model, and, if so, how do we shift from playing catch-up to proactively preventing cyberattacks?**

The reason the cybersecurity/anti-malware industry exists is to prevent malware from disrupting operations and inflicting harm. However, as I pointed out in Chapter 3, one super helpful way to do this is to protect the flow of data into an organization in the first place. That's the mission of a Firewall for Data. Below is what the data flow into most organizations looks like.

The journey I described in Chapter 3 led me to a whole new architecture that employed 30 anti-malware engines and sandbox technology. Though the diagram on page 87

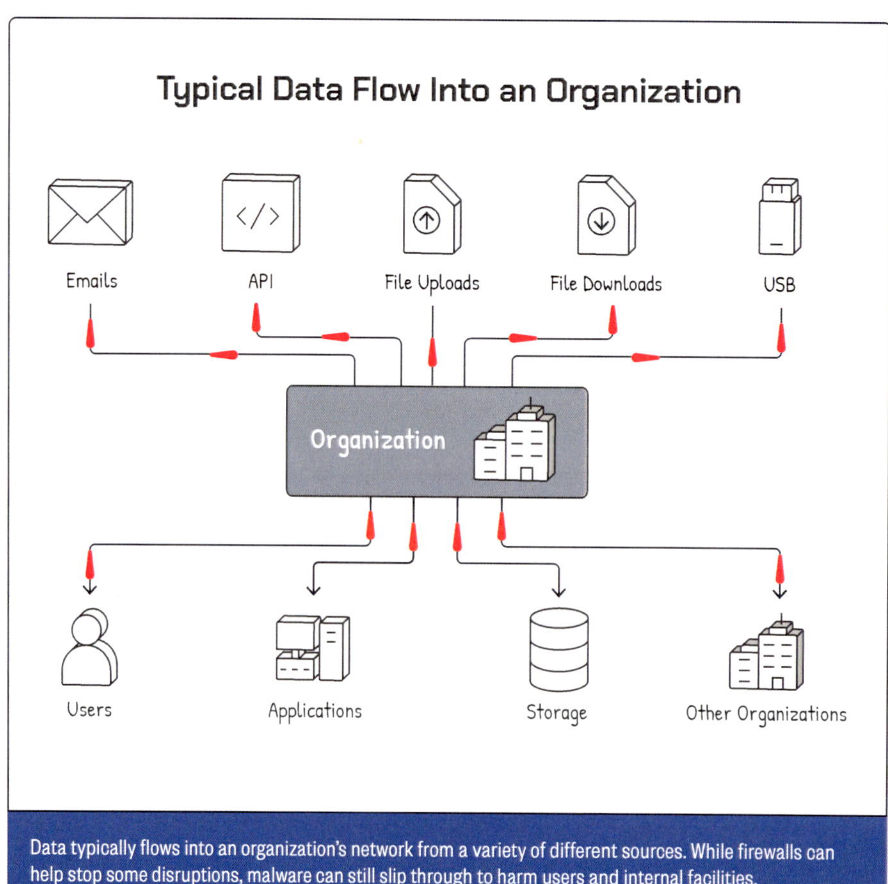

Data typically flows into an organization's network from a variety of different sources. While firewalls can help stop some disruptions, malware can still slip through to harm users and internal facilities.

represents an ideal deployment of a firewall for data protection, it quickly became apparent that such a system may not be practical for everyone due to the costs involved to implement it.

Unfortunately, this architecture leaves us with a flawed approach to detecting and preventing malware from entering systems. Multiscanning and sandboxes have advantages over basic file-scanning, but too much malware still gets through and problems like zero-day vulnerabilities are not addressed.

So, if detection is flawed, can we discard it ? And if we eliminate detection, what do we replace it with?

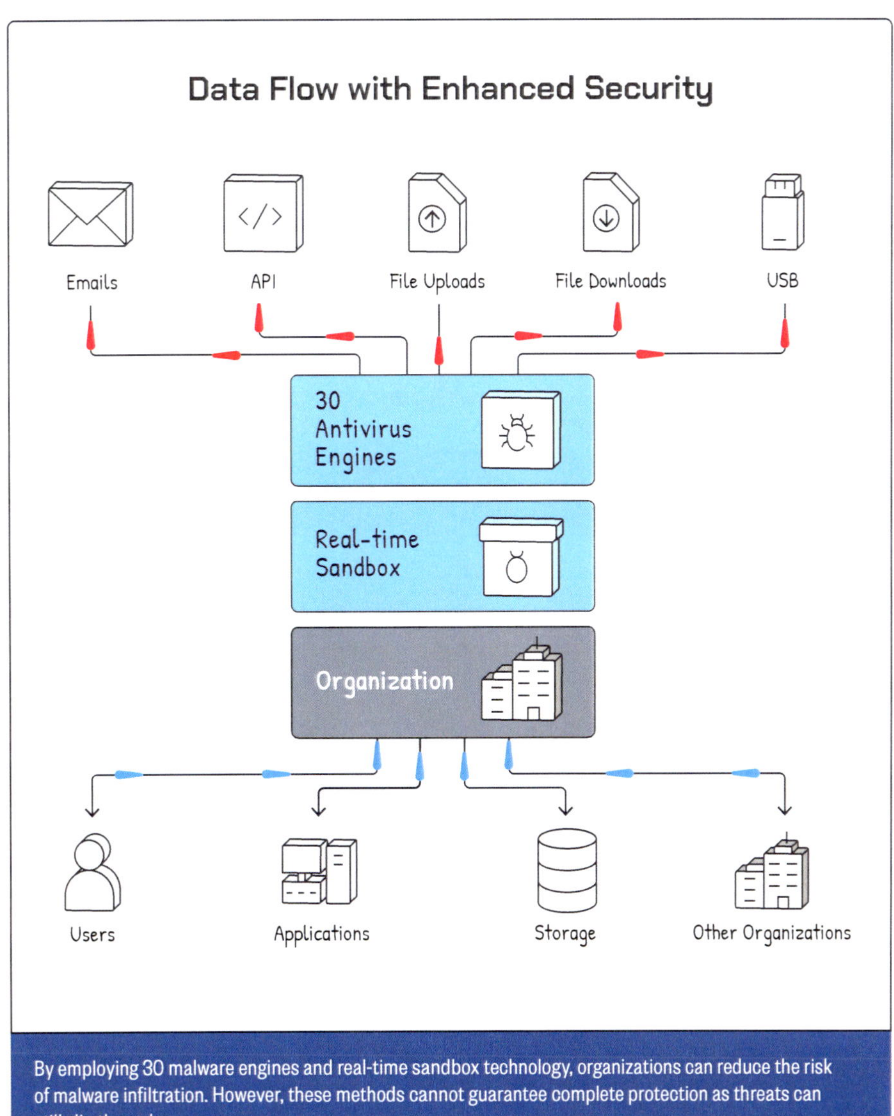

By employing 30 malware engines and real-time sandbox technology, organizations can reduce the risk of malware infiltration. However, these methods cannot guarantee complete protection as threats can still slip through.

This Breakthrough Moment Changed Everything

Once I abandoned the "detection-first" mindset, I had my aha moment and the breakthrough that led to the development of Content Disarm and Reconstruction (CDR), a sanitization technique that changed everything technologically. It happened when I stopped thinking about detection entirely and started envisioning cybersecurity without having to constantly worry about identifying threats. Instead of detecting malware, I began exploring more fundamental questions:

- What is the actual purpose of data flow? I realized that the goal isn't to deliver files; it's to deliver the data within the files.

- What if we assumed that every file is malicious? If we let the concept of detection go, we may then assume that all files are compromised. This was the early establishment of what we now call a "zero-trust" philosophy.

- Could we extract and deliver usable data, completely eliminating malware, without relying on detection?

For a long time I felt stuck; caught in an endless loop of trying to replace detection, unplug it, and swap in something better. But looking back, I see now that I was still trapped in a "detection-first" mindset. I wasn't truly rethinking the problem. I was just searching for ways to improve detection rather than finding a way to eliminate the need for it altogether.

Fortunately, my previous work to understand and rigorously test vast quantities of malware, combined with our team's comprehensive analysis of file-scanning mechanisms, equipped me with all the necessary background I needed to delve deeply into this last question.

Once I thought it through, I realized I had moved beyond the need for detection altogether. It didn't matter whether malware was present in a file or not. By regenerating a file in a safer way, I could solve the problem entirely. I got really excited, and my mind was racing. This was the thinking that eventually led me to the concept of **"data sanitization" (CDR).**

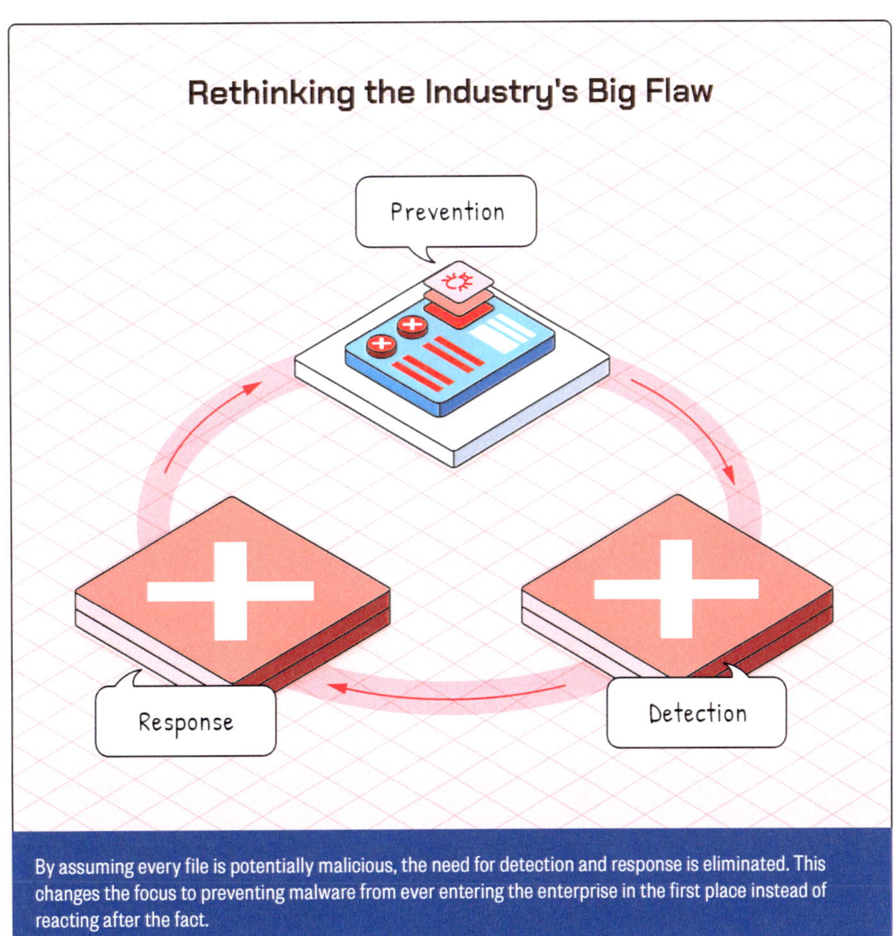

By assuming every file is potentially malicious, the need for detection and response is eliminated. This changes the focus to preventing malware from ever entering the enterprise in the first place instead of reacting after the fact.

CDR: A Look Behind the Name

I have a strong aversion to the term "Content Disarm and Reconstruction" (CDR). In fact, I hate the name. I much prefer "data sanitization" as a description because Content Disarm and Reconstruction implies that content must first be detected before it can be disarmed.

This detection mindset is exactly what we need to eliminate from cybersecurity thinking, given the inherent flaws and limitations of detection-based systems. CDR, on the other hand, is a more deterministic approach that does not rely on detection. It represents a process that ensures safety by transforming data into a secure state without needing to explicitly identify malicious content.

The only reason the name CDR has gained traction in our industry is because Gartner adopted and promoted the term early on in its writings. Gartner's influence in the cybersecurity industry is undeniable, and its terminology often becomes the industry standard. However, just because the name is widely used doesn't mean it's the best or most accurate term for the technology. It's frustrating to see such a flawed term gain acceptance purely based on industry clout.

OPSWAT's holistic approach to data sanitization aligns much better with the zero-trust philosophy and the evolving needs of cybersecurity strategies, moving us away from the flawed reliance on detection. In essence, data sanitization is not only a more precise and accurate description of the process, but it's also more practical for communication. This shift in terminology is crucial for accurately conveying the proactive and deterministic nature of the approach we should be taking.

Despite my strong preference for "data sanitization," I eventually adopted the term "CDR" as more and more people in our industry embraced it, finally accepting that sometimes aligning with a term that has become an industry standard is a pragmatic choice, even if it means compromising on terminology.

How Regeneration Works

When I began working on regeneration, I had not yet built the product. My first priority was figuring out how to explain it. That may seem counterintuitive, but I knew from experience that a groundbreaking technology without a clear and compelling explanation would fail to gain traction.

Breaking free from the traditional "detection first" mindset in cybersecurity had taken me years. Most people, whether engineers, customers, or partners, were still locked into it. They viewed anti-malware strictly through the lens of finding and blocking threats. Regeneration, which we now call CDR, operates on a completely different principle.

The challenge was twofold: first, getting people to understand what regeneration is, and second, convincing them that it works. Even today, this remains the hardest part of the sales process.

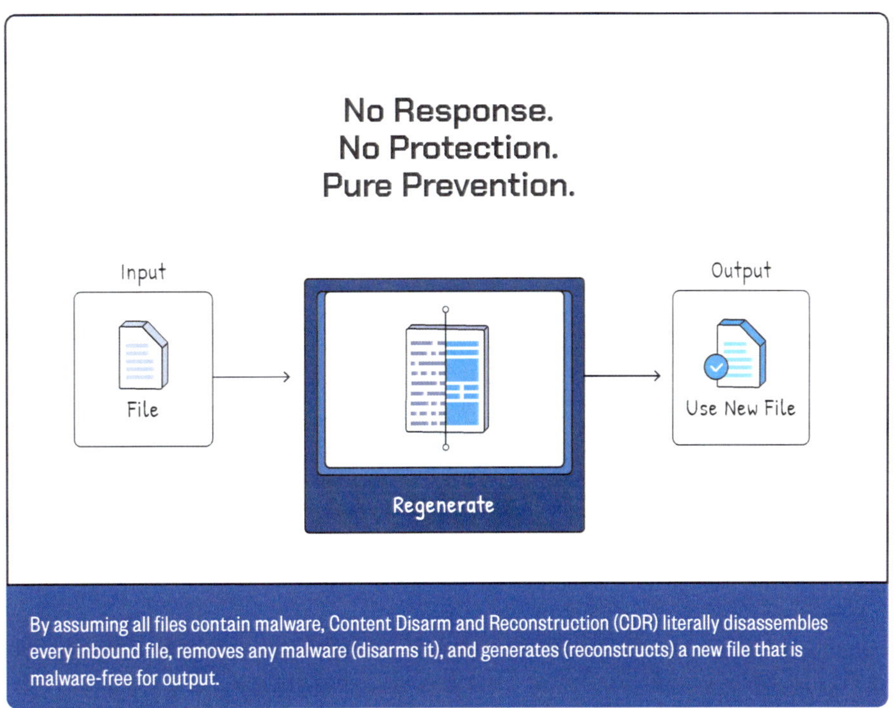

By assuming all files contain malware, Content Disarm and Reconstruction (CDR) literally disassembles every inbound file, removes any malware (disarms it), and generates (reconstructs) a new file that is malware-free for output.

Two examples helped me shift mindsets.

Cloning Animals:

The first example, and I apologize to vegetarian readers, came from Dolly the sheep, one of the first cloned animals. Suppose you wanted to eat some lamb, but you were unsure if the sheep was safe for consumption. Testing the animal might help, but you could never guarantee every possible problem was found.

Instead, imagine cloning the sheep in a sterile, controlled environment. You would get the same wholesome qualities of the original animal without the risk of contamination. This is regeneration. Instead of trying to detect every possible threat, you simply create a clean version of the file from its safe components.

Sanitizing Water:

Imagine you are camping and need to drink from a stream. You could run many tests for bacteria and other contaminants, which is similar to multiscanning for malware. However, at the end of all that testing, you would still be thirsty if the water was deemed unsafe. The better option is to distill the water.

As the illustration on page 92 shows, distillation works by evaporating and then condensing the water, leaving all contaminants behind and producing pure, clean water. It doesn't matter what was in the original source. The process rebuilds the water itself into a safe form. In cybersecurity terms, this is what regeneration does. It rebuilds a file from trusted components, guaranteeing its safety without the need to detect every threat first.

While neither of these examples perfectly matches the technical details of how regeneration works, both illustrate something more important. They shift people out of the detection mindset. Once that shift happens, the value of the concept hopefully becomes clear.

My Journey to Build a CDR Engine

Building a CDR engine was one of the most challenging and rewarding journeys of my career. On the surface, the idea sounded simple: take files in, regenerate them, and deliver something safe and usable. This is elegant in theory, but once we started digging into the details with our team, we quickly realized just how complicated it would become.

In this section, I want to take you with me on a step-by-step journey to show you how we finally built a CDR engine that was fully functional. My goal is not just to explain the mechanics, but to share the excitement I felt while piecing together the vision of the Firewall for Data discussed in Chapter 3. This was not just an engineering project; it was an exploration full of lessons, surprises, and the occasional dead-end that forced me to think differently.

The first step in designing such an engine was to classify the kinds of files that move into and across an organization. At the highest level, they fall into two categories:

1. **Executable Files:** Files containing code that a computer runs
   to perform actions.
2. **Productivity Files:** Files containing information people use to do their
   jobs—documents, spreadsheets, images, presentations, and videos.

Each category came with its own unique challenges and demanded a distinct approach. Executables were raw power and high risk. Productivity files carried the lifeblood of

Why Different Types of Executables Matter

You might wonder why I have taken the time to go over so many different forms of executables. The reason is clarity. Too often people hear ".exe" and think only of Windows applications. In reality, executables take many shapes across every operating system. A screensaver, an installer package, or a shell script can be just as dangerous as a traditional application file. By showing the variations, I want to make the risk visible. Blocking only one or two extensions is not enough. Attackers will always find another form to exploit. Here are some of the more common variations:

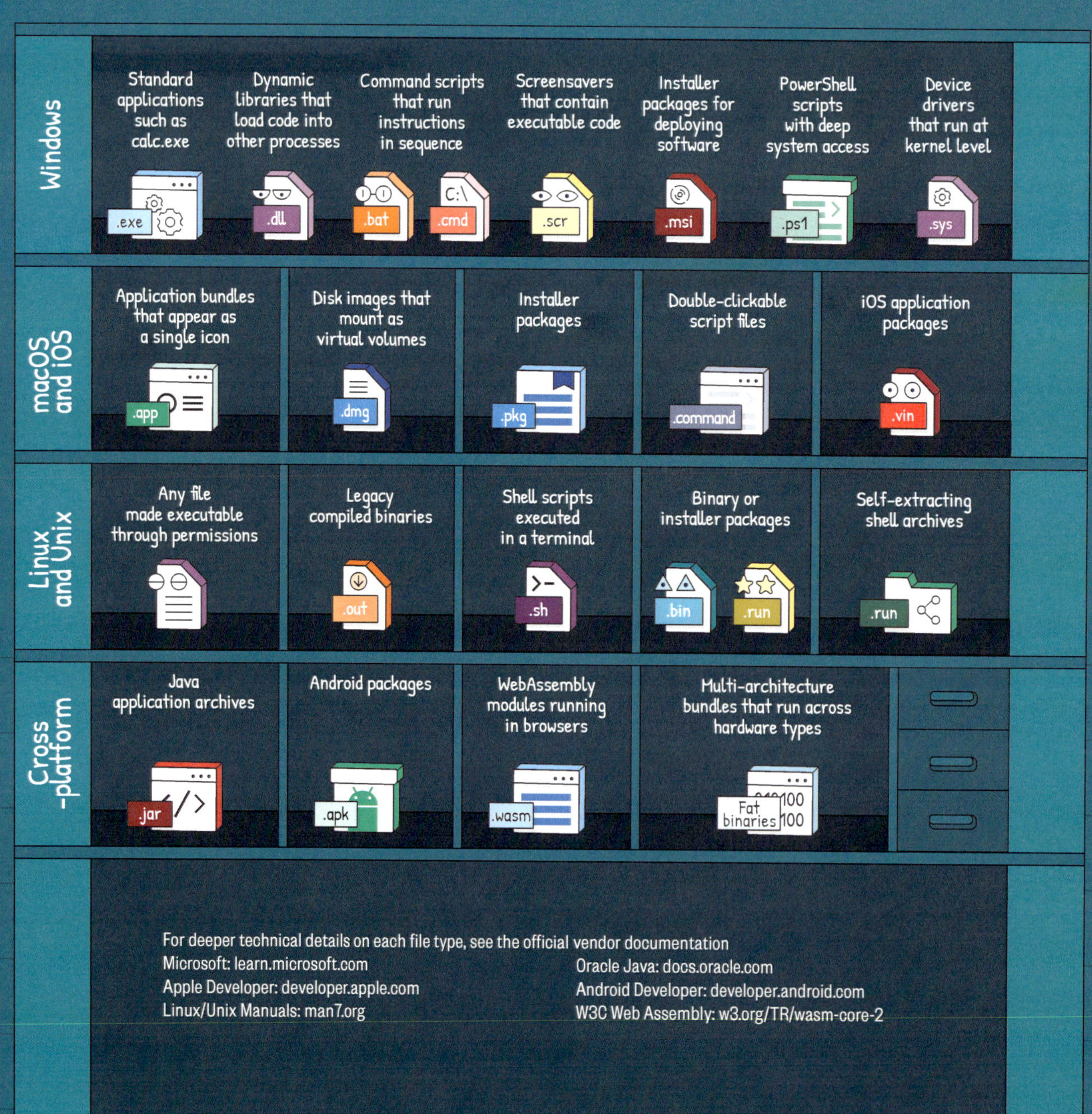

For deeper technical details on each file type, see the official vendor documentation
Microsoft: learn.microsoft.com
Apple Developer: developer.apple.com
Linux/Unix Manuals: man7.org
Oracle Java: docs.oracle.com
Android Developer: developer.android.com
W3C Web Assembly: w3.org/TR/wasm-core-2

business but also hid dangerous opportunities for attackers. To build a complete CDR engine, I knew I had to deal with both worlds head-on.

Can Executables Be Regenerated?

One of the first questions I'm asked about regeneration is: What about executables?

Executables are programs. They contain instructions that a computer runs directly. Once executed, those instructions can do almost anything: install software, change settings, steal data, or hold a system hostage. Unlike a Word document or an image, an executable cannot be taken apart, sanitized, and rebuilt in a way that guarantees a clean file. The regeneration concept does not apply here.

Why Executables Are a Different Class of Risk

Executables are the most abusable file type in the history of cybersecurity. Attackers rely on them because they do not just contain data, they contain power. A single file can deliver ransomware, spread worms, or trigger a zero-day exploit. They are also widespread, appearing in phishing campaigns, USB drops, downloads, and API submissions.

The real truth is that executables do not belong in most business workflows. No one needs an installer showing up through email, a random upload, or a casual download. Installing software should be done through a controlled process, handled by authorized IT teams. This is why the rule is simple and non-negotiable in our model: Executables are stopped by the Firewall for Data not because the technology cannot try to regenerate them, but because it should not.

Why Blocking Works Without Hurting Business

Blocking executables at the Firewall for Data does not harm productivity. Executables make up only a small fraction of the files moving through organizations, and when they are needed, they should come through IT in a controlled process. Stopping them in open channels prevents unnecessary risk without interfering with the everyday flow of business.

The End of the Road for Executables

Executables bring raw power, but with that power comes unacceptable risk. They cannot be safely regenerated, and they should never be allowed to move unchecked through data flows. The Firewall for Data exists to protect against that threat and with executables the answer is final: They are always blocked.

Why Isolation Alone Didn't Solve the Executable Challenge

In the early 2010s, endpoint security innovators tried a different path: isolating executables and threats instead of detecting them. One of the most ambitious was Bromium, founded in 2010 by former Citrix and HP engineers. Their idea was bold: run every risky action in its own hardware-enforced micro-virtual machine (micro-VM) on the user's device. Each browser tab, email attachment, or document lived inside its own temporary container, supposedly preventing even zero-day exploits from breaking out into the host system.

The approach sounded like the perfect answer to malicious executables. If a user clicked on an .exe, .dll, or a booby-trapped script, it would detonate inside the micro-VM and stay trapped. In theory, the system outside remained untouched.

Bromium raised more than $75 million from investors, including Andreessen Horowitz, Intel Capital, and Highland Capital Partners.[1] Its Secure Platform was hailed as a pioneer in the cybersecurity world and caught the attention of governments and Fortune 500 companies.

But adoption lagged.[2] Enterprises cited performance hits, high resource use, and integration hurdles with legacy IT as negatives. More critically, isolation created a usability paradox: files viewed inside micro-VMs could not easily rejoin the workflow. If a spreadsheet ran inside isolation, how could a user safely copy data back into their normal environment without reintroducing risk? This problem was especially painful with executables, which, by design, could never be released safely. Users were forced to choose between security and productivity, and most chose productivity.

By 2019, growth had stalled. HP Inc. acquired Bromium for an estimated $30–$50 million, well below the amount of capital they raised, and folded the technology into HP Sure Click, which is now offered on HP enterprise laptops. The stand-alone Bromium platform was discontinued.

Other isolation companies followed similar paths. Invincea, which built container-based endpoint protection, was acquired by Sophos in 2017 for about $100 million. Authentic8 pivoted to niche markets with its secure remote browser. The pattern repeated: Technology was strong for trapping threats, but weak on usability when dealing with day-to-day files and executables.

The lesson is clear: Isolation without reconstruction leaves a gap. Virtual containers can stop a malicious executable from breaking out, but they do not solve the challenge of delivering clean, usable files back to the user. In contrast, CDR tackles the problem

---

1 TechCrunch – "Bromium Rraises $40 Mmillion For Security Technology That Traps Malware And Limits Attacks": https:// techcrunch.com/2013/10/23/bromium-raises-40m-for-security-technology-that-traps-malware-and-limits-attacks
2 Forbes – "Why Bromium Didn't Take Off" (archived reference, 2019)

at the root. It rebuilds files at the point of entry, removing active content and delivering safe, business-ready versions before they ever touch the endpoint.

Bromium's downfall was not about weak security; it was about misalignment between security and usability, especially around executables. CDR closes that gap by offering prevention that scales, securing email, web, cloud, and collaboration systems without sacrificing the flow of business.

The Real Mountain: Productivity Files

After drawing a hard line on executables, the real mountain came into view with productivity files.

Unlike executables, productivity files could not simply be blocked. These were the files everyone needed to do their jobs: documents and spreadsheets, presentations, photographic images, videos, and CAD drawings. Without them, business stops. And that was the real challenge. If I wanted to build a sanitization engine that organizations could actually use, I had to find a way to let these files flow while still keeping them safe.

At first, I underestimated the problem. I thought, *How bad can it be? We just need to handle a few dozen formats—Word, Excel, PDF, maybe JPEG and PNG.* But when I dug deeper, it felt like falling into a rabbit hole. I spent hours inside **MetaDefender Cloud**, analyzing file flows and submission patterns. I compared what I saw with catalogs like **file.org** and **fileinfo.com**. Instead of a few dozen formats, I was staring at thousands. FileInfo alone documents over **10,000 file types**, and file.org catalogs thousands more. Some were familiar. Many I had never even heard of. Yet each one was in use somewhere, and each one could become a weapon if the wrong person decided to exploit it.

Scrolling through those lists was overwhelming. I remember pausing at obscure entries like **.sgy** (seismic exploration data), **.nc** (NetCDF scientific datasets), or **.indd** (Adobe InDesign publishing files) and realizing that if an organization relied on them, our engine would have to support them. There was no shortcut. If we were serious about building a true Firewall for Data, we had to face the full complexity of the file ecosystem.

What was even more troubling was realizing that the deeper I looked, the more it became clear that each format carried not just a single risk, but often multiple potential attack vectors. Some formats had not been exploited yet only because attackers had found easier targets. But that would not last forever.

At this stage I realized curiosity had to become discipline. It was not enough to glance at file types or skim through research papers. I had to dig, catalog, and understand every angle.

I leaned on industry events like AVAR, Virus Bulletin, and AMTSO, where the best minds in cybersecurity shared their latest findings. I spent long calls with peers across anti-malware companies, trading notes and hunting down edge cases. And inside OPSWAT, I worked hand in hand with our engineers, tearing files apart, building test cases, and discovering risks that were hiding just beneath the surface.

That work reshaped how I saw productivity files. They were not safer than executables. They were simply dangerous in different ways. A photo, a PDF, or a spreadsheet may look harmless, but each can carry threats as serious as any program. To make this clear, I collected a set of attack vectors that, to me, represented the fundamentals of how attackers shape productivity formats into weapons.

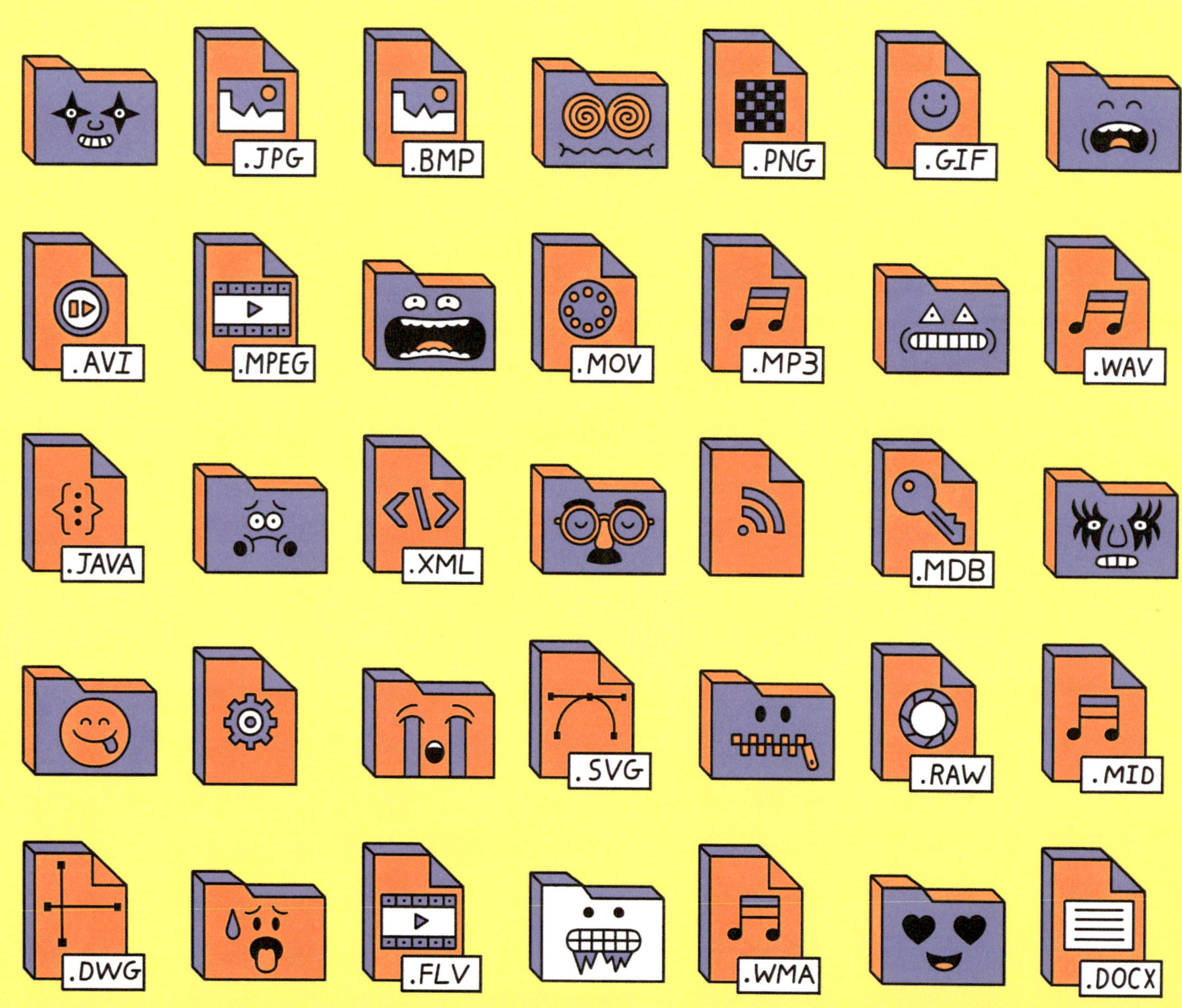

Buffer Overflows

Some files are built to break the rules. When an application opens a file, it expects the data to fit neatly into memory. Attackers deliberately craft files that don't fit. They overload the program until the extra data spills into places it should never reach. That overflow is more than a crash. It can rewrite instructions, hijack execution, and give the attacker control of the system.

Steganography

Attackers hide malicious code inside images, audio files, and videos, so the file looks normal on the surface. The hidden content is invisible to the user, but it can be extracted and executed by malware already on the system.

Scripts

Formats like PDFs, MS Office files, or SVG images support built-in scripting for interactivity. Attackers use this capability to hide code that runs silently when the file is opened, turning a useful feature into a delivery mechanism for malware.

Macros

Office files like Word and Excel support macros to automate tasks. Attackers exploit this feature by embedding code that begins running the moment a file is opened, often downloading or executing malware under the guise of normal productivity.

Embedded Objects

Many file formats can carry other files inside them, such as PowerPoint slides with spreadsheets, PDFs with scripts, CAD drawings with linked images, or design files with fonts and layers. Attackers use this nesting to smuggle malicious content inside otherwise trusted files.

Malicious Links

Files often include hyperlinks, but attackers disguise them so the visible text looks safe while the link leads to phishing sites, malware downloads, or exploits hidden behind a single click.

Metadata

Files carry hidden details like author names, comments, file paths, or GPS tags. Attackers can exploit these fields to inject malicious data into parsing tools, or the metadata itself may leak private and confidential information. Without control, metadata becomes both an exploit surface and a data loss channel.

Containers and Archives

Formats like ZIP, RAR, or ISO are used to package and share files. Attackers use the same convenience to conceal malware, often layering or encrypting archives to bypass defenses until the contents are extracted.

I chose these attack vectors because I believe they represent the fundamentals. They help explain the risks that hide inside productivity files and, just as importantly, they illustrate the lessons I learned while building the sanitization engine.

With that in mind, let's go deeper. In the following sections, I will walk through specific examples for each attack vector, showing how they work in practice and why they became so central to my thinking as I shaped the Firewall for Data.

Buffer Overflows: When a File Quietly Takes Control

When I first started digging into productivity file risks, buffer overflows hit me hard. They showed me that even something as simple as a picture or a song could be turned into a weapon.

The concept is straightforward. Software expects a file to be neatly packed. But an attacker deliberately stuffs it with more data than the program can handle. That extra data doesn't just break the application; it spills into memory where it doesn't belong, overwriting instructions and giving the attacker control of the file.

For the coders among us, it might be easier to understand with a simple example:

```c
#include <stdio.h>
#include <string.h>
void vulnerable(char *input) {
    char buf[8];              /* only 8 bytes */
    strcpy(buf, input);       /* no bounds check */
    printf("%s\n", buf);
}
int main(int argc, char **argv) {
    if (argc > 1)
        vulnerable(argv[1]);
    return 0;
}
```

Run this code with a short string and it behaves as expected. But if you pass in a long string, the data spills beyond buf, overwriting memory. With the right payload, an attacker can change where the program returns and point it straight at their own code.

That is exactly what happened with one of the most famous buffer overflow flaws: the Windows GDI+ JPEG vulnerability, known as MS04-028. Simply opening a JPEG in Explorer or Word was enough to compromise the machine. No clicks, no prompts. The Huffman tables inside the JPEG were tampered with to overflow memory and redirect execution. At the time, Microsoft reported that hundreds of millions of Windows systems were affected. Security analysts noted that attackers could gain the same privileges as the logged-in user, meaning they could have full control of the endpoint in many corporate environments. The bulletin described the issue as "critical," with the potential for global exploitation at scale.

Here are some key sources:

- Microsoft Security Bulletin MS04-028: https://learn.microsoft.com/en-us/security-updates/securitybulletins/2004/ms04-028

- CISA Alert: https://www.cisa.gov/news-events/alerts/2004/09/16/micro-soft-windows-jpeg-component-buffer-overflow

This wasn't ancient history, either. More recently, **libjpeg-turbo** had a heap overflow (CVE-2023-2804). It impacted countless applications because libjpeg-turbo is embedded in major browsers, imaging tools, and enterprise systems. The National Vulnerability Database (NVD) rated it as "high severity."[3]

- FFmpeg suffered a heap overflow (CVE-2022-2566), which was first published in 2022. FFmpeg is one of the most widely used multimedia frameworks in the world, powering streaming services, media players, and even enterprise surveillance systems. Exploitation could lead to full system compromise if a crafted AVI file was opened.[4]

The damage from these productivity file exploits has been immense. MS04-028 alone forced emergency patch cycles across governments and industries, costing hundreds of millions in lost productivity, IT overtime, and system downtime.

The FFmpeg flaw in 2022 was cited by enterprise security teams as one of the most disruptive remediation campaigns of that year, given the sheer number of dependent applications. And libjpeg-turbo's vulnerability affected products across both consumer and enterprise ecosystems, forcing software vendors worldwide to issue urgent updates.

3 NVD: https://nvd.nist.gov/vuln/detail/CVE-2023-2804
4 NVD: https://nvd.nist.gov/vuln/detail/CVE-2022-2566

This is where I like to pause and bring it back to something current. Netflix recently released a limited series called *Zero Day*[5]. The show imagines a global cyberattack unfolding in real time. It is fiction, but the idea at its core resonates with me: many attacks start with unknown vulnerabilities that defenders have not patched and cannot even detect yet.

That is what buffer overflows teach us.

- Known vulnerabilities are the ones like MS04-028. They get a CVE, a patch, and a flurry of updates.

- Unknown vulnerabilities, or zero-days, are the ones still hiding in code we trust. Attackers find them first, then weaponize them before vendors even know they exist.

In Chapter 1, I talked about the sheer number of operating systems and applications in the world. Each OS, app, plugin, and library is a parser waiting to be stressed. And with over 10,000 documented file types across catalogs like fileinfo.com and file.org, each format is a potential entry point. The attack surface is vast, and many vulnerabilities are still unknown.

The Netflix series Zero Day, starring Robert De Niro, underscores the fact that many cyberattacks start with unknown vulnerabilities that those defending organizations are not yet able to detect.

5 Official page: https://www.netflix.com/title/81598435

That is the lesson buffer overflows left me with: File structure itself is an attack surface that can be bent, twisted, and abused.

Steganography: When Files Whisper in Secret

Another turning point for me was realizing that attackers do not always need to crash an application to win. Sometimes they hide their payloads in plain sight, inside files that look and behave exactly as they should. This is steganography.

The word comes from the Greek *steganos,* meaning "covered," and *graphein,* which means "writing." It means concealing one message inside another. In the digital world, it means burying malicious instructions in images, audio, or video where no one can see them. To the human eye, the photo of a sunset is still a sunset. The song plays without distortion. The video looks normal. But within the pixels, waveforms, or frames, an attacker has left instructions waiting to be unpacked by malware already present on the endpoint.

Over the years, I saw three common carriers abused again and again:

Images (JPEG, PNG)

Malicious code hidden in pixel data, padding bytes, or metadata fields like EXIF.

Audio (MP3, WAV)

Payloads tucked into silent segments or shifted frequencies that human ears cannot detect.

Video (MP4, AVI)

Code hidden in large containers, spread across frames, or embedded in stream metadata.

What makes this powerful is that the files remain valid. They are still perfectly good photos, songs, and clips. Signature-based detection tools do not see anything wrong, because technically, there is nothing wrong with the format. That is why steganography became one of those moments for me where I knew detection would always be too late.

Steganography is all about hiding one message inside another. Images may look perfectly normal, but malicious code can be hidden in pixel data, padding bytes, or metadata fields like EXIF.

Real-world cases drove this lesson home:

- The **ZeusVM** banking trojan hid its configuration data inside PNG images, allowing infected systems to silently fetch instructions without raising alarms. (IBM X-Force, 2014)

- The **Lurk** trojan evolved into a multi-purpose espionage tool by hiding scripts in PNGs, which let it avoid detection even during lateral movement inside enterprise networks. (Group-IB, 2016)

- The **Triton (Trisis)** malware targeting industrial safety systems also leveraged steganography, embedding payloads in images to disrupt operations in critical infrastructure. (FireEye and Dragos, 2017)

For me, steganography was not just a clever trick. It was proof that the file format itself is not neutral. Attackers can bend even the simplest file into a delivery mechanism. And with over 10,000 documented file types, the number of hiding places is staggering.

Steganography reminded me that files are not just containers of data. They can also carry secrets. And in a world where attackers innovate faster than patches, the only way to trust a file is to rebuild it.

Scripts: When Code Hides in Plain Sight

Productivity tools actually paved the way for attackers. Microsoft Office, Adobe Acrobat, and many other editors were designed to empower users. Microsoft built in scripting to make life easier to automate workflows, validate data, or make files interactive. But that same convenience created one of the easiest and most effective attack surfaces in the history of cybersecurity.

In Word, Excel, and PowerPoint, Visual Basic for Applications (VBA) is right there in the product. Anyone can open the editor and add a script in minutes. Excel lets scripts run when a workbook is opened or even when a single cell changes. PowerPoint allows scripts tied to slide actions. Adobe PDFs support JavaScript inside form fields, buttons, and annotations. These were intended as productivity features, but to an attacker, they are ready-made weapons.

That ease is what makes script attacks so dangerous. An attacker does not need to discover a vulnerability or invent a zero-day. They can simply use the tools already provided by the software itself. In some cases, the effort is trivial: a handful of lines pasted into a macro editor or a small JavaScript snippet inside a PDF.

The end result is a file that looks completely ordinary, like a report, slide deck, or an invoice, but it carries hidden instructions that execute as soon as it is opened.

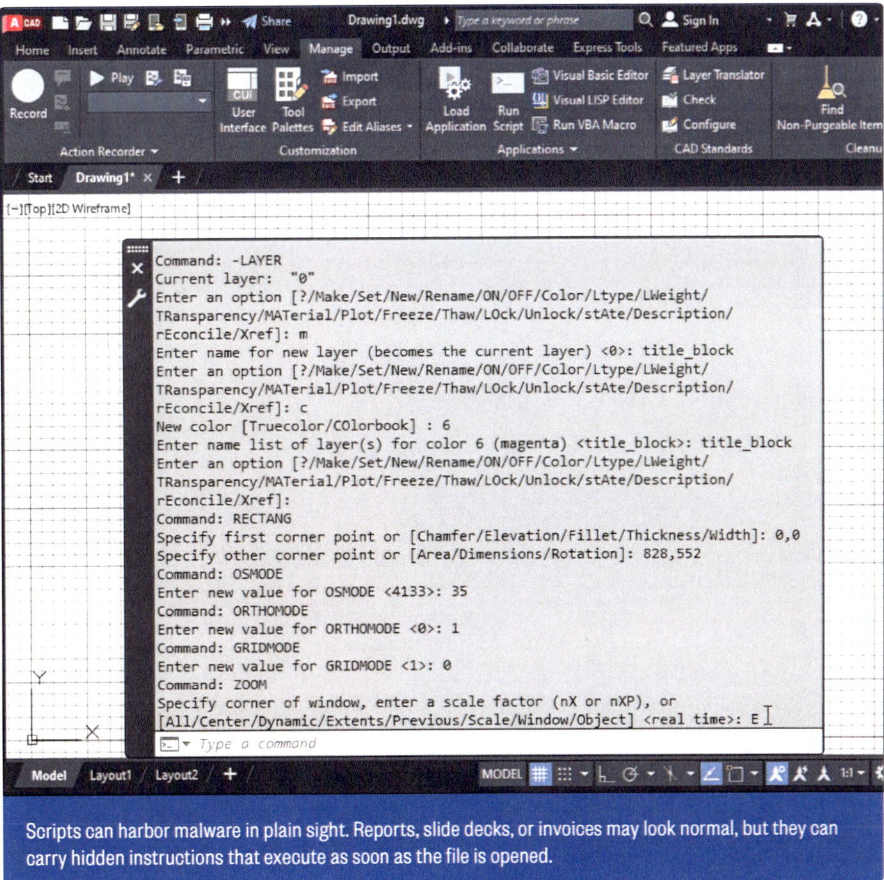

Scripts can harbor malware in plain sight. Reports, slide decks, or invoices may look normal, but they can carry hidden instructions that execute as soon as the file is opened.

History shows how effective this simplicity can be:

- **Dridex** spread globally through Word files carrying script-based instructions to download banking malware. The attachments looked like invoices but cost organizations more than **$100 million in fraud losses.**

- **Emotet** became one of the most destructive botnets of the last decade by abusing scripts in Office attachments to fetch its loader. From there it raided inboxes and replied to real conversations with new infected files, spreading faster than defenders could keep up. Cleanup costs often exceeded **$1 million per incident**, according to the Department of Homeland Security.

- **Donoff** relied on script-laden Word documents that quietly pulled down obfuscated JavaScript payloads. It was not elegant, but it was effective, infecting millions of machines simply because the files looked harmless.

What makes this so humbling is that attackers didn't need to think too hard. They didn't have to chain exploits or break cryptography. The software itself provided the channel. Attackers merely supplied the intent.

Scripts taught me that sometimes the most powerful cyberattacks come not from sophistication, but from simplicity. When everyday tools make it easy to embed code, attackers do not need to be brilliant. They only need to be opportunistic.

Macros: When Convenience Becomes a Weapon

Macros were designed to save time. Microsoft wanted to give users a way to automate boring, repetitive work in Word, Excel, and PowerPoint. With just a few clicks, anyone could record a macro to reformat text, update a chart, or generate a report. Behind the scenes, these macros ran in VBAs, a scripting engine built right into Office.

The problem was that the very same simplicity that helped workers also helped attackers. Embedding a malicious macro into a file required almost no skill. Open the macro editor, paste in a handful of lines, and set it to run automatically when the file opens. That is it. No exploit chain. No zero-day. Just the features Office shipped with by default.

That ease is why macros became one of the most abused attack vectors in history. Attackers did not need to break into systems. They just needed a victim to open a document and click "Enable Content."

Microsoft eventually added guardrails with security prompts, warning banners, and restrictions on macros from the internet. But it created a dynamic we have all seen before. It was like putting a big red button on the screen with a warning sign: "Do not press." And yet, under pressure, curiosity, or habit, people pressed it. Attackers

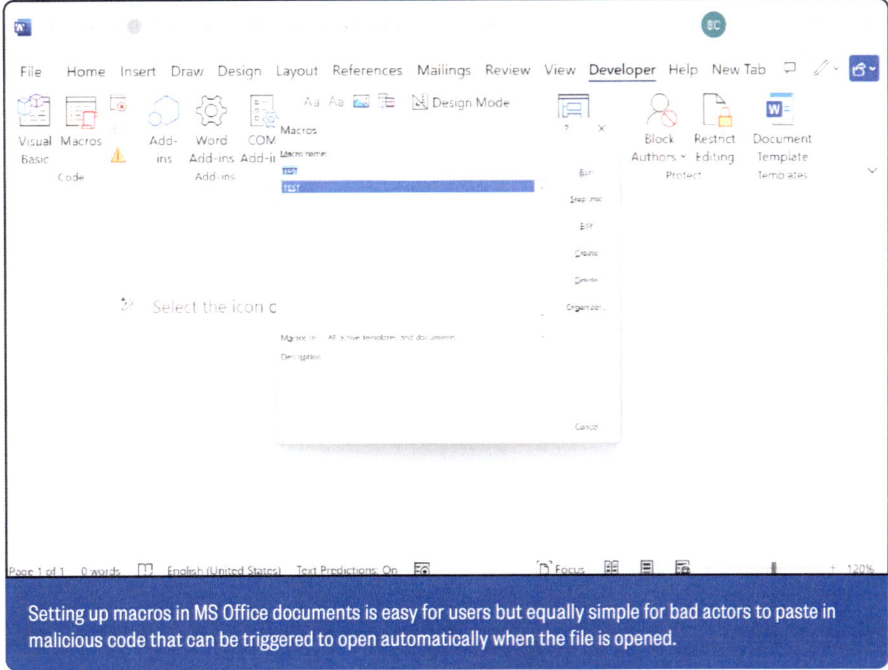

Setting up macros in MS Office documents is easy for users but equally simple for bad actors to paste in malicious code that can be triggered to open automatically when the file is opened.

knew this, and their phishing campaigns were designed to push victims right past those warnings.

The results were devastating:

- **GoldenEye Ransomware (2016):** Delivered through Excel attachments. Victims opened what looked like an HR spreadsheet, clicked to enable macros, and instantly triggered PowerShell commands that downloaded and executed ransomware. Entire corporate networks were locked within hours.

- **Fareit Trojan (2014):** Spread through Word files with embedded macros. Once opened, Fareit harvested stored passwords from browsers and FTP clients. It was lightweight, easy to spread, and became one of the most common infostealers of its time.

- **Ursnif (Gozi) Banking Trojan (2015–2018):** Phishing campaigns used macro-laden Word documents to silently install Ursnif, which harvested banking credentials and personal data. Losses reached tens of millions across Europe.

- **Hancitor (2017–2020):** A loader almost entirely dependent on malicious macros. Victims clicked "Enable Content" on Word attachments, and Hancitor immediately downloaded additional payloads, such as ransomware.

What all of these had in common was not sophistication but simplicity. Anyone with basic knowledge of Office could weaponize a file. The macro editor was right there, waiting to be used. A macro that once automated formatting could just as easily automate compromise.

That realization hit me hard. Attackers did not need research labs or months of work. They could take advantage of tools built for convenience, paste in a short script, and let the software do the rest. It was not only possible to weaponize files quickly; it was trivial.

Macros taught me a lesson I could not ignore. When you tell people "do not press the red button," someone will press it. And in cybersecurity, we cannot afford to build defenses that rely on perfect human behavior. We sometimes need to remove the button entirely.

Embedded Objects: When Files Carry Hidden Passengers

Another feature designed to make life easier turned out to be a gift for attackers: embedded objects. Microsoft Office, PDF editors, and many other productivity tools allow users to insert one file inside another. The idea was convenience. A presentation could carry a supporting spreadsheet, or a Word document could hold a reference chart or even another document. On the surface, it made collaboration smoother.

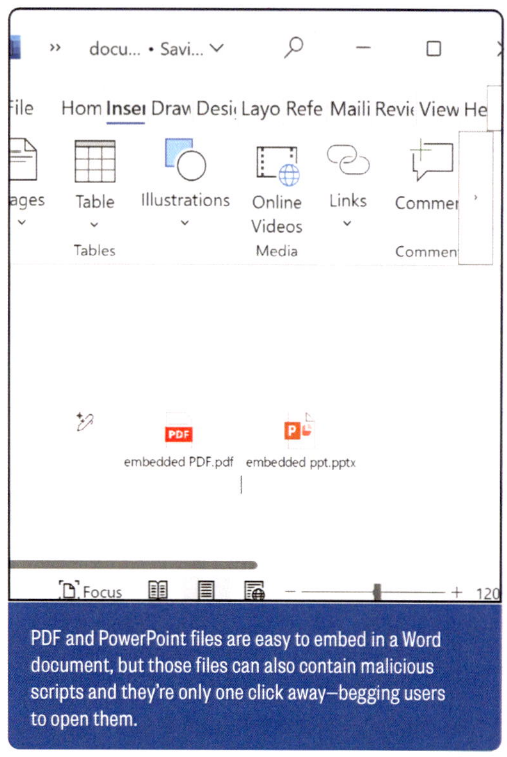

PDF and PowerPoint files are easy to embed in a Word document, but those files can also contain malicious scripts and they're only one click away—begging users to open them.

The problem is that embedding one file inside another also makes it trivial to smuggle in something dangerous. An attacker can take a malicious executable, script, or payload, wrap it as an embedded object, and hide it inside a file that looks ordinary. To the recipient, the attachment seems harmless; it opens as a presentation, report, or contract. But the hidden object is there, waiting to be triggered.

At its core, the underlying primitive is the same as what we see with scripts or macros: trick the software into running instructions that the user never intended. What embedding did was make that attack easier to disguise. Instead of sending a suspicious-looking file directly, attackers could layer it. For example, a malicious script could be

hidden in a PDF, and that PDF could be embedded inside a Word document. Now the lure looked more convincing. The file seemed to carry supporting evidence, reference material, or documentation, providing a perfect setup for social engineering.

What made this so dangerous is how productivity editors handled it. They gave users the ability to double-click an embedded object to "activate" it. That meant the attack was only a click away. Like the dynamic for macros, it was like putting a red button in the middle of the document and telling users, "Only click if you trust it." We know how that story ends. Attackers crafted their lures precisely to encourage users to click and they did. The results were ugly:

- **Equation Editor Exploit (CVE-2017-11882):** Attackers used embedded objects in Office documents to exploit a decades-old component. Victims only had to open the document for the exploit to trigger, giving attackers full code execution. Nation-state and cybercrime groups weaponized it worldwide.

- **CVE-2017-0199:** A flaw in how Office handled embedded OLE objects allowed RTF files to fetch and run external HTA scripts. This exploit became a favorite in phishing campaigns because the victim did not have to click anything beyond opening the file.

- **Malicious PDFs:** Embedded files in PDFs have been used repeatedly to smuggle executables or scripts. Once extracted or launched, they gave attackers a direct foothold on the system.

For me, embedded objects reinforced the same lesson I learned with macros. Features that make work easier often make attacks easier, too. And just like with the red button problem, we cannot expect users to always choose correctly under pressure.

Embedded objects taught me that the most dangerous thing about them was not just the technical trick, but how easily they could be disguised as legitimate content. When attackers can wrap one file inside another, social engineering becomes part of the exploit itself.

Malicious Links: When the Trap Is Just a Click Away

Another feature that seemed harmless on the surface but turned into a weapon was hyperlinks inside documents, presentations, and PDFs. Links were designed for productivity. They made it easy to reference a website, share supporting material, or connect a report to an online source. But for attackers, links became one of the simplest ways to trick people into opening the door themselves.

In essence, the primitive is the same as with other attacks: deliver something harmful by disguising it as something useful. Links just made it easier to pull this off. Instead of embedding code directly, the attacker could hide a trap behind a convincing text link.

The document shows "https://microsoft.com," but the actual destination might lead to a fake login page, a malware download, or a browser exploit. Presentations and PDFs make it even simpler by allowing links to be hidden in buttons, images, or annotations.

The social engineering angle makes links especially dangerous. People expect links in reports, proposals, and slides. They are predisposed to automatically click on them. It is the ultimate red-button problem. Attackers know this, so they craft their documents to push users right past hesitation.

We have seen this play out repeatedly:

- **OneNote Campaigns (2022–2023):** Attackers used embedded links disguised as buttons inside OneNote files to deliver malicious executables.

- **PDF Phishing Kits:** Emails carried PDFs with links to fake login portals. Because the PDF itself looked static and harmless, many passed through filters. Victims clicked and handed over credentials.

- **Business Email Compromise:** Fraudsters often embed links in contracts or invoices that redirect executives to malicious sites, leading to credential theft and multi-million-dollar wire fraud.

But links present a special challenge for sanitization. Unlike macros, scripts, or embedded objects, you cannot always "regenerate" a link into something safe. The file may need its links to remain functional.

The role of sanitization, therefore, is to eliminate links altogether when they pose a risk, or to subject embedded URLs to deeper analysis and testing during regeneration. Sometimes the safest path is to strip them out. Other times, the engine can rewrite them to go through a controlled inspection service before they are used.

Malicious links reminded me that sometimes the simplest click is the most dangerous. And in those cases, the job of regeneration is not to make the link safe, but to make sure the user never steps on the trap in the first place.

Metadata: When the Details Betray You

Many files carry more than what you see. Behind the visible text, numbers, or images lies a hidden layer called "metadata." It is designed to be helpful: recording who created the file, which program was used, when it was saved, and sometimes even where it was created.

A Word document might quietly preserve author names and revision history. A spreadsheet can contain deleted cells or confidential comments. A photo may silently embed GPS coordinates of where it was taken.

At first, metadata feels harmless, almost invisible. But over time, I came to see it as one of the most underestimated risks in productivity files. The danger falls into two categories: exploitation and exposure.

Exploitation: Each time software reads metadata, it has to interpret those details—and that process is fragile.

In 2021, a critical flaw was discovered in ExifTool, a widely used image analysis utility (CVE-2021-22204). Attackers found that they could embed malicious code inside image metadata, and simply scanning the file was enough to trigger remote code execution.

This resembles a buffer overflow: a parser expects tidy fields, but if attackers stuff them with malformed or oversized data, the software spills over into memory or corrupts its own logic. What should be harmless content becomes an entry point for compromise.

Similar weaknesses have been uncovered in libraries like LibTIFF, ImageMagick, and even Microsoft Office, showing this is not rare but systemic across ecosystems.

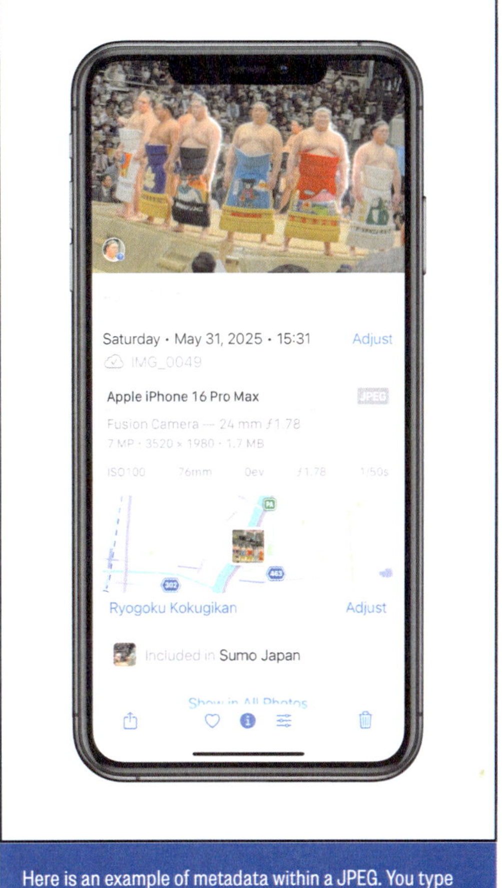

Here is an example of metadata within a JPEG. You type "Ryogoku Kokugikan," the National Sumo Arena in Tokyo, Japan, into the Maps app on your iPhone and up rolls the location along with a photo of professional sumo wrestlers. You can't tell, but there could be malware hidden in the wrestler's image.

Exposure: Even when metadata isn't weaponized, secrets are often divulged that were never meant to leave the file. For example, GPS tags in photographs have exposed the locations of military bases when soldiers casually uploaded personal snapshots of themselves and friends.

In 2003, journalists discovered that parts of the UK's Iraq dossier had been plagiarized from a student's thesis, revealed through metadata in the Word document.

In 2012, John McAfee's hiding place in Belize was uncovered when a photo posted online carried embedded GPS coordinates. Governments, corporations, and journalists alike have accidentally published sensitive drafts, redlined comments, or confidential deliberations simply because they overlooked the hidden data inside files.

For attackers, metadata is a gift: both an additional attack surface and a treasure trove of intelligence. For defenders, it is a silent liability, creating avenues of compromise that bypass the main content entirely.

Containers and Archives: When the Package Hides the Threat

Packaging files together is something we all do. ZIPs, RARs, ISOs, and other archive formats make it easy to bundle content, share projects, or deliver software in one neat package. They save space, they simplify transfers, and they have been part of business life for decades.

Attackers saw the same value, but for very different reasons. Archives gave them the perfect way to wrap malicious files in a clean-looking package. On the surface the archive appears harmless. Email filters and scanners often see it as a single, compressed object, not the individual files inside. The danger only shows itself when someone extracts the content.

The concept is the same as with other attack vectors. The attacker needs a delivery vehicle. Archives make it easier to disguise malware. A malicious executable can be zipped up and attached to an email. A harmful script can be packed inside an ISO and passed off as a document bundle. Even password-protected archives are used, with attackers supplying the password in the email to trick the victim into unlocking the trap themselves.

Examples are everywhere. IcedID used ISO files to bypass Microsoft's security controls in 2022. QakBot campaigns regularly shipped in ZIP attachments posing as invoices. Ransomware operators have long relied on archives to smuggle droppers into corporate environments.

For defenders, this created one clear challenge that needed to be addressed: a ZIP file is not just one file, it is a container that can house multiple files. Unless you look inside and validate every component of that container, you will never really know what is coming in. The most dangerous threats often hide inside what looks ordinary. A ZIP file represents convenience to one person and camouflage to another.

Cracking the Code of File-Borne Threats

When I set out to understand file-borne threats, I was not just chasing theory. I wanted to know exactly how malware gets into files, how it hides, and how it maps to the formats people rely on every day. What I found was not just a list of attacks, but a pattern. And once I could see the pattern, the way forward became clearer.

Some attacks are universal. Buffer overflow, steganography, and metadata abuse do not care what the file looks like on the surface. A JPEG can crash an image parser.

Attack Vectors Across File Types

Some readers may point out that formats like MP4 or MKV can technically include clickable annotations or external references in metadata. That is true, but it is not the same as embedding a link directly into a Word document or PDF. Still, sanitization has to treat them carefully, because even metadata-based references can become a backdoor.

File Type / Format	Buffer Overflows	Steganography	Metadata	Scripts	Macros	Embedded Objects	Malicious Links	Notes on Complexity / Inheritance
Word/Excel/PowerPoint (DOCX/XLSX/PPTX)	Yes	Yes	Yes	Yes	Yes	Yes	Yes	Complex
PDF	Yes	Yes	Yes	Yes	No	Yes	Yes	Complex
TXT / CSV	Yes	Yes	Yes	No	No	No	No	Simple
JPEG / PNG / BMP / TIFF	Yes	Yes	Yes	No	No	No	No	Simple
SVG	Yes	Yes	Yes	Yes	No	No	Yes	Complex
MP3 / WAV	Yes	Yes	Yes	No	No	No	No	Simple
MP4 / AVI / MKV	Yes	Yes	Yes	No	No	No	No*	Simple
PSD (Photoshop)	Yes	Yes	Yes	Yes	No	No	Yes	Complex
AI (Illustrator)	Yes	Yes	Yes	Yes	No	Yes	Yes	Complex
INDD (InDesign)	Yes	Yes	Yes	Yes	No	Yes	Yes	Complex
DWG (AutoCAD)	Yes	Yes	Yes	Yes	No	Yes	Yes	Complex
SKP (SketchUp)	Yes	Yes	Yes	Yes	No	Yes	Yes	Complex
HDR / HDP / HTD / EXR	Yes	Yes	Yes	No	No	No	No	Simple

A WAV can carry a hidden payload in silence. Even a plain TXT file can betray secrets through metadata or overwhelm a weak parser. These vectors appear everywhere, across the simplest formats.

Other attacks are tied to richer formats. Scripts, macros, embedded objects, and malicious links only show up in families of files designed for productivity: Word, Excel, PowerPoint, PDFs, CAD drawings, and Photoshop projects. These features were meant to make work easier with automation, interactivity, and embedding. But attackers exploited the same features and turned them into weapons.

That was when the distinction between **simple files** and **complex files** became clear.

Simple files hold raw data. A JPEG, WAV, or TXT file has fewer moving parts, but that does not mean they are safe. They still overflow, they still carry hidden payloads, and they still leak metadata.

Complex files are layered. They do not just hold their own data, they pull in other files, link to external content, and execute processes. A Word document can run macros and hide embedded PDFs. A PDF can carry JavaScript and attachments. A DWG drawing can reference fonts, images, and models outside the file. And, most importantly, complex files inherit the risks of the simple files inside them.

That inheritance effect was the breakthrough. A Word file with a JPEG inside is not just one risk, it is two. Word brings macros, links, and objects. The JPEG adds overflows or steganography. Stack them together and the attack surface multiplies. The same holds true in design and engineering. A DWG may look like one drawing, but it can quietly include textures, scripts, and linked models. Each layer adds another opportunity for compromise.

Once I recognized this pattern, I had a framework. CDR was no longer about treating every file the same. It was about breaking the problem down: apply universal protections everywhere, then apply targeted strategies where richer features exist. That is what turned a messy challenge into something we could implement.

The picture snapped into focus. CDR could not stop at the surface. It had to take every file apart, strip out the risks, and rebuild the content so it stayed useful while closing the door on attackers. The consistency I was looking for came from treating every vector the same way, no matter which file carried it. And that realization gave me the blueprint to start implementing CDR in a structured, scalable way.

Bringing CDR to Life

As I said at the start of this chapter, my aha moment stretched out over a long period of time and required a lot of analysis and experimentation. While it is not easy to summarize the process of creation, the four steps described in this section will give you an idea of how CDR came together as a mature concept.

Step 1: We Take Primitive First Steps With File Flattening

When I first started exploring how to stop file-based threats, I wanted something simple that worked. My goal was to reduce risk without slowing users down. That's where the idea of **file flattening** came from.

The concept was straightforward. If I could convert a risky file into a cleaner, safer format, I could eliminate most of the attack surface in one move.

For example, converting a Word document to a PDF removed any macros. Turning an Excel file into a CSV stripped out embedded scripts. Flattening a JPEG into a BMP broke common exploit techniques tied to compression.

By changing the file type, I could break the attacker's assumptions and remove functionality that didn't belong.

I wanted to get this into the real world quickly, so I rolled it out as a beta feature to all Metascan customers with no barriers and at no extra cost. I wanted honest feedback, so I stayed close to it, asking our sales and support teams to funnel insights back to me. I also reached out to customers directly to understand how they were using it and what they were seeing.

The early feedback was strong. Customers saw fewer threats, cleaner files, and more predictable behavior. Flattening stripped away macros, scripts, and embedded content. It reduced the surface area attackers could use and simplified security across email, file uploads, and web gateways. But it didn't take long to see the limits.

The more feedback I received, the clearer it became: File flattening was safe, but it wasn't always usable. Interactive forms, animations, media, and other important elements were lost in the process. For some workflows, that was fine, but for others, it broke functionality the users needed, so I pushed further.

We built a dedicated flattening engine inside Metascan with more control and smarter options. That gave some customers what they needed, especially in high-security environments. But something still didn't feel right to me.

I started asking a harder question: Was flattening enough? The answer was "no." Flattening removed a lot of vulnerabilities, but it didn't remove everything. Advanced malware could adapt to new formats. In rare cases, threats like steganography could survive the conversion and still cause harm. That wasn't a risk I was comfortable accepting.

That was the turning point at which I realized flattening was only the first step. To stay ahead, we needed to go deeper. We had to move from format conversion to real content-aware file regeneration. That meant understanding the structure of each file, separating what was safe from what wasn't, and rebuilding it with purpose.

That mindset shaped everything that came next. It became the foundation for our approach to CDR and how we think about prevention today.

Step 2: Implementing Intermediate Formats to Increase File Safety and Usability

After working through the limitations of basic file flattening, I started looking for a better way to reduce risk without sacrificing usability. That led to our next idea.

We began experimenting with a method that used intermediate formats to regenerate files. The concept was to convert a file into a safer format, clean it, and then convert it back to its original form.

We tested this with common file types. JPEG images were converted to BMP, cleaned, and then returned to JPEG format. Word documents were rendered as PDFs and then converted back into Word format. This method helped disrupt malware that relied on file structure or embedded logic while preserving the usability of the file. It also felt like a step forward from flattening, which often broke functionality.

We added this capability into our existing Metascan product and rolled it out to our customer base. Just like before, we made it available to everyone and encouraged feedback. Customers responded quickly. Many appreciated having cleaner files that still retained most of their original format and function. It felt more usable than pure flattening, and in many cases, the security outcomes were stronger. But it wasn't perfect.

Some reverted files didn't meet usability standards. Formatting would occasionally break. In some cases, interactive features stopped working. And while this approach improved security, it wasn't foolproof. Advanced malware and hidden content could still survive, especially if they were cleverly embedded or carried through the conversion process.

What we realized was that flattening and reformatting, while useful, were still fairly unsophisticated. These methods removed obvious threats, but they didn't fully understand the structure of the file. As we kept exploring, we discovered that file formats had layers of complexity we hadn't addressed. Within those layers were components that attackers often used to hide malware.

That realization sparked a new idea. If we could understand those internal structures, we could start giving security teams control over which parts of a file to keep and which to remove. This approach would allow for selective sanitization based on actual threat potential, not just a change in format.

By late 2008, it was clear that we needed more than format conversion. We had an opportunity to create something more advanced—something that could truly reshape the way we think about file security. That insight pushed us toward building what would become one of our most transformative innovations: a real CDR engine built on secure file regeneration.

Step 3: Building an Effective CDR Engine

To truly protect data, we had to stop thinking in terms of blocking or flattening and start thinking like the file itself. Every file format has a structure. Every piece of content has a place. I realized that if we could fully understand how files store data, and identify exactly where the threats could be hidden, we could surgically remove the risk and keep everything the user needs intact.

It felt like building a compiler, but in reverse. We weren't just parsing files. We were learning how to take them apart, clean them, and rebuild them from the ground up—safely and at scale.

We outlined three core steps to make it real:

A. **Identify the File Format**

   This came first. Before we could do anything else, we had to know exactly what we were dealing with. Misidentifying a format could mean applying the wrong rules or missing a threat entirely. So we built a robust file identification layer that could distinguish not just extensions, but true format signatures.

B. **Build a Reliable Parser**

   Once we knew the format, we needed to unpack it safely. For simple formats, this meant decompressing data, analyzing structure, and extracting raw content. For complex formats like DOCX, PDF, and PPTX, it meant parsing macros, URLs, media files, and embedded components with full awareness of how they interact.

We treated every format as its own ecosystem and built parsers that could walk through them without triggering anything dangerous.

C. Create the Regeneration File

This was the breakthrough. After parsing a file, we began reconstructing it from scratch. We used clean building blocks—validated text, images, layout structures, and metadata—and we rebuilt the file under strict configuration policies set by admins. Every macro, every script, every hidden URL was intentionally left out. Even image files and media were re-encoded to neutralize steganographic payloads or buffer overflow triggers.

But we weren't just focused on safety. We wanted the output to work. We wanted users to open regenerated files and not even notice a difference. To get there, we carefully preserved structure and layout, while eliminating every element that posed a risk.

When we saw the first files come out clean, fully functional, and threat-free, it was a moment of real validation. This wasn't flattening but something entirely different. **This was regeneration—the ability to take an untrusted file, rebuild it, and give it back to the user in a form they could trust.**

For simple formats, this eliminated risks like buffer overflows without breaking the file. For more advanced threats like steganography, we introduced slight distortions to disrupt hidden data while keeping the content visually unchanged.

What started as a technical project quickly became something much bigger. It became a way to restore confidence in data without slowing people down. We had built something that didn't just stop threats; it rebuilt safety into the fabric of every file.

CDR in Action: The JPEG Example

Now that we have walked through the attack vectors and the logic behind regeneration, I want to show you what CDR actually looks like in practice. Let's take the JPEG file, one of the most common formats in the world, and one of the most abused.

Imagine a JPEG arriving from an untrusted source. It could be attached to a phishing email, uploaded through a web form, or dropped on a USB stick during a targeted campaign. On the surface, it is just a photo. But inside its structure, the attacker may have planted malicious instructions. These can hide in EXIF tags, IPTC fields, or custom metadata blocks. They can even be encoded through steganographic tricks buried in pixel data. To the user, the image still looks like a sunset or a headshot. But to an attacker, it is a delivery mechanism. This is where the CDR engine goes to work.

1. File Identification

We never trust the extension alone. Attackers can rename a file from .exe to .jpg in seconds. Even the so-called "magic bytes" at the header like FF D8 FF for JPEG are not enough. A real CDR engine checks deeper. It verifies that the internal structure actually matches the JPEG specification: valid markers, segment order, quantization tables, and proper end-of-image markers. We also validate that the file is not masquerading as multiple formats at once, a common trick in polyglot files. Only when these consistency checks pass do we confirm that we are working with a true JPEG.

2. Parsing the Structure

Once identified, the file is broken down into its components. A JPEG is not just pixels. It has segments for compression, Huffman tables, quantization matrices, and embedded metadata like EXIF, IPTC, and XMP. Each of these pieces is read and analyzed. Attackers know this and abuse them, including EXIF fields carrying malicious payloads, oversized Huffman tables triggering buffer overflows (for vendors using outdated sanitization technologies), or thumbnail images stuffed with code.

3. Regeneration (Policy-Driven)

This is the heart of the process. **The engine extracts what is safe (the raw pixel data) and discards what is not. Then it rebuilds the file according to defined policies**. This means you can decide on the:

- **Compression level:** keep original quality, apply lossless compression, or re-encode to reduce file size.

- **Image dimensions:** enforce maximum width and height to stop oversized files that could be weaponized.

- **Metadata handling:** strip all metadata, or selectively remove sensitive fields like GPS coordinates, author names, or device IDs while keeping useful tags like orientation.

- **Format normalization:** standardize the file to a baseline JPEG spec version to eliminate unusual encodings.

- **Validation:** Before releasing the file, we run integrity checks. Compression ratios, color space, and image size are validated. If the file fails to meet structural expectations, it does not pass. If it succeeds, it is delivered. From the user's perspective, nothing looks different. From a security perspective, everything has changed.

The regenerated JPEG looks identical to the user but it is built clean, with only the allowed elements preserved. It is safe by construction, not by detection.

JPEG Sanitization

Before and After CDR

Component	Before CDR Untrusted JPEG	After CDR Regenerated JPEG
Pixel Data	May contain hidden payloads or manipulated values	Cleaned, re-encoded pixels only
EXIF Metadata	Device info, GPS coordinates, software version, user tags	Removed or scrubbed (per policy)
IPTC/XMP Metadata	Author, comments, editing history; embedded scripts possible	Removed or scrubbed (per policy)
Huffman Tables	Can be oversized or malformed to trigger buffer overflows	Rebuilt to match JPEG spec, safe defaults
Thumbnails	Can carry hidden payloads or obfuscated code	Regenerated or discarded
Compression Markers	Could be manipulated to crash parsers	Normalized to safe and standard structures
File Header/Footer	Can be spoofed or malformed to disguise file type	Verified and rebuilt clean

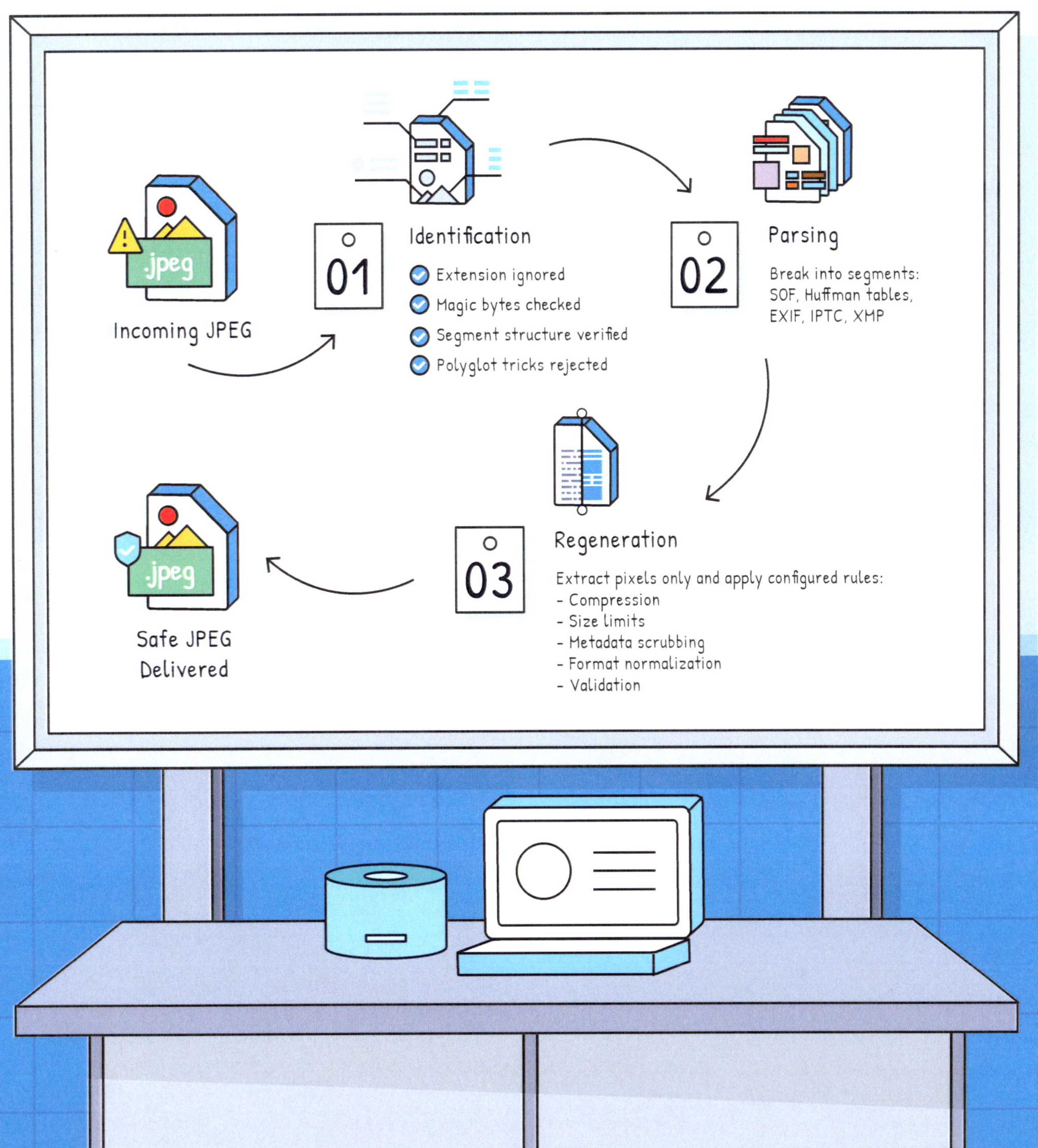

JPEG CDR Flow
Incoming JPEG
.jpeg
Identification
01
Extension ignored
Magic bytes checked
Segment structure verified
Polyglot tricks rejected
Parsing
02
Break into segments:
SOF, Huffman tables,
EXIF, IPTC, XMP
Regeneration
03
Extract pixels only and apply configured rules:
- Compression
- Size limits
- Metadata scrubbing
- Format normalization
- Validation
Safe JPEG
Delivered
.jpeg

Tackling the Hidden Dangers of
Recursive File Structures With Deep CDR™

Shortly after our first CDR deployments, our understanding of file formats had evolved significantly. Initially, we had categorized files as being simple or complex.

We soon discovered, however, that many common file formats used in business and personal communications, such as Word documents and PDF files, function more like containers or archives. These complex formats could contain other file formats that could also be complex or simple. For example, a PDF might contain embedded images or even additional PDFs, vastly increasing the original file's complexity.

This insight into what we call "the recursive nesting of data" led us to recognize that more files than we'd anticipated functioned as archives. The recursion in these file formats (i.e., their ability to contain instances of themselves or other files) presented unique challenges, as each embedded file within the original could potentially harbor additional risks or malicious content. This discovery made the CDR process exponentially more complex.

We recognized we needed an even more comprehensive approach to file sanitization, so we improved our CDR engine to function recursively, enabling it to apply the sanitization process to itself. We called this **"Deep CDR,"** and its development was an exciting technical breakthrough and a pivotal step in managing and mitigating risks associated with nested file structures.

One significant challenge was addressing the potential for an "archive bomb," which occurs when a file is designed to exhaust system resources during the extraction process by nesting files hundreds of levels deep. This approach effectively creates a denial-of-service attack from within. To combat this danger, we gave our CDR engine the ability to recognize and unpack these nested structures, applying stringent security checks to each extracted layer.

Our recursive CDR approach ensures that every layer, no matter how deeply it's embedded, is thoroughly cleaned and secured according to the same high standards set for top-level files. This capability allowed us to offer a more robust defense against complex cyber threats hidden in multi-layered file formats.

The development of Deep CDR marked a significant advancement of our cybersecurity capabilities. With it, we provided unprecedented protection against sophisticated threats lurking in the modern digital environment, ensuring our clients' data remains secure in an increasingly complex digital landscape.

Deep CDR: Success Stories and Skeptics

As Deep CDR gained traction, we received numerous success stories from customers who integrated CDR into their data firewall frameworks. Organizations reported significant improvements with CDR after finding that traditional antivirus and sandboxing solutions offered inadequate protection against continuous attacks. These customers also noted CDR's effectiveness in thwarting cyber threats that had previously bypassed conventional security measures.

One notable case involved a large manufacturing company that had initially viewed CDR merely as a "nice to have." Their perspective shifted dramatically, however, after a ransomware attack shut their facilities down. This incident led them to adopt CDR across their entire data flow, transforming their security posture and effectively mitigating the impact of such devastating attacks. This experience reinforced the importance of proactive content disarmament.

Despite numerous success stories, the path toward universal acceptance and implementation of Deep CDR has not always been smooth. Some clients remain hesitant, fearing that integrating file regeneration into their security protocols will be too complex, even though it's really not. Sometimes we just need to do a better job of explaining how CDR works.

Other times, organizations are reluctant to deviate from familiar, traditional security solutions. Notably, such hesitation is most pronounced among organizations that have yet to experience the impact of a severe cybersecurity breach. Unfortunately, they view the transition to CDR as unnecessary or overly complex until they encounter a critical incident that traditional defenses cannot mitigate. This disparity highlights the need for ongoing education and advocacy to demonstrate the benefits and necessity of advanced file sanitization techniques like Deep CDR.

At OPSWAT, we are committed to demonstrating CDR's effectiveness through case studies, educational outreach, and direct engagement with potential clients. Our goal is to emphasize the security CDR offers and its role in fostering a more resilient and secure operational environment.

By continually sharing success stories and addressing the reservations posed by skeptics, we continue to expand the adoption of Deep CDR, ensuring that more organizations are equipped to handle ever-evolving cyber threats.

The Hidden Dimension: File Versions

Just when I thought I had a grip on file types, another layer of complexity revealed itself: file versioning. It was one of those moments where the ground shifts under you. A PDF is not just a PDF and a JPEG is not just a JPEG. Each format evolves over time, adding features, embedding new capabilities, sometimes maintaining backward compatibility, and sometimes breaking it. That evolution adds an entirely new dimension to the challenge of CDR.

This realization hit me during testing. At first, we were validating that our CDR engine could correctly detect and regenerate file formats. But soon I noticed something: file detection was not enough. You also had to know which version of the format you were dealing with. Regenerating a PDF 1.0 file is not the same as regenerating a PDF 1.7 with embedded Flash objects and AES-256 encryption. The same is true for images, audio, video, and design files. If you miss the version, you miss the rules. Some extend older capabilities or patch flaws, and many leave behind a trail of semi-compatible debris. From a sanitization perspective, this means the parser cannot just ask, "Is this a PDF?" It must ask, "Is this a PDF 1.0, a PDF 1.5, or a PDF 2.0, and what tricks can each one hide?"

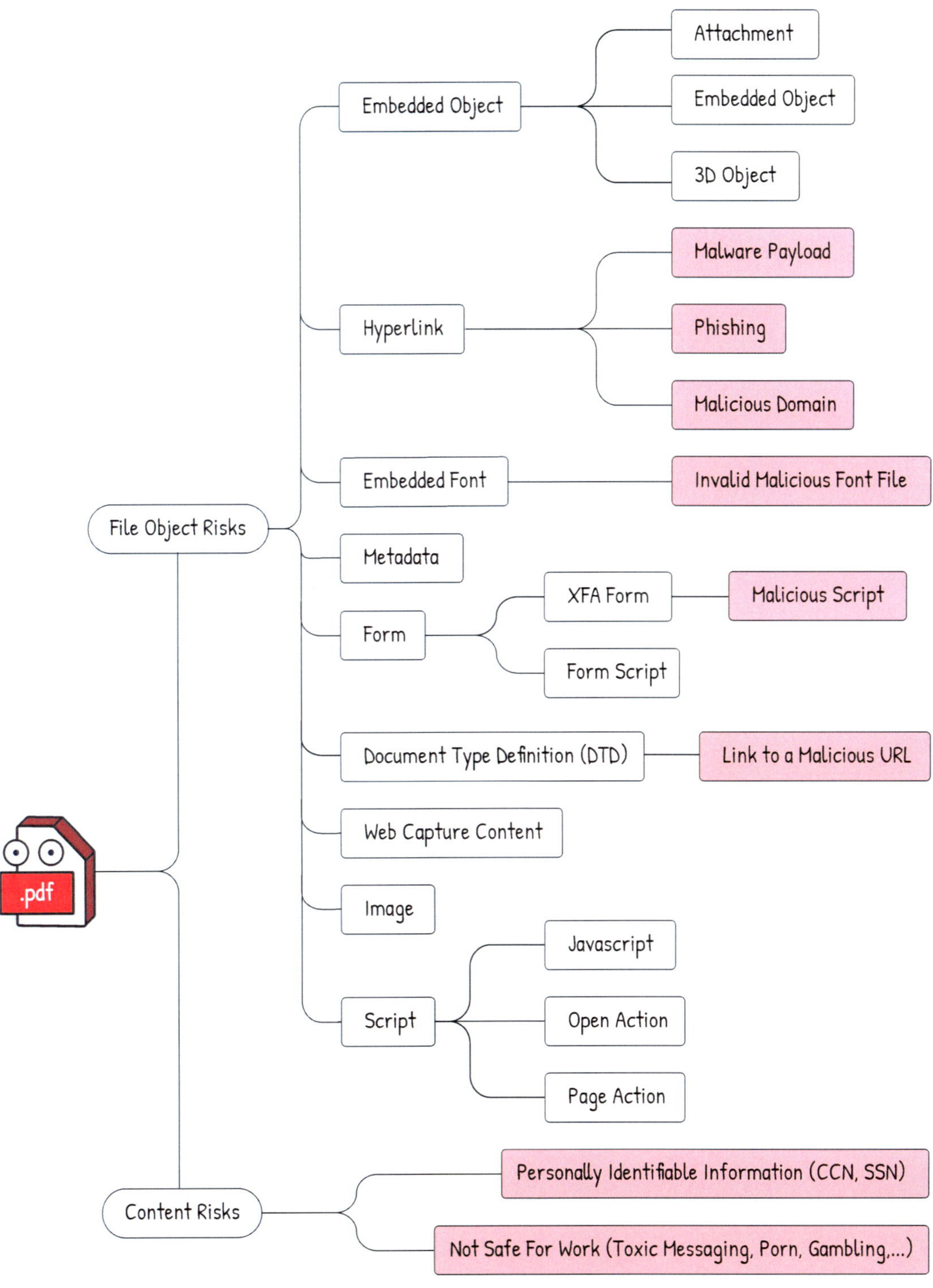

I discovered that many common file formats function more like containers or archives, providing a convenient place for bad actors to hide malicious content.

This complexity is not theoretical; it is right there in the history of common formats. This is why CDR cannot be a one-size-fits-all process.

A PDF 1.0 file might only need basic text and image validation. But a PDF 1.7 with embedded JavaScript and attachments requires a much deeper sanitization workflow. Similarly, a JPEG with only baseline compression is simpler to regenerate than one with extensions like SPIFF or JFIF, which may introduce extra structures.

In other words, versioning adds another axis to the problem. It is not just file type versus attack vector. It is file type and file version versus attack vector. Testing and validation must confirm not only that a file is identified correctly, but that it is parsed according to the right specification version.

This was one of the insights that shaped how I thought about the sanitization engine. It was not enough to think about executables versus productivity files, or simple versus complex. I also had to think about old versus new, and baseline versus extended. Each one had its own security story.

The lesson I carried forward was clear: CDR must be version-aware. Without that, you are not rebuilding files, you are gambling with them.

A Business Case and Market Opportunity for CDR

While the technical validation of CDR was already in motion, I quickly saw the opportunity to take it further. The engine we built was not just a powerful layer of security; it had the potential to stand on its own. We made the decision to license the technology as a separate engine and began embedding it across multiple products using different business models tailored to customer needs.

The market response was strong. CDR offered something organizations were not getting from traditional detection-based tools. It gave them confidence that files could be used safely without relying on signatures, threat feeds, or reactive scanning. It was more than just a new security feature; it represented a shift in how companies could think about prevention.

We positioned it as a core capability—a safeguard that would protect users, applications, and data flows in real time. Companies started viewing it as a critical layer in their defense strategy. It didn't replace their existing tools; it simply made everything they had more effective.

What started as a focused engineering effort turned into a true growth engine. CDR unlocked new revenue streams, created new licensing opportunities, and gave us a way to meet different customer needs across industries. Most importantly, it delivered measurable protection and became a cornerstone of trust in every product it touched.

PDF Version History

Version	Year	Key Features	Acrobat Reader Support
1.1	1994	Passwords, MD5/RC4 40-bit encryption, device-independent color	Acrobat 2.0
1.2	1996	Interactive forms (AcroForm), FDF data, Unicode, compression, external sound and movie support	Acrobat 3.0
1.3	2000	Digital signatures, embedded file streams, JavaScript actions, smooth shading	Acrobat 4.0
1.4	2001	JBIG2, transparency, XML form submissions, XMP metadata, tagged PDFs	Acrobat 5.0
1.5	2003	JPEG2000, multimedia embedding, cross-reference streams, XFA forms, public-key encryption	Acrobat 6.0
1.6	2004	3D artwork, OpenType embedding, AES encryption, improved signatures	Acrobat 7.0
1.7	2006	ISO standardization, extended multimedia, multiple attachments, stronger crypto	Acrobat 8+
Extensions 8.1-9.1	2008-2009	XFA extensions, AES-256 encryption, Flash/JavaScript integration	Acrobat 9+
Later Revisions	2011+	Newer scripting, multimedia, and security changes	Varies

Source: Adobe ISO 32000-1:2008, Wikipedia PDF specification history

JPEG Version History

Part	Standard	Year	Title	Description
1	ISO/IEC 10918-1:1994	1992	Requirements and Guidelines	Original JPEG Standard
2	ISO/IEC 10918-2:1995	1994	Compliance Testing	Rules for Conformance
3	ISO/IEC 10918-3:1997	1996	Extensions	Still Picture Interchange Format (SPIFF)
4	ISO/IEC 10918-4:1999	1998	Registration	Registration of JPEG Profiles and Markers
5	ISO/IEC 109185:2013	2011	JFIF	JPEG File Interchange Format Standardization
6	ISO/IEC 10918-6:2013	2012	Printing Systems	JPEG Subset for Printers
7	ISO/IEC 10918-7:2023	2019-2023	Reference Software	Official Reference Implementations

Source: International Organization for Standardization, IEC JPEG Standard History

FILES
EMAILS
ENDPOINTS
PERIPHERAL MEDIA
CLOUD/WEB
CODE
FIREWALL
FOR DATA
USER ENDPOINTS
APPLICATIONS
STORAGE
OTHER ORGANIZATIONS
RECURSIVE SANITIZATION
INVOICE.DOC
HIDDEN.PDF
PICTURE.JPG
CORPORATE.PPT
IMAGE.JPG
EM
DASHBOARD
AUDIT
REPORTING
SECURITY
SETTINGS
USER
LICENSE
LOCATION
DEEP CDR REPORT
BEFORE SANITIZATION
AFTER SANITIZATION
PDF
INFECTED 2/42
NO THREATS 0/42
DOC
INFECTED 12/42
NO THREATS 0/42
XLS
INFECTED 17/42
NO THREATS 0/42
RESULT FILE TYPE
USERS
I.T
LEGAL
LAB
MARKETING
USERS
FINANCE
ENGINEER
CYBERSECURITY
CREA
BLOCKED
ATASCAN DEEPSCAN PROACTIVE DLP ASSESS FILE
.PDF
.DOC
.DLL
.GIF
.AI
.MOV
.EPS
.AVI
.XML
.WAV
SEARCH
USAGE
DASHBOARD
HISTORY
WORKFLOW
USER
INVENTORY
SETTINGS
BLOCKED OBJECTS
264
PROCESSED OBJECTS
5.4K
SUMMARY
ALLOWED
PROCESS ADMIN VULNERABILITY F
.ISO
.RAW
.MID
.FLV
.DWG
.SVG
.RSS
.MDB

Building the Engine That Could Rebuild Everything

Our technical vision was clear from the beginning. We wanted to create an engine that could securely rebuild every file, no matter how simple or complex. We started with the most common productivity formats: DOCX, XLSX, PDF, JPEG, and ZIP. These were the everyday files flowing through inboxes, upload portals, and collaboration tools. And they were also the formats most frequently abused in real-world attacks.

To take this on, I began building a team that believed in the mission: not just engineers, but people who were genuinely excited about solving hard problems and redefining how security could work. We weren't just creating a security layer. We were reimagining the relationship between productivity and protection.

From the start, we knew scale would be our biggest challenge, so we created a shared internal language—a framework of parsing logic, transformation rules, validation models, and policy controls. This gave us a foundation that allowed each new file type to be added faster, tested more efficiently, and hardened against new threat patterns. It also let us handle different versions and subtypes of formats like PDF 1.3, 1.7, or MS Office documents with legacy macro support.

Speed and security had to scale together, however. Every time we added a new file type, we optimized for performance without compromising integrity. We tuned the parser, improved the regeneration logic, and integrated secure validation checkpoints to ensure clean output every time.

But we also knew that not every user needed the same level of strictness. Some customers wanted maximum protection and were fine removing all active content. Others needed interactive features to remain functional. So we started building flexible configuration layers. With these controls, users could move along the spectrum from fully locked down to fully usable, based on their risk profile and business needs.

Once we introduced Deep CDR...we were regenerating files, stripping out risk, and delivering trusted, safe content before anything had a chance to do harm.

This wasn't just about rebuilding files. It was about rebuilding trust in the data that powers modern organizations. We knew we had something that could go beyond traditional detection. And we kept going with more formats, options, precision, and a relentless focus on doing it better, faster, and safer each time.

Evolving Metascan Into MetaDefender

When we first built Metascan, the name made sense. Our focus back then was scanning. We were identifying threats and helping customers detect what shouldn't be there. But as our technology evolved, our thinking did, too.

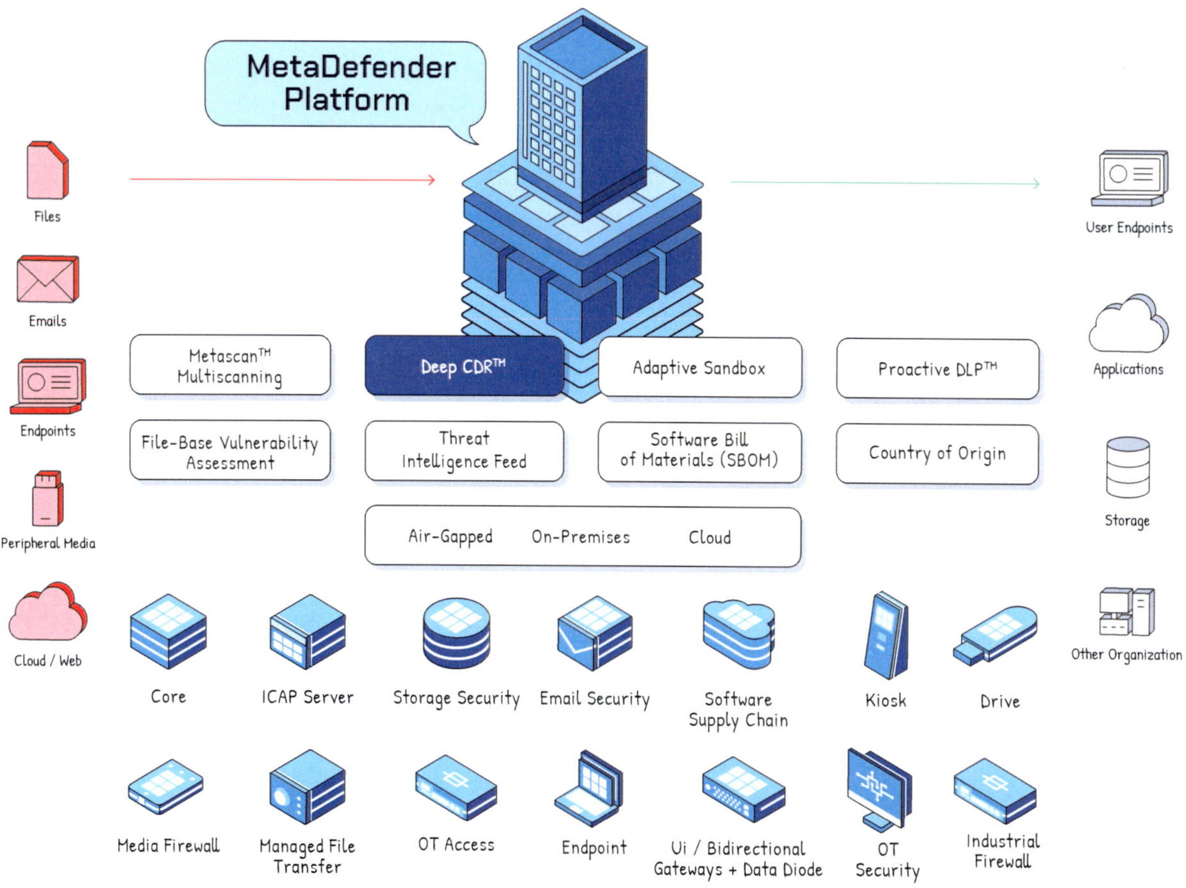

Once we introduced Deep CDR, everything changed. We were no longer simply scanning. We were regenerating files, stripping out risk, and delivering trusted, safe content before anything had a chance to do harm. Our work moved from detection to prevention; from scanning to defending.

It became clear that the name Metascan no longer fit. It sounded passive and it was tied to an old mindset. We needed something that better reflected what we had built and where we were going, so we renamed the product "MetaDefender."

MetaDefender wasn't just a new label; it was a new identity. It spoke to the real power behind our engine—the ability to defend files, users, and infrastructure by removing threats before they exist. It also captured the idea of standing between data and danger; of creating clean, usable content that teams could trust.

We also wanted customers to hear the name and understand immediately that this was not just another tool that waits for something to go wrong. This was a platform built for preemptive protection—a way to stop threats before they become incidents.

Ultimately, the name change was part of something bigger. It was the moment we stopped explaining what we used to do and started showing what we were truly capable of doing. With sanitization at its core, MetaDefender became more than a product; it became a promise.

Looking Ahead—How CDR Changes the Cybersecurity Equation

CDR reshaped how we thought about cybersecurity. Instead of chasing alerts and reacting to breaches, we now had a way to neutralize threats before they caused any damage. That shift didn't just improve security; it made it stable. It gave organizations a way to predict risk and budget with confidence. No more constant cycles of emergency patches and reactive spending.

CDR lets teams focus on building, not just defending. It turns security into something proactive, measurable, and reliable. And it's just the beginning.

The next chapter goes deeper into what CDR and file sanitization actually mean for security leaders. It covers the decisions that matter, the controls that drive adoption, and the steps that are needed to bring this technology into a modern enterprise. Transitioning from detection to prevention requires a fundamental change in mindset and architecture—in the next chapter, we will explore what that looks like.

100%
BATTLE
READY
SANITIZATION
PREVENTION

CHAPTER FIVE

ADVANCED CDR

A CISO's guide to deployment, trade-offs, and reality.

Back in 2008, we based the development of our cybersecurity solution on a simple idea: What if files could be rebuilt to be safe before we ever opened them? That basic file-conversion tool has since grown into a fully-engineered CDR (Content Disarm and Reconstruction) Platform, trusted by thousands of organizations—from power plants and banks to manufacturing facilities and defense installations—in 80 countries.

Looking back, the journey has been revealing. When we introduced this technology, responses ranged from interest and curiosity to hesitation and skepticism. Some dismissed it entirely; others reached out only after experiencing a serious incident. Ironically, it was often the most resistant teams who later became the strongest supporters.

We learned quickly that selling CDR was never just about listing features. It required strong relationships and a shared belief in what the technology could do. That's why we built the OPSWAT Academy, which has certified more than 200,000 professionals. We also changed our mindset about staffing by hiring solution architects instead of salespeople. And we changed the conversation from product to strategy.

In this chapter, I want to share what we learned, starting with what I call "the 10,000-foot view for CISOs." We'll then zoom in closer to address the architects and engineers who helped make it all work.

Highlights in this chapter include:

1. **Prepare the Team: Cultural and Technical Buy-In**
   Why some teams embrace CDR early—and how to lead the ones that don't.

2. **Map Your File Flows: The First Step to a Real Deployment**
   You can't secure what you haven't mapped. This is always the first real step.

3. **The Business Case for CDR**
   How to talk to leadership about ROI, security operation center (SOC) relief, audit wins, and privacy enforcement.

4. **Detection: You Can't Rely Solely On It, and You Can't Live Without It**
   Why CDR doesn't replace detection, but absolutely complements it.

5. **A Practical Process for Rolling Out CDR**
   Start focused. Show results. Build confidence. Expand wisely.

We'll also touch on how to choose the right CDR engine and how to verify that your CDR protocol is effective based on real-world testing, dataset validation, and spotting false bravado in marketing claims.

Finally, we'll discuss:

- **Comprehensive and Responsive File-Type Support**
  Why file version support is critical—and what most vendors won't tell you.

- **Securing the CDR Process**
  Hardening the engine itself: file spoofing, parser exploits, and regeneration vulnerabilities.

- **Designing CDR Policies That Actually Work**
  How to move beyond defaults and tailor your policies for file types, use cases, and user roles.

- **Ensuring the Speed and Scalability of CDR**
  How to avoid performance issues before they happen.

- **Preserving File Usability**
  Safety doesn't mean much if the output breaks. Users must trust the result.

- **Operational Trade-offs in the CDR Architecture**
  What changes? What breaks? What's not covered? And why it's important to be transparent early?

My goal is simple: to help your team move faster, avoid common missteps, and get it right the first time.

Setting the Table for CISOs

Your security posture lives and dies with your people. It's not the engine—it's the team behind it. Tools help, but people protect. And sometimes, when it comes to implementing CDR, the biggest challenge isn't technical, it's cultural.

1. Prepare the Team: Cultural and Technical Buy-In

Deep CDR isn't just another detection engine. It doesn't wait for a threat to trigger an alert. Deep CDR assumes every file is suspicious and rebuilds it to be safe before it's ever opened. This approach assumes risk is always present—not just when an alert is sounded. For many teams, this takes time to digest.

Let's be honest: Resistance is normal. Some people worry about hashes changing or files looking different. Others fear an influx of support tickets or usability complaints. Dig deeper, however, and you'll often find something more personal. You might be challenging professionals who've spent their entire career mastering detection tools, such as antivirus, sandboxing, and EDR. For them, having to accept a new concept like CDR can feel as if you're tossing aside years of experience and implying that their life's work isn't good enough.

Sometimes it's not even about the tech itself. People get attached to brands. They follow AI hype, they invest in certifications, and they lean on analyst frameworks that prioritize detection. In many cases, CDR hasn't shown up on those checklists yet, so it feels unfamiliar and can even be perceived as threatening.

This is where leadership matters most.

Start by creating curiosity. Don't lead with slides; lead with real examples. Show your team instances in which files that passed traditional scanners would have been blocked or neutralized with CDR. Use internal incident data if you can. Those are the stories that change minds. Once you have their interest, run a pilot. Keep it small and low-risk: one use case, one channel. Let the team see how it works.

Back it up with hands-on workshops, training, and peer case studies. Invite your engineers to join threat forums, or CDR user groups. Let them hear from others who've made the shift. This builds trust. Present them with short success stories and run analyses on malware incidents that CDR could have prevented.

If there's a regulatory incentive, highlight it. Even near-misses can help create momentum. Compliance is rarely the sole reason teams adopt CDR, but it's often a helpful boost.

Most important, show empathy. Change is hard, especially when it challenges someone's foundational understanding. Recognize their experience. Make it clear that CDR is not replacing what they've built (at least for now)—it's expanding it by filling in the blind spots detection was never meant to uncover.

Once your team understands the "why," they'll come around. And once they take ownership, the shift becomes theirs, not just yours. That's when things begin to click—not because CDR is a better tool, but because your team believes in the problem it solves.

2. Map Your File Flows: The First Step to a Real Deployment

Rolling out CDR in a large organization isn't something you just switch on, however. It's a shift, and only when it reaches scale does it become a real program. What's worked well for me is breaking the implementation down into two tracks.

The first track is all about understanding the data flows—what's coming in, what's going out, and how it moves internally. That often means sitting down with the CISO's team, whiteboarding workflows, and asking some basic-but-revealing questions:

- Where do files enter the environment?
- Who's sending them?
- How are they being used?

You'd be surprised how often even mature teams don't have full visibility. Most organizations track devices and users but not the actual flow of files and data. So, we map it. This can sometimes be a painful process, but it pays off.

The second track is about infrastructure. We review what security and IT systems are already in place and figure out how CDR fits in. This is where things get real. We start spotting overlaps, gaps, and opportunities to embed CDR into existing workflows without causing friction.

Both steps matter. Miss the data flow, and you'll leave openings. Miss the architecture fit, and your rollout will stall. Together, they give you the foundation to build something that actually works and sticks.

Below is a summary of the common data channels I usually review during these early conversations. Each one has its own quirks, but they're all places where unsafe files

Data Flow Channel	Description	CDR Integration Strategy
Email Systems	Main channel for external file delivery	Sanitize attachments and links using an SMTP proxy or Graph API (Office 365).
Web Traffic	Files downloaded via browser or apps	Use ICAP (Internet Content Adaptation Protocol) with a web proxy to clean files before delivery.
APIs	Software-to-software file transfers	Redirect file flows through a CDR-enabled API gateway.
Cloud Services	File uploads and downloads from SaaS or storage platforms	Integrate CDR via API, agent, or cloud tunnel.
Mobile Apps and Devices	File exchange from managed or unmanaged phones and tablets	Sanitize through your MDM or secure mobile gateway.
Network File Sharing	Internal file transfers on shared drives or SharePoint	Add CDR to your storage protection layer.
Databases	Data pulled into or from databases, often file-based uploads	Sanitize files before insertion using an API.
Physical Media	USBs, DVDs, external hard drives, etc.	Sanitize with endpoint agents or kiosk stations.
IoT Devices	Smart devices exchanging files (e.g., cameras, printers)	CDR supports file-based sanitization to prevent overflow or logic injection.
Remote Access	RDP, VPN, or virtual browsers	Scan incoming files at ingress before saving or opening.
Social Media and Messaging	Files shared through LinkedIn, WhatsApp, and similar tools	Sanitize files on download through browser proxy or endpoint tools.
FTP Transfers	File transfers using older FTP systems	Inject CDR into FTP flows via custom scripts or middleware.
Slack/Teams/Chat	Files shared via corporate chat apps	Sanitize via inline. proxy, API, or bot-based upload handler

can creep in unnoticed and where CDR, if applied right, can quietly neutralize threats before anyone ever sees them.

Once you visualize your file flows like this, it's no longer overwhelming—it becomes actionable. Start where it matters most. Prove it works. Expand with confidence and with clear priorities. You don't need to do it all at once. Start where the risk is highest, prove it works, then expand.

It's not just about switching on CDR. It's about turning it into something your organization can trust and grow with.

CDR doesn't replace your tools— it complements them by protecting against file-based threats.

Integrating CDR Into Existing Security Infrastructure

Once we understand and prioritize how data flows through the organization, the next step is figuring out where CDR fits.

Most companies already have a solid security stack—firewalls, endpoint protection, email gateways, data loss prevention (DLP), and security information and event management (SIEM). The real question is: Where does CDR amplify what's already working, and where does it cover what detection can't? The challenge isn't starting from zero—it's finding where CDR can be added to strengthen what's already working.

CDR doesn't replace your tools—it complements them by protecting against file-based threats before they're even detected.

When deciding where to begin CDR integration, I usually suggest starting with the areas that handle the most files. Email, file uploads, and web downloads are high-volume/high-risk areas. Starting here makes it easy to show value quickly.

That said, some teams prefer to ease into it. In these cases, starting with a small use case—such as a public-file-upload form or internal file exchange—is a great way to build trust. Starting this way also gives your team and users a chance to see how the system works without overwhelming them.

Where CDR Adds Value

Here's a table I often use when mapping out integrations with CISOs and their teams. It gives
a clear picture of where CDR adds value, and where it doesn't need to be involved.

Security System	What It Does	CDR Integration
Firewalls and Load Balancers	Block and filter network traffic.	Can integrate via ICAP to sanitize files entering or leaving the network, some firewalls and load balancers support Rest API.
Antivirus, EPP, EDR	Detect and stop known malware.	Integration is rare, and to protect the endpoint, a sanitization client may need to get this installed.
IDS (Intrusion Detection System)/IPS (Intrusion Prevention System)/NDR (Network Detection and Response)	Monitor network behavior and detect threats.	Not applicable here. These tools look at patterns, not files.
Data Loss Prevention (DLP)	Prevent sensitive data from leaving the network.	Sanitizes outbound files before they are transferred, supporting DLP accuracy.
Security Information and Event Management (SIEM)	Centralize and analyze security alerts.	Not directly integrated, but logs from the CDR engine can feed into SIEM.
Email Security	Block phishing and email-borne malware.	One of the top use cases. Integrate via SMTP relay, Graph API, or cloud email gateway.
Web Security Gateways	Protect users from unsafe websites and downloads.	Sanitization can scan downloaded files through ICAP or Rest API.
Identity and Access Management (IAM)	Control access to applications and data.	Not a direct fit, but works in parallel to protect files being accessed or uploaded.
VPN or SDP	Provide secure remote access.	Integration is rare, and to protect the endpoint, the sanitization client may need to get this installed.
Mobile Device Management (MDM)	Secure mobile devices and control apps.	Can sanitize files on mobile devices via API connection with MDM.
Network Access Control (NAC)	Restrict devices based on compliance.	Not typically used here.
Cloud Access Security Broker (CASB)	Monitor and control cloud app usage.	Sanitizes uploads and downloads from cloud platforms using API or ICAP.
Security Awareness Training	Train employees to recognize threats.	Not a technical integration, but you can show users how files are regenerated to reinforce awareness.
Encryption Tools	Protect data confidentiality.	Apply CDR before encrypting files or after decryption.
Secure File-Transfer Tools	Transfer files securely across systems.	Sanitize files before transfer using an API or ICAP integration.
Vulnerability Management	Identify software vulnerabilities.	Not applicable here. This area focuses on patching, not file safety.
Penetration Testing Tools	Simulate attacks to test defenses.	Doesn't integrate directly, but can highlight the need for CDR during risk analysis.

Every organization is different. The right approach depends on what systems you already have in place, how much risk you're facing, and how quickly your team is ready to move. The best rollouts I've seen combine technical readiness with user adoption. Communicate clearly, show the value early, and keep everyone involved.

CDR doesn't compete with your existing tools—it strengthens them by filling a critical gap that detection-based systems can't always cover, giving you an extra layer of protection where it counts most.

How CDR Saves Money

1. Direct Cost Reduction
- **Incident Response:** Fewer active breaches mean fewer hours spent on forensics, fewer war rooms, and reduced third-party incident response (IR) retainers.
- **Legal and Compliance:** Avoid fines, investigations, and regulatory escalations by stopping incidents before they trigger reporting thresholds.
- **Notification Costs:** If there's no incident, there's nothing to disclose to customers, partners, or regulators.
- **Remediation and Recovery:** No malware means no image rebuilds, no patch scrambles, and no user disruption.

2. Indirect Cost Savings
- **Brand Trust:** Quiet security is powerful. Avoiding public breaches protects your company's reputation and long-term customer relationships.
- **Operational Continuity:** Keep your business running smoothly without shutdowns or "all hands" fire drills.
- **Cyber Insurance:** Some organizations have negotiated lower premiums due to the reduced risk profile CDR brings.

3. Security Impact
- **Intellectual Property Protection:** Most targeted attacks don't come in as executables– they come in as files. Sanitizing those files protects your sensitive data from being exfiltrated or weaponized.
- **Fewer False Positives:** CDR regenerates clean versions of files, which means fewer alerts from downstream tools, less noise, and fewer SOC headaches.
- **Faster Incident Response:** Many IR teams now rely on sanitized versions of suspicious documents to analyze intent without delay. There is no sandbox lag and no risk of detonation.

The Business Case for CDR

Before you pitch ROI, think about this: What would you give to remove 80 percent of the noise from your SOC overnight?

Don't evaluate CDR as a replacement. Evaluate it as a multiplier that reduces noise, lowers response times, and stops the threats your current stack wasn't built to catch. Most importantly, don't start by comparing CDR to another detection product. Start by thinking about everything you wish your current stack could stop.

Think about all the zero-day exploits that detection engines miss. Think about all the malware noise your SOC has to dig through daily. Think about how many productivity files flood your email gateway, only to get kicked to a sandbox or, worse, delivered and detonated by accident. CDR gives you a way to flip the model. Instead of chasing threats, you prevent them outright by rebuilding every file before it lands on your endpoint.

This isn't about replacing your security stack—it's about reducing its stress. It's about clearing out the noise so your detection tools can focus on what they're actually good at—finding real anomalies, not fighting embedded macros or malformed JPEGs pretending to be clean.

Detection: You Can't Rely Solely on It Alone, but You Can't Live Without It

During a recent roundtable with several CISOs, we had a conversation that comes up every time I talk about CDR. One question in particular stood out: "What do I do with files I'm not allowed to change?"

It's a fair question, and in a perfect world, we'd sanitize everything. But in reality, certain files—due to legal, operational, or regulatory reasons—need to stay exactly as they are. You can't regenerate them, redact them, or even adjust their structure. In these cases, CDR won't help. But that doesn't mean you're stuck.

This is where detection still plays a critical role. Antivirus, IDS, and behavioral analytics tools remain essential for visibility. When you can't sanitize, you rely on monitoring, logging, and alerting. It's not about choosing one over the other—it's about combining both in a smart way.

Another common question involves unsupported file types: "What about the files your vendor doesn't support?"

The truth is, no engine covers everything. There will always be gaps—executable files, rare formats, legacy systems that don't fit into the CDR process. That's when traditional defenses step in. Multiscanning, sandboxing, and sometimes even manual review are the right answer. These tools still add value. They just require more time and vigilance.

In looking at **CDR versus detection**, it's important to be honest about what CDR is and isn't. CDR doesn't detect. It doesn't raise alerts. It doesn't tell you who's attacking or where the malware came from. It simply removes risky elements from files based on structure and policy. That's its strength, but also its limitation. (Although CDR's primary purpose is not malware detection, we have leveraged the file type detection and the CDR parsing engine to improve additional detection layers within our MetaDefender platform.)

Detection is what tells you when something is going wrong. It's how you measure your exposure, investigate incidents, and meet compliance obligations. Detection helps your teams understand where the threats are coming from and how they behave.

Even in a fully-sanitized environment, detection still matters. Threat research, incident response, and forensics all depend on it. It gives you the broader picture that prevention alone can't provide.

So, no, we're not replacing detection. And we shouldn't try to. What we're doing is shifting the burden. Let CDR also take the unknown, the non-predictable, and the new AI-generated malware that traditional tools struggle with. Then let your detection tools focus on what they do best—finding the truly suspicious activity, fulfilling compliance requirements, and handling the cases your team actually wants to investigate.

That's how you get a more resilient stack—not by choosing one path, but by combining both where they work best.

A Practical Process for Rolling Out CDR

One thing that's important to understand from the beginning: **CDR is not an on-off switch**. Unlike traditional (anti-malware) tools, which are often binary in nature (they allow, block, detect, or ignore), CDR is nuanced. It requires thoughtful configuration based on how your organization actually uses files.

For example, you might allow macros for one internal group but strip them for everyone else. Or you might allow embedded images in marketing materials but block them in finance. These kinds of choices matter. And they're what make CDR powerful when deployed correctly.

I've seen a lot of projects over the years. Some were beautifully planned, others were held together with duct tape and adrenaline. But even the messiest implementations have a few common characteristics.

If you're just starting out, here's a simple process that I've seen work across different industries and environments. You don't need to change everything at once—you just need to get the sequence right.

Step 1: Build Internal Buy-In and Train Your Team

Start with your people. They need to understand why CDR matters, what makes it different, and where it fits in your security stack. Use real-world examples. Offer a quick workshop or run a hands-on demo. Once the team gets it, the rest will fall into place.

Step 2: Map Your File Flows

Look at all the entry points where files come in—email, web downloads, cloud apps, partner uploads, etc. Don't assume you've covered everything—audit it. You'll likely discover flows that were never documented. The goal is to understand which files are coming in, where they're coming from, and how they're being used.

Step 3: Build a Deployment Plan

Focus on your high-risk or high-volume areas first. For many companies, that means email, followed by web downloads and file-upload portals. Don't overextend yourself. Choose one or two use cases, select a vendor, and start from there.

Step 4: Configure for Your Environment

This is where things get real. Policies should always be tailored to match their business usage. Maintain a small allowlist of trusted, validated macros for your automation teams, and then block all other macros, especially in files that arrive from outside of the organization. Teams that genuinely need macros should document them first and then have them reviewed before adding them to the allowlist instead of turning macros on globally.

Step 5: Learn, Tune, and Expand

Once live, monitor everything. What's getting sanitized? What's being rejected? Where are users seeing friction? Use this feedback to fine-tune your setup. Then expand to more channels and file types as your team's confidence grows.

Step 6: Maintain and Improve

CDR isn't a set-it-and-forget-it technology. Update your engine. Evolve your policies. Add support for new formats as your business changes. Keep the system current so it continues doing its job without getting in the way.

How Do You Verify That Your CDR Is Effective?

In the last few years, we've seen a surge in new companies claiming to offer CDR. That may sound like progress, but in many cases, it's created more confusion than clarity.

Some vendors simply offer file conversion and call it "sanitization." Others remove a macro and market it as a complete solution. I've even seen cybersecurity executives talk confidently about how their platform adopts malware signatures as part of their "data sanitization strategy." That completely misses the point. CDR isn't detection or containment. It is prevention achieved by regenerating the file, not by trying to analyze it.

For CISOs, the challenge now is cutting through the noise. What's real, what's marketing, and what actually protects the organization?

In this section, I'll walk you through how to evaluate a vendor, what to test, and how to know if you're working with a partner who understands the real mission behind data sanitization.

1. Is My CDR Solution Working?

This is the first question a CISO should ask—and the one most vendors answer with slides instead of proof. My take? Show me the file, show me the output, and let me run it myself.

In Chapter 4, we covered the difference between simple and complex file formats and walked through examples in which threats—such as buffer overflows, steganography, macros, and embedded scripts—can hide in seemingly harmless files. **It's important to remember that simply converting or modifying a file doesn't mean the threat has been eliminated.**

As the CDR market grows, so do the marketing claims. Everyone says they sanitize "deeply." But in reality, only a few products show consistent results. That's not unusual; it happens with every valuable technology. Counterfeits only show up when the real thing has impact.

This is where the journey to total data security really starts: finding a solution that does what it claims to do, and a partner you can trust to protect the way data flows into your organization.

2. Approaches to Testing

You don't need a glossy brochure. You need proof.

Before committing to any data-sanitization platform, hands-on testing is the single best way to validate that it works for your environment, file types, and risks. Without it, you're operating on trust alone.

Start with a plan that includes testing both simple and complex files across realistic use cases. A strong dataset should cover threats such as malformed headers, embedded scripts, macros, malicious links, nested objects, and even obscure attacks like steganography. The more diverse your test set, the more confidence you'll have that the system works not just in theory, but in practice.

If your budget allows, consider purchasing a malware feed from a reputable cybersecurity vendor. These usually include a broad mix of formats and real-world threats. Running them through the engine gives your team something tangible they can see, inspect, and learn from. In my experience, this kind of testing sparks real engagement from quality assurance (QA) and security teams. It encourages creativity and brings out good questions, which almost always leads to a stronger deployment.

You can also take malware samples your organization has already flagged—especially those embedded in productivity files such as Word, Excel, and PDFs—and run them through your CDR engine. Once they're sanitized, rescan the output with your existing detection tools. If they're no longer flagged as malicious and the functionality is preserved, that's a powerful signal that the CDR process is working as intended.

For teams that don't have the time or resources to test deeply in-house, third-party labs can help. SE Labs regularly publishes performance reports on sanitization solutions. These aren't just checkbox reviews. They go into threat removal, file usability, and false positives. Just make sure the tests reflect your reality, because file types, data channels, and workflows all matter.

When evaluating any CDR solution, a key question to ask is: Can it reliably sanitize the files your people use every day?

Whether testing happens inside your walls or through a trusted partner, this is the moment at which marketing claims become measurable outcomes. It's your first chance to see if the product truly performs and to build the confidence your team needs before rollout.

Once you see it work with your own data, the conversation changes from "Does it work?" to "How fast can we get this running?"

3. Comprehensive and Responsive File-Type Support

One of the most overlooked but absolutely critical challenges in deploying CDR is file-type coverage. There are anywhere from 10,000 to 15,000 known file types in use today. No single organization uses them all, but most use far more than they realize. And the mix varies widely depending on your industry, geography, and the tools your teams rely on.

Design and architecture firms often depend on AutoCAD or Adobe Creative Suite. Legal teams may handle older Microsoft formats, while financial institutions exchange zipped archives with embedded spreadsheets. In South Korea, the .hwp format is everywhere. In Japan, .jtd files from JustSystems' Ichitaro are still more common than Microsoft Word. These aren't edge cases—they're mission-critical for daily work in those regions.

When evaluating any CDR solution, a key question to ask is: Can it reliably sanitize the files your people use every day? If it can't, that's not a small gap—it's a blind spot. And blind spots are where threats hide and get through.

Unsupported or partially supported formats create holes that attackers can exploit. Worse yet, they create frustration among users who may bypass CDR altogether when it breaks something they need.

4. Start With What You Use

Before selecting a vendor:

- Map out the file types used across your organization.
- Ask the vendor for a complete and current list of supported file types and versions.
- Then, pressure-test that list against what matters to your teams.

Don't just stop at "PDF" or "Office" support. Dig deeper. If you are not sure what you use, a large language model (LLM) query on your security information and event management (SIEM) system, your firewall logs, or Office 365 might reveal most of them.

Also, ask how support is maintained. Are new types added regularly through structured research, or only when customers complain? The ideal answer would be both.

Here's a reference table I often share with teams during evaluations:[1]

Type	Version	Release Date	Key Updates
.doc	1.0, 1.1, 1.2, 1.3, 1.4, 1.5, 1.6, 1.7, 2.0	1993–2017	Standardized by ISO Introduced transparency and metadata Transitioned to PDF 2.0 for ISO-only control
.jpeg	JPEG, JFIF, Exif, JPEG-LS, JPEG 2000, JPEG XR, JPEG XT, JPEG XS, JPEG XL	1992–2021	Added wavelet compression (JPEG 2000) Introduced HDR support (JPEG XR) Improved compression and backward compatibility (JPEG XL)
.png	1.0, 1.1, 1.2	1996–2003	Replaced GIF with lossless compression Standardized by ISO
.doc	1.0, 2.0, 6.0 / 95, 97, 2000, 2002 / XP, 2003	1990–2003	Introduced binary DOC format Transitioned to XML-based DOCX format
.xlsx	2.0, 4.0, 5.0, 95, 97, 2000, 2002 / XP, 2003	1987–2003	Introduced BIFF8 format Transitioned to XML-based XLSX format
.pptx	1.0, 2.0, 3.0, 4.0, 95, 97, 2000, 2002 / XP, 2003	1987–2003	Introduced binary PPT format Transitioned to XML-based PPTX format
.html	1.0, 2.0, 3.2, 4.0, 4.01, XHTML 1.0, HTML5	1993–2016	Standardized web structure Introduced multimedia and APIs Adopted Living Standard model
.mp4	Version 1, Version 2, 2020, 2022	2003–2022	Established as standard container Enhanced streaming and metadata support Integrated modern video codecs (HEVC, AV1)
.zip	1.0, 2.0, 4.5, 6.3	1989–2019	Added 64-bit (ZIP64) support Enhanced encryption and metadata features
.hwp	1.0, 2.0, 3.0, 5.0, HWPX	1989–2010	Transitioned to XML-based format (HWPX) Improved cross-platform compatibility
.jtd	1.0, 2.0, 3.0, 4.0, 5.0, 6.0, JTDX	1985–2013	Introduced rich text support Adopted XML structure for modern versions

1 "File.Org - We Help You Open Your Files!," file.org, accessed July 9, 2025, https://file.org/

5. Version Support Matters Just as Much

Choosing the right vendor isn't just about the file types they cover—it's about the versions, too. File formats evolve over time. Some get more secure. Others introduce complexity. If a CDR engine doesn't keep up, its sanitization logic can fall out of sync with the files it's meant to protect.

Take PDFs, for example. Adobe introduced PDF 1.0 in 1993. Since then, the format has undergone more than a dozen significant updates. PDF 1.3 introduced digital signatures; 1.5 brought in layers and new metadata fields. PDF 2.0, released in 2017, became an ISO standard and brought major changes to how interactive content and encryption are handled. A CDR engine that supports only "PDF" as a label doesn't tell you much. You need to know which versions are covered and how well.

This versioning challenge applies across the board to DOCX, XLSX, ZIP, HTML, and more. Each new version can change how scripts are embedded, how metadata is structured, and how file content is rendered. All of these differences affect how files should be parsed and rebuilt during sanitization.

A. What to Press the Vendor On

When you're in the evaluation phase, here are a few practical questions I always ask:

- Can you provide your full list of supported file types and their specific versions?

- How quickly do you add support for emerging or obscure formats?

- Is your engine version-aware? Can it parse and sanitize based on version-specific logic?

- How do you handle malformed or corrupted files?

- Can I test your system against the actual file mix we use, including older documents?

This is not just a technical checkbox—it's foundational as to whether the system works in the real world. The broader and more responsive the file type coverage, the fewer exceptions you'll encounter, and the more consistent your protection will be.

B. Service Level Agreements for New File Types and Versions

One of the easiest ways to future-proof your CDR deployment is also one of the most often overlooked: Negotiate a service-level agreement (SLA) that guarantees timely support for new file types and evolving format versions.

Think of it the same way antivirus software handles new threats. Just as AV engines push daily updates to stay ahead of new strains, your CDR solution should be backed by a process that tracks file format evolution and adapts in real time. Formats don't stay static. PDFs, Office files, ZIPs, and media files are always changing, and new types emerge every year.

Without an SLA in place, you're relying on goodwill or customer escalation to drive updates. That's not good enough.

A strong SLA gives you leverage. It sets expectations and, most importantly, it tells you something about the vendor: whether they're proactive or reactive.

What to Ask:

- Can you share recent examples of file types or versions you've added?

- What's your current roadmap for file format support?

- Do you guarantee timelines for critical updates or new format support?

- How do you track emerging file types? Is it research-led or customer-driven?

If a vendor is serious about maintaining effective protection, they'll be ready to put it in writing. If they hesitate, that's your signal to either press harder or walk away.

C. Securing the CDR Process

We tend to evaluate CDR engines by asking: "Does it remove malware?" But we shouldn't stop here. Attackers don't just try to sneak a threat through. They look for ways to attack the sanitization engine itself—to confuse it, crash it, or use it as a pivot.

That's why, when you're planning a deployment or evaluating vendors, you should be asking a different question: "What are you doing to protect the sanitization process itself from being exploited?"

This answer is important because if a malicious file breaks your engine or slips past due to a weak parser, you haven't just failed to sanitize the file—you've introduced a new attack surface.

I've added some notes from my experience and some from working with the OPSWAT engineering team on this subject.

1. File-Type Identification: Securing the First Step

Before a file can be parsed or rebuilt, we need to know what it actually is. That sounds simple, but attackers know how easy it is to confuse those taking this step.

Spoofing the file type isn't just evasion, it's a way in. It gives the attacker a shot at triggering a parser crash or even a buffer overflow. That's why we don't take this part lightly.

Let me put it in perspective: If your file-type detection is 97-percent accurate and someone else's is 99.9 percent, that may not sound like a big difference. But run 1,000 files through each engine and the 97-percent engine will misclassify 30 of them, while the 99.9-percent engine might only miss one. That's 30x more exposure. And it only takes one misclassified file to cause real damage, especially if it ends up in front of the wrong parser.

This isn't just a technical detail. This is an attack on the sanitization process itself.

I recommend going deeper into file-type detection when evaluating or building your sanitization pipeline. Don't stop at the classic methods: file extensions, MIME types, and magic numbers. Those are useful for logging and quick triage, but attackers have figured out how to manipulate them in all sorts of ways.

Without going into too much detail, I will say this: We found machine learning to be very effective. It's not perfect, but it has consistently outperformed traditional, rule-based approaches in catching spoofed, malformed, and polyglot files, especially on adversarial samples. The reason is simple. Many files that organizations treat as harmless are nothing more than plain text. PowerShell scripts, shell scripts, JavaScript files, and Python files all fall into this category. They carry no meaningful structure, which means mime-type checks, basic magic numbers, and simple validators offer almost no real protection.

A malicious script wrapped inside a friendly looking file extension will slip through any system that trusts extensions. Modern operating systems even warn users when a file's content does not match its extension and recommend updating it. That alone tells us how fragile extension-based trust has become. Security decisions must be based on what the file truly is, not what the filename claims.

We also introduced **schema validation** before and after CDR. If a file claims to be a DOCX, it should structurally behave like one. After CDR, that structure should still be valid and the file should still work. This extra step has helped us catch structural inconsistencies and format manipulation early, before they become user-facing issues.

What's Worked for Us

- Combine multiple detection methods: extension, magic number, MIME, entropy, heuristics, and machine learning.

- Log and alert on any mismatch between declared and detected file types.

- Validate file structure (e.g., XML schemas, PDF object models, ZIP directory layouts) before and after CDR.

- Run file-type detection inside isolated containers so there is no shared memory, no persistent state, and no shortcuts.

2. Secure Parsing: The Heart of the System

Once a file is identified, the next step is parsing—breaking it down so it can be analyzed and sanitized. This is where structure really matters. If the parser expects one format but gets another, you're now in dangerous territory: Memory corruption, logic errors, or full-on parser crashes can occur.

Regeneration is the final step in the CDR process. It's where we rebuild a clean version of the file that's safe, usable, and free of anything that shouldn't be there.

The reality is that to properly execute CDR, you need to rely on multiple parsers. Some you'll license, some may be open-source, and some might be built in-house. Based on my experience, the moment we started asking vendors about parser-level patching, software bill of materials (SBOMs), and common vulnerabilities and exposures (CVEs) tracking, the answers got fuzzy. That's when we realized we needed more control over this stage.

3. How We Hardened Parsing

Parsing is the stage attackers go after when detection fails them. If they can exploit the parser, they can destabilize the entire system. Worse yet, they may be able to pivot even deeper. However, if you isolate the parser, monitor it, and treat it like the high-risk component it is, you can cut off that attack path entirely. Here are some tips to defend your system:

- Require a full software bill of materials—SBOMs for every parsing component—so you know exactly what's inside.

- Track and monitor CVEs associated with each parser or dependency.

- For any in-house parser, enforce static code analysis and fuzzy testing as part of the build process.

- Run all parsers in isolated containers, spun up per file, with no persistent state, and reset automatically after use.

- Treat parser crashes as security events, not just engineering bugs. If something breaks here, it gets investigated like an incident.

- Log parser activity.

In the end, securing your data isn't just about parsing files. It's about defending the system that's parsing them.

4. Safe Regeneration: Think of It Like a Clean Room

Regeneration is the final step in the CDR process. It's where we rebuild a clean version of the file that's safe, usable, and free of anything that shouldn't be there.

In theory, this step should happen in an isolated, stateless environment, such as a clean room, where no trace of the original file can leak through. In practice, however, I've seen regeneration engines reuse shared memory, retain leftover object references, or quietly carry forward structures that were supposed to be removed. Sometimes it wasn't even a bug—it was just the system assuming the output was "probably safe enough."

That's not how I wanted to think about safety, so we changed our approach.

Every time we regenerate a file, we now spin up a fresh environment—a disposable environment that starts clean and ends clean. After that, we validate the output's schema to make sure it still conforms to expected standards—DOCX, PDF, XML, or whatever it claims to be. Then we hash and sign the output, so we know exactly what was delivered and can trace it later if needed.

In more sensitive deployments, we sometimes go one step further and pass the output through a second, independent CDR engine that ideally comes from a different vendor. If both engines agree, it gives us added assurance that nothing was missed.

What's Worked for Us

- **Regenerate files in isolated, disposable environments**. Don't reuse memory or containers between files.

- **Validate the output's structure after regeneration**. Make sure it's clean, usable, and conforms to the format it claims to be.

- **Hash and digitally sign sanitized files** to ensure integrity and traceability.

5. Infrastructure and Runtime Hardening:
Don't Let the System Become the Weak Link

It's easy to focus so much on the file that you forget about the environment that's processing it.

If the OS running your CDR engine is out of date, if your patching depends on someone remembering to check, or if your containers live too long and accumulate risk, your system will quietly drift into vulnerability.

What's Worked for Us

- Secure boot and signed container images for everything related to the CDR stack. No unsigned components. No guesswork.

- Automate CVE tracking and patch management, especially for shared libraries and parsing tools. We don't wait for vendors to notify us—we monitor it ourselves.

- Redeploy core CDR containers regularly, not just when something breaks. If a container's been running for weeks, that's a red flag.

- Red-team your CDR system specifically. It's tempting to concentrate red-teaming efforts on user access, cloud exposure, or firewalls, but if you trust CDR to protect your last mile, it deserves its own scrutiny.

Advice for Anyone Building or Buying Data CDR

If you're deploying CDR at scale, you're not just securing the content—you're building a processing system that lives inside your infrastructure. This is why you need to treat it accordingly. The best place to start is by asking your vendors the following questions:

- How long do their scanning containers live?
- How do they update their base OS images and patch their libraries?
- Does their system support signed builds and secure boot?

If they hesitate when you bring up red-teaming their CDR logic, that should be a red flag.

Auditability and Traceability: You Can't Defend What You Can't Prove

At some point, someone always asks:

- "Was this file sanitized?"
- "Which engine touched it?"
- "What version was running at the time?"

And in that moment, you either have the answer or you don't.

We learned early on that if you want to build real confidence in your CDR process, you have to treat logging and traceability as a critical part of the system, not just something you do for compliance.

We log every file, engine, and decision not just for troubleshooting, but because sometimes those logs tell you something you didn't expect.

In fact, some of our earliest indicators of anomalies in files that shouldn't have gotten through, including unexpected parser behavior and emerging zero-days, were picked up not because of real-time detection, but because our audit logs told the story in hindsight.

Paying this much attention to detail in logging everything made us better. And more than once, it's helped us spot weak points in the system before they turned into actual breaches.

What We Log (and Why)

For every file that goes through the system, we track:

- Input hash—so we can prove what came in.
- Detected file type—and how it was classified.
- Parser invoked—including the exact library or engine used.
- Schema validation result—both pre- and post-sanitization.

- CDR engine ID and version—critical for historical traceability.
- Output hash—so we know exactly what left the system.

All of this is stored in append-only, digitally signed formats. No one can tamper with it quietly. And, yes, we've used this audit trail to prove internally and externally that a file was processed safely, even when questions were raised long after the event.

Why It's More Than Just Logs

Scrutinizing details like this isn't about checkbox compliance—it's about building trust in the CDR process. The more automated the pipeline becomes, the more critical it is to have a record of what really happened.

We've also fed audit trails into our Security Operations Center (SOC) dashboards, so that anomalies in file flows, unexpected file types, schema mismatches, and parsing failures get flagged automatically. Sometimes that's the first sign that something's wrong. It might be a configuration drift or it might be a zero-day being probed. Either way, we'd rather know sooner than later.

What's Worked for Us

If you're designing a secure CDR deployment or evaluating a vendor, build this into your expectations:

- Demand full-audit logging, including file-type detection, parsing behavior, engine version, and output integrity.
- Insist on cryptographic signing and immutability for logs. Being tamper-proof isn't optional.
- Push for integration with your SOC or SIEM, so your security team can see anomalies in real time.
- Ask vendors how long they retain logs, and whether customers can access the full trace for incident investigation.

If you can't trace what happened to a file, you can't explain it. And if you can't explain it, you can't trust it.

Auditability doesn't just help you investigate incidents—it's what builds confidence that the system is doing what it says it does...every day.

If CDR is going to be a foundational layer in your security architecture (which it should be), you need to treat it like any other mission-critical system.

It's not enough to simply clean files—you need to defend the cleaning process itself. Cyberattackers will try to exploit misclassification, crash your parsers, trick your regenerators, or live in the blind spots within your infrastructure. Your job is to ensure those doors are closed.

This section wasn't built from theory. It's the result of dozens of rollouts, real-world testing, and learning from when things didn't go perfectly. If you apply even half of these safeguards, you'll be way ahead of where most organizations are today.

And if you're evaluating vendors, start with this question: What are you doing to protect your own sanitization engine from attack?

Designing CDR Policies That Actually Work

One of the most overlooked strengths of CDR is how much control it gives you. This isn't like antivirus, where the engine just says "malicious" or "clean" and you're expected to live with the result. Here, you get to define what safe looks like, down to the level of embedded scripts, macros, links, and even image metadata.

That makes configuration not just a technical task—it makes it a strategy.

Every file that comes through is rebuilt. How it's rebuilt is entirely based on the policies you apply. If that policy is too strict, users will complain. If it's too loose, you risk malware slipping through. You can't rely on a default setting to balance that. You need to configure based on how your organization actually uses files by format, by department, and even by role.

1. Start With What Your Files Are Doing

To configure effectively, you first need to understand two things:

- What file types you use.
- How those files are used inside your organization.

For example, an accounting department might work with heavily formatted PDFs but never need embedded JavaScript. A research team might rely on macros for automation in Excel, while HR doesn't touch them at all. These differences matter and they should drive how you configure your CDR engine.

Simple file formats, such as JPEG or PNG, may require extra configuration to remove hidden metadata or prevent steganography. For more complex files—such as DOCXs, PPTXs, or PDFs—you'll want to focus on what scripts, links, or embedded content should stay and what should go.

2. Default Settings Are Just the Starting Point

Most vendors will offer a default configuration. That's fine for getting started, but in real-world use, defaults rarely align with actual business needs.

You might need:

- Different policies for different teams (e.g., marketing versus finance)
- Allow lists for known-safe content, such as approved domains or templates
- Allow-listed macros or scripts from known templates that users rely on

Good configuration isn't about turning everything off; it's about making intentional trade-offs—security without breaking the workflow.

3. Common Configuration Techniques

Here are a few practical examples I've seen in real environments:

JPEG and Image Files

- Adjust image compression to balance quality and file size.
- Strip all metadata (EXIF, GPS, comments) to avoid hidden content.

Complex Document Formats

- Strip macros unless specifically allowed for certain roles.
- Remove or rewrite embedded links.
- Validate structure against format schema (e.g., PDF object layout, OOXML standards).

Archives

- Limit unpacking depth to prevent archive bombs.
- Flag files with extreme compression ratios.
- Reject files containing embedded executables or nested archives beyond policy limits.

How Policies Become Configuration Rules

A Policy is a general statement of what should be done to sanitize files

Configuration Rules Implement That Policy

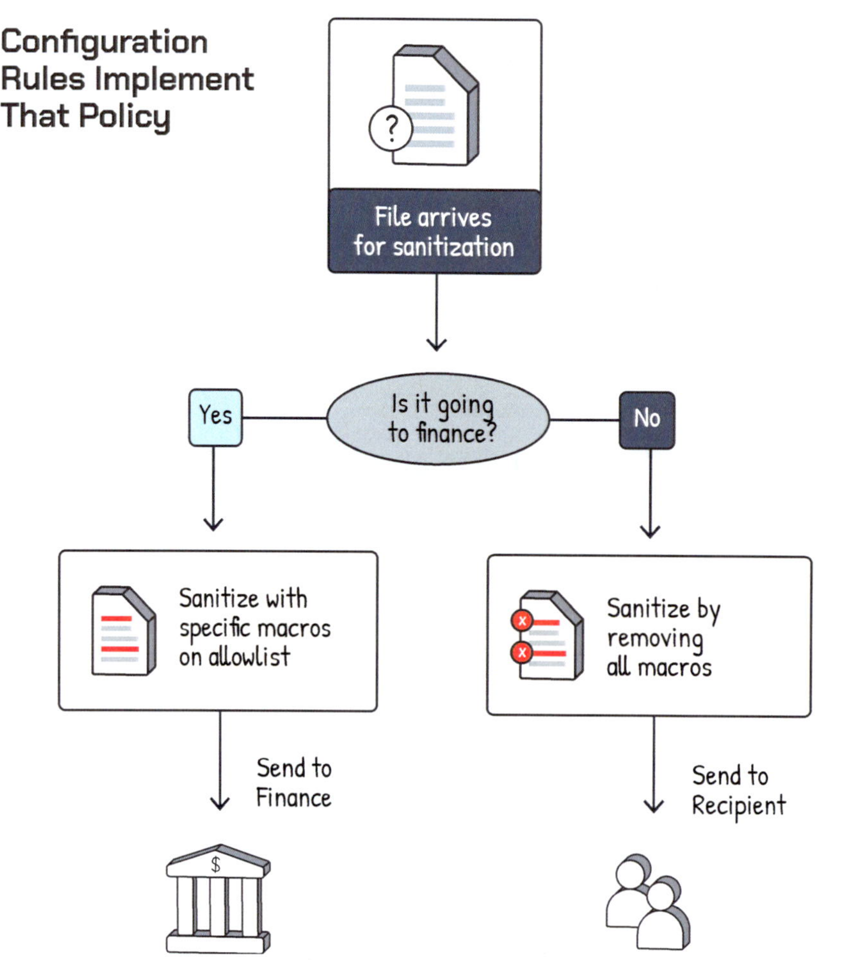

Real-World Policy Examples

A recruiting firm handling thousands of résumés realized macros were never needed. They configured their data sanitization policy to strip them out entirely, so the problem was solved and there were no user complaints.

A financial services company required sanitized W2s and tax forms but needed to preserve layout for compliance. Their configuration removed scripts and active content but retained formatting.

In another case, a data analytics team required macro functionality for automation, so the policy was adjusted to allow macros only from internal templates.

These decisions weren't made by the vendor—they were made by the security team, because CDR gives you that control.

Unlike traditional detection tools, CDR doesn't just say "yes" or "no." It asks, "How?"

That's the power and the responsibility. Every configuration choice reflects your organization's real-world balance between security and usability. Get it right, and users barely notice. Get it wrong, and they start looking for ways to work around the system.

So don't treat configuration as an afterthought. It's where the real value of CDR gets unlocked. And it's where your team will show whether they're just checking boxes or building something that will last.

Ensuring the Speed and Scalability of CDR

Speed and scale matter. Users expect files to open fast, so your system needs to keep up, especially under a load. A lot of the performance depends on the vendor, but you're the one who takes the heat when things slow down.

I get asked these questions frequently: "How fast is CDR?" or "How quickly will the file be regenerated?"

My answer depends on who's asking.

- **For nontechnical teams:** Sanitized files should arrive almost instantly. If there's a noticeable delay, users will complain.

- **For technical teams:** CDR is a bit slower than antivirus, but much faster than sandboxing.

- **For ultra-technical folks:** It depends. Speed varies by file size, file type, and how complex the policies are. A small image with no active content can be checked fast. A large PDF with macros, embedded links, and layered structure is going to take longer.

If you want the real answer, test with actual data. Run big batches and tune each file type. That's the only way to know what your setup can really handle.

You also need to be realistic. If you're sanitizing a 1TB file, it's going to take time. Most systems will skip or fail silently. CDR doesn't. It actually processes the file, and that, honestly, comes at a cost. That's I/O, not magic. Most antivirus or sandbox tools will skip or flag huge files. CDR doesn't skip, it secures. And securing large files means putting in the work.

Preserving File Usability

Security doesn't succeed if the user can't open the file. If they can't trust what they receive, they'll bypass the system—and that's a bigger risk than that posed by the original malware.

After CDR, users won't care how safe a particular file is. That's the balance we have to get right. Nobody wants to explain to a business unit why their files are suddenly broken. Sanitization that breaks usability doesn't solve a problem—it creates one.

For simple files—such as images, videos, and plain documents—expectations are clear: A 4K video should stay 4K and an invoice should still look like an invoice. These files should pass through CDR untouched from the user's point of view. With complex files, things get harder.

A PowerPoint presentation might include animations, videos, or embedded objects. If the timing, layout, or sequence changes even slightly, the whole file will feel wrong. That leads to frustration, workarounds, or, worse, people trying to bypass CDR altogether.

At OPSWAT, we've used a deep-learning technique called a "convolutional neural network" (CNN). It's a machine-learning model trained to recognize patterns in visual content mostly used in tasks such as image comparison, object detection, or layout verification.

We use CNNs to visually compare a file before and after CDR. This includes layout, formatting, clarity, and other subtle changes. The goal isn't to catch malware—it's to catch broken usability before users do.

What's Worked for Us

If your team deals with visual content or heavily formatted files:

- Run visual comparison tests on your most common complex file types: DOCX, PPTX, PDFs, XLSX. Test files that include macros, links, charts, and embedded media.

- Test actual videos before and after CDR. Confirm that resolution, playback speed, and duration stay the same. A 4K video shouldn't come out at 720p.

- Watch for layout drift tables shifting, charts misaligning, or slides playing out of order. These small details create big issues.

- If your vendor offers AI-based usability testing, ask to see it in action. It won't replace manual QA, but it helps scale the process.

- Ask for a test plan from the data sanitization vendor.

Perfection isn't the goal; practical trust is. Know where CDR shines, know where it leans on detection, and deploy it with your eyes wide open. That's how you win adoption—and keep it.

Operational Trade-Offs in the CDR Architecture

Every security technology comes with trade-offs, and CDR is no exception. If you're a CISO or security leader rolling this out, it's important to set the right expectations internally and externally. Here are a few key realities to be upfront about:

- **Digital signatures won't survive.** CDR creates a new file, so any digital signature tied to the original file will be broken or stripped. This matters in workflows where signed PDFs, contracts, or forms are exchanged. If your process depends on preserving original cryptographic signatures, you'll need to manage around this either by re-signing or handling those files differently.

- **Files will change.** CDR creates a new file. Workflows that rely on hash matching or unchanged documents need extra handling either by re-signing or establishing bypass policies.

- **Not all file types are supported.** CDR is file-type-specific. If the format isn't supported, it can't be safely processed. That leaves you with two options:

1. Block the file outright.

2. Pass the file to detection-based tools (multiscanning, sandboxing, etc.).

I've seen teams overlook this step and assume everything is covered—it's not. You still need a fallback for unknowns.

- **CDR doesn't detect attacks**. This is important to understand: CDR is attack-agnostic. It doesn't care whether a file is malicious or not, it just rebuilds the structure based on policy. That means it won't raise an alert when an attacker targets your organization. It won't track malware families. And it won't tell you if you're under attack. You'll still need detection tools for that.

CDR can feed into detection systems by routing flagged files, triggering workflows, or correlating metadata, but it doesn't generate that intelligence on its own.

- **CDR is not 100% effective**. No security tool is absolutely foolproof. There are still file types we don't fully support, edge cases we haven't seen, and technical limits in what today's engines can sanitize reliably. Any vendor claiming 100-percent coverage is overselling.

As I write this, there are specific file types that neither we nor the Department of Homeland Security know how to fully process. That doesn't mean it's impossible; it just hasn't been solved yet.

I like how tennis great Rafael Nadal put it: "I try my best." That's how I see CDR. You configure it, test it, monitor it—and keep improving. No system is flawless—you just keep making it better.

These trade-offs don't mean CDR isn't worth it, but it works best when it's deployed with clear expectations. Know what it can do, know where it needs help, and make sure your team understands both.

You don't need perfection—you need coverage, clarity, and control. That's what you're aiming for.

Using CDR to Protect Privacy

Security isn't just about blocking threats. It's also about controlling what your files reveal when they leave the organization. Most people think of CDR as a way to remove malware, but it's just as powerful for protecting privacy.

I really started noticing this during broader defense deployments when we looked not just at email, but across general file flows. When we began sanitizing files across endpoints, portals, and internal workflows, what we saw was eye-opening: documents leaking GPS coordinates, author names, edit history, internal timestamps, and even server paths. All were invisible to the user, but they were right there in the metadata.

That's when it clicked: CDR isn't just about providing safety from malware—it's about protecting the organization from accidental data exposure.

Common File Formats That Leak More Than You Think

These are some of the most common formats that silently carry private information. These leaks don't show up in the UI, but they're still there. When files leave the organization, that metadata goes with them.

GPS coordinates, timestamps, camera models, metadata

  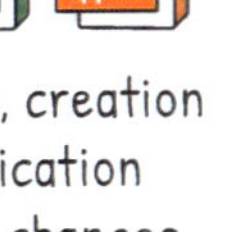

Author name, creation and modification dates, track changes, comments

Embedded JavaScript, hidden layers, printer paths, revision history

GPS data, editing timestamps device metadata

Author name, creation and modification dates, track changes, comments

Layer history, internal notes, version metadata

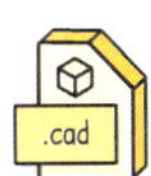 

Object properties, drawing scale, embedded comments

Email headers, IPs, routing history

Hidden tabs, formula history, filter state, author tags

How CDR Helps

CDR gives you control. You define what gets stripped, what gets rebuilt, and what stays.

- Strip GPS, device information, and EXIF data from images and video.
- Remove author names, timestamps, and editing metadata from Office files and PDFs.
- Eliminate comments, tracked changes, hidden fields, and scripts.
- Flatten visual layers and animations.
- Scrub printer paths, internal links, and embedded metadata.
- Apply privacy policies automatically to outbound documents.

When to Use CDR

Use CDR for privacy anytime files will leave your organization, especially if they come from:

- HR (résumés, internal forms, candidate profiles)
- Legal (contracts, drafts, discovery files)
- Marketing (media files, product visuals, creative assets)
- Finance (reports, forecast docs, board materials)
- IT (logs, technical exports, support escalations)

It's also wise to sanitize before publishing or sharing files with partners or during audits or external reviews.

Implementing CDR the Right Way

After deploying CDR in hundreds of environments—including defense agencies, banks, manufacturers, critical infrastructure, and everything in between—here's what I've come to believe: **This technology works. But only when it's implemented with care, clarity, and commitment.**

It's not about checking a box or dropping another tool into your tech stack. It's about seeing files for what they are: the single most common way threats move, the most underestimated source of privacy leakage, and—when handled right—one of the easiest places to cut risk at scale.

How to Scale Your CDR Solution

A good CDR setup should be able to process thousands or even millions of files a day without failing.

Here's how to scale:

- Vertical: Add more CPU or memory.
- Horizontal: Add more engines and load-balance the traffic.
- Hardware acceleration: Offload some workloads to FPGAs or GPUs, if available.

You can also tune performance with smart policy decisions:

- Lower recursion depth on archive files.
- Skip or defer large image/video sanitization during peak hours.
- Prioritize high-risk or sensitive flows ahead of routine traffic.

Your vendor should be able to help guide your scaling strategies, but don't rely on them alone. Benchmark everything under your own conditions, tune aggressively, and keep iterating.

Throughout this chapter, I've tried to share the lessons I've learned: the real deployment patterns, the trade-offs that matter, the mistakes that cost time and trust, and the wins that stick.

If you're just starting out, start small. Focus on one channel, prove that it works, get the team on board, and then scale. If you're already deep into the process, double-check the pieces that get overlooked—parsers, logs, usability, and policy drift. Tighten where needed and improve what you can. If you're leading the initiative, don't just sell the product—sell the purpose. Help your team understand the why, not just the how. When they believe in what they're building, they'll carry it further than any roadmap ever could.

CDR isn't magic—it's engineering. When done right, however, it changes the game. Employ it, and you'll stop chasing threats and simply reacting. You'll also start building a safer, quieter, and more resilient file pipeline—one that protects people before they even know they needed it. And that, in the end, is what makes it worth doing.

As I look ahead, I see CDR becoming as essential to cybersecurity as firewalls once were—quiet, effective, and invisible to the user, but foundational to resilience.

THOU SHALT NOT TRUST A FILE.
THOU SHALT NOT RELY ON DETECTION ALONE.
THOU SHALT REBUILD, NOT REPAIR.
THOU SHALT CLEANSE ALL ACTIVE CONTENT.
THOU SHALT VALIDATE WHAT THOU REBUILDS.
THOU SHALT NOT FORSAKE SECURITY FOR USABILITY.
THOU SHALT LOG ALL ACTIONS TAKEN.
THOU SHALT ADAPT THY POLICY TO THY WORKFLOW.
THOU SHALT ALWAYS STUDY DATA SANITIZATION.
THOU SHALT PLACE DATA SANITIZATION AT THY PERIMETER.

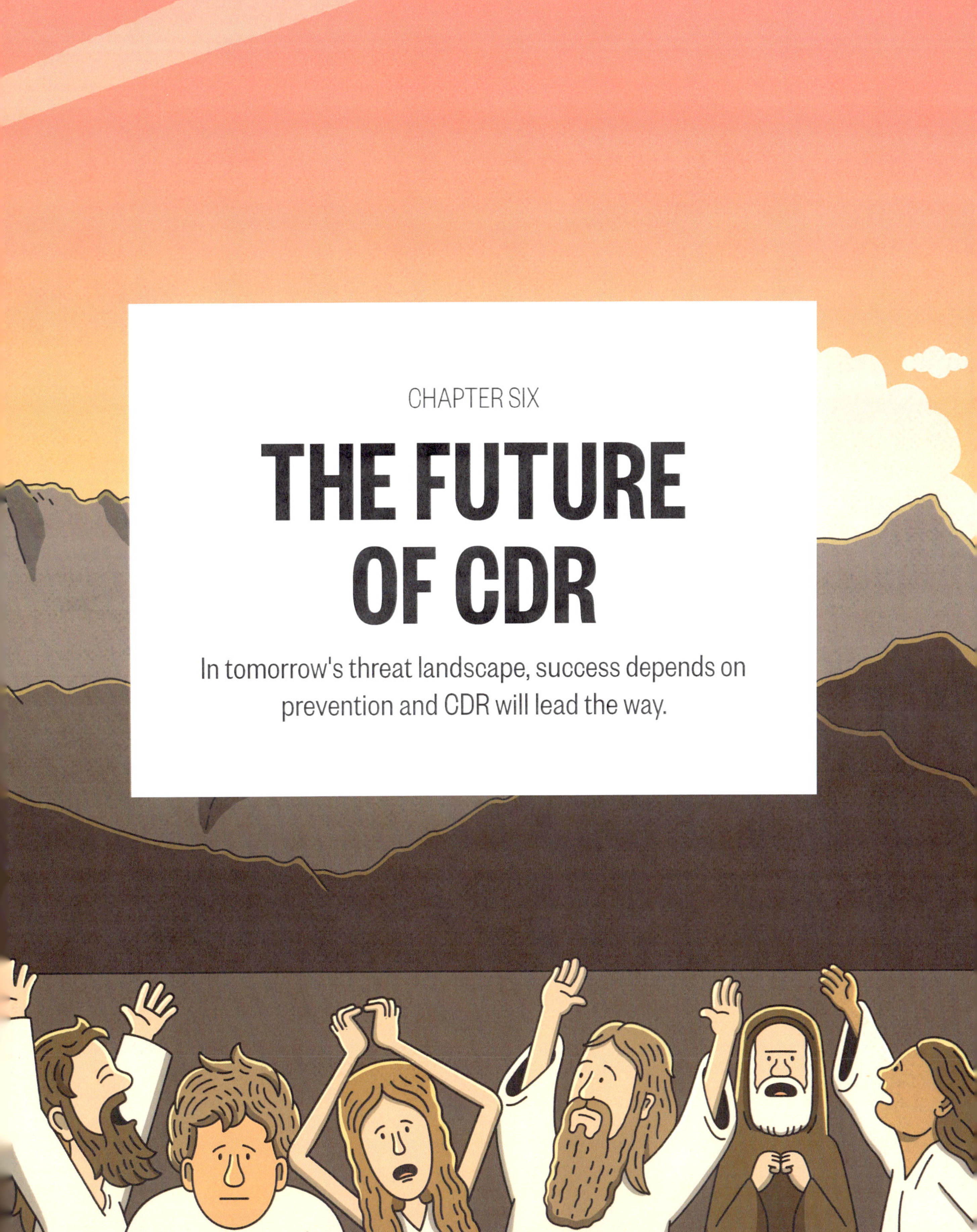

THE FUTURE OF CDR

In tomorrow's threat landscape, success depends on prevention and CDR will lead the way.

After years of building, deploying, and advocating for CDR, I'm convinced of one thing: We're just getting started. CDR isn't just a clever way to strip macros or clean up PDFs—it's a foundational shift in how we think about malware prevention, privacy protection, and secure collaboration. What started as a workaround is becoming a baseline. Yet even with everything we've achieved, I believe this technology hasn't come close to realizing what it can become.

This isn't about theory—it's about what I've built, tested, and validated through its use in the field inside banks, power plants, government agencies, and Fortune 100s. I've watched teams go from skepticism to full-on reliance, not because they believed the marketing, but because the results made believers out of them. And still, I find myself hoping for more.

In my wishful moments, I imagine a world where every major cybersecurity framework treats file sanitization like it treats encryption—as non-negotiable. I imagine cloud storage platforms with built-in CDR, where every email attachment is rebuilt before it lands, every developer pipeline auto-sanitizes test data, and every AI input is cleaned before it ever hits a tokenizer. I see a world where, "Was this file sanitized?" is no longer a question because every file will be cleaned before it ever enters a network. We're not there yet, but we're getting close.

In this chapter, I want to share where I think we're headed next. I've seen what this technology can do when it's properly deployed. Now I want to imagine what it can do when it's integrated everywhere.

CDR as a Native Security Layer

When we first started deploying CDR, it was treated like an afterthought—something you bolted on after you'd already been burned by a macro or a zero-day slipped through your filters. We'd patch it into a gateway or drop it into an upload flow, hoping it didn't break too much. It worked, but it never felt native. It felt like I was trying to patch something together with duct tape after the breach. That's the shift I believe is finally starting to happen. Sanitization is moving from a reaction to a foundation.

In the future I see, and I say this not just from hope but from watching where the industry is already heading, CDR will be embedded everywhere. It will be **baked directly into cloud storage platforms** like OneDrive, Dropbox, and Google Drive. Files will be rebuilt automatically before anyone even opens them. You won't have to enable it; it will just be on part of the trust layer.

Email providers will follow, integrating CDR alongside spam filters and phishing protection. Attachments won't just be scanned; they'll be rebuilt, silently, before they ever hit your inbox. You won't notice a difference except that there will be fewer incidents, fewer incident response calls, and fewer "was-this-safe" Slack messages at 2 a.m.

DevOps pipelines will evolve, too. Right now, those pipelines ingest files from all over, including artifacts, datasets, open-source modules, and AI models. Every one of those is a vector. Soon, sanitization will be part of the build process. Test data will be rebuilt, external packages will be cleaned before they're committed, and all of it will happen in real time, without slowing the team down.

APIs and developer tools will offer CDR as a flag. You won't need a separate security team to integrate CDR. It'll be as simple as setting sanitize: true in your upload SDK. Just like we flipped the switch for HTTPS or how we added OAuth, CDR will become like personal hygiene—expected and non-negotiable.

At that point, safety won't feel like an add-on anymore—it will be part of how we work, how we share, how we store, and how we collaborate. And just like backups, encryption, and SSO, it will be invisible, automatic, and built into everything by default.

That's the world I want to help build—where CDR isn't something we'll need to explain—it's something we'll assume. In this new world, every file will be clean not because we checked it, but because it was rebuilt before it ever touched us. Ultimately, safety won't feel like a feature, it will simply be there.

CDR in Academia: The Missing Layer in Cybersecurity Education

I've always been a big believer in education. I believe academia still plays a critical role not just in producing research papers or degrees, but in shaping how we think, how we approach problems, and how we build the next generation of cyber defenders.

Universities don't just teach students how to use tools—they help form instincts. They create the first mental models that young professionals will carry into every SOC, every code review, and every decision. That's why it's more important than ever that CDR, specifically file sanitization, becomes part of the standard cybersecurity curriculum.

Today, the typical academic cybersecurity path is predictable. You study networks, cryptography, access control, risk, and compliance. You get hands-on with familiar tools: firewalls, antivirus, IDS, SIEM, and maybe some AI and EDR if the program is progressive. That's all fine, but something fundamental is missing.

Most students can finish a degree in cybersecurity and never hear the word "sanitization" mentioned—not in a lecture, not in a lab, not even in a vendor demonstration. That's not just an oversight—it's a blind spot because sanitization isn't just practical, it's rooted in deep computational truth.

Here's what most textbooks don't explain: A significant portion of malware detection problems are NP-complete. That means, in plain terms, that there's no known algorithm that can determine with certainty in polynomial time, whether a given file is malicious. Determining if a file contains a threat, especially when it's packed, obfuscated, layered, or hidden using steganographic techniques, is not just challenging—it's mathematically intractable at scale.

Antivirus and behavioral detection tools try to approximate this with signatures, heuristics, and machine learning, but they're ultimately just educated guesses, because they can be bypassed, delayed, or defeated by novel threats. This is not theoretical—it's foundational computer science. (For those interested in the academic underpinning, look into the Rice Theorem and the Halting Problem in undecidability theory. They illustrate how general-file analysis inherently hits the wall of computability.)

Now consider what that means at enterprise scale. If the problem is unsolvable in real-time for arbitrary inputs, you have two choices—you can keep trying to guess what's bad, or you can change the rules. That's where CDR comes in. It sidesteps the entire complexity by reframing the problem. Instead of asking, "Is this file safe?" it says, "Let's rebuild this into something that's definitely safe." It's not about catching the bad; it's about extracting and preserving only what's known to be good. This is a mindset shift—and that shift belongs in the classroom.

This is already happening in some corners of academia. I've started to see Ph.D.-level research and master's theses focusing on advanced file sanitization, schema validation,

When you start from the assumption that no file is trustworthy until it is rebuilt, everything else in your security model gets stronger.

polyglot detection, and even AI-enhanced sanitization workflows. It's encouraging, but we need more. This kind of thinking needs to bleed into undergraduate programs, cybersecurity bootcamps, and online certifications. If it doesn't, we'll keep producing graduates who can design a firewall rule but don't know that a DOCX file can carry an embedded command shell.

CDR is already protecting some of the most sensitive environments in the world, including critical infrastructure, defense networks, border control systems, and high-assurance supply chains. It's being used where detection is too slow, too noisy, or just not good enough. The only rational move is to rebuild the file before trusting it, and yet the concept of CDR is absent from most classroom discussions. This has to change.

CDR should be core to cybersecurity education, not a fringe topic. CDR should be covered in a vendor-led workshop. It should be a foundational layer, just like encryption, access control, or secure coding. Students should be learning early on that files lie and that a DOCX isn't just text—it's XML, macros, embedded media, linked templates, version history, and more. They should also be learning that a PDF can carry JavaScript, that metadata can leak secrets, and that ZIP bombs are still real.

They should be running malformed files through real CDR engines—analyzing what gets stripped, testing usability of output, and comparing before-and-after hashes. They should be understanding schema validation and evaluating where prevention outperforms detection. Most importantly, they should understand the mental shift from "Can I detect what's bad?" to "Can I rebuild what's good?"

That shift matters because once you've internalized it once, it's part of how you think. You don't need to justify it anymore—it becomes obvious, like encrypting traffic, enabling multi-factor authentication (MFA), or patching a vulnerability. When you start from the assumption that no file is trustworthy until it is rebuilt, everything else in your security model gets stronger.

By embedding CDR into cybersecurity education, we're not just teaching students about a tool; we're teaching a mindset and a model of trust that starts with skepticism and ends with clean, validated content. And maybe one day, when someone in a boardroom says, "Should we be sanitizing files before we open them?" a new hire will answer with a quiet smile, because they've already been doing it since their second semester in college.

That's how we change the industry—not with a product, but with a principle that's been missing from the classroom for far too long. The signs are there. Early research, doctoral dissertations, and a growing number of labs are starting to test malformed files instead of just scanning them. It's slow, but it's happening. We just need to accelerate this thinking in educators because when education leads, the rest of the industry will follow.

The Evolution of Cybersecurity Toward a CDR Mindset

Before we talk about where cybersecurity frameworks are headed, we need to step back and talk about what they are and why they matter.

A cybersecurity framework is a structured guide—a map, a set of best practices and controls that help organizations protect what matters most. Think of it as the blueprint a CISO uses to build a security program without having to reinvent the wheel. Frameworks create a common language between practitioners, vendors, auditors, and regulators. They also take the chaos of daily threats and turn it into a structured defense model.

These frameworks were invented to solve a problem that every organization faces: How do you implement security without relying on gut instinct or isolated product choices? How do you scale trust? Frameworks were the answer. They brought order and introduced shared expectations. Over the years, they've helped define the playbooks we now take for granted. These frameworks helped bring cybersecurity into the boardroom. They created structure where ambiguity once reigned. But here's the truth: Most of them were designed in a world where the threat was assumed to come from the outside, where files were trusted by default, and where "scan for malware" was considered good enough.

The list on page 173 list a mere sampling of the many frameworks that are out there and each was born from a different pain point.

That world is gone and these frameworks need to evolve. Let's take a closer look at how a few of the leading frameworks are beginning to address this challenge and how I believe they need to grow to meet the reality we're living in today.

NIST Cybersecurity Framework (CSF)

The NIST Cybersecurity Framework (CSF) has become the global standard for organizing security programs.[1] It's built on five core functions: Identify, Protect, Detect, Respond, and Recover. These pillars provide a structured path for improving cybersecurity posture across any sector. And in practice, this framework has shaped how entire industries, from finance to healthcare to the energy sector, prioritize controls, budget resources, and speak a common security language.

For all its strengths, however, NIST CSF is still a product of its time. It reflects a mindset built around breach detection and incident response. The "detect" function has become so central to how security is measured that it risks overshadowing what should be the real focus: **prevention.**

---

1 "Cybersecurity Framework," NIST, November 12, 2013, https://www.nist.gov/cyberframework

Common Frameworks

NIST CSF (Cybersecurity Framework): Created by the U.S. government to help protect critical infrastructure.

ISO/IEC 27001: An international standard for building an auditable, certifiable information security program.

NERC CIP: The North American Reliability Corporation's Critical Infrastructure Protection standards.

PCI DSS: Written to protect cardholder data in the retail and financial world.

SOC 2: A flexible auditing framework used by SaaS providers to demonstrate security to customers.

HIPAA: Created in the U.S. to safeguard sensitive health information in digital form.

GDPR/CCPA: Built to protect data privacy and enforce consumer rights across digital platforms.

Let's be specific: CSF includes categories like PR.DS (Data Security) and PR.IP (Information Protection Processes and Procedures). This is precisely where CDR belongs. But today, those sections talk about access controls, backups, encryption, and scanning—not reconstruction. Malware protection is mentioned, but it's vague and tilted toward detection technologies like antivirus and EDR.

Here's where I believe it needs to evolve.

CDR should be explicitly added under the "protect" function and be positioned not as a replacement for detection, but as a prerequisite step that ensures files are trustworthy *before* they enter detection pipelines or storage environments. In PR.DS, CDR should align with secure content handling, metadata removal, and file-level transformation. In PR.IP, it should support documented, enforceable processes for sanitizing inbound and outbound content—not just scanning it, but rebuilding it.

But it can go deeper.

While NIST CSF lays out high-level categories, it stops short of prescribing *where* sanitization should happen across the data lifecycle. That's the next step. A future NIST CSF could include granular guidance by data channel. For example:

- Apply CDR at file upload points: APIs, web portals, email gateways
- Rebuild files passing through storage synchronization systems like cloud sync or document collaboration platforms
- Require sanitization for files transferred between network zones or trust boundaries
- Sanitize content leaving the enterprise for compliance with privacy regulations and secure exchange

By introducing channel-aware recommendations, the framework can help organizations embed CDR more precisely, mapping it to real flows instead of leaving it open to interpretation.

We need the framework to evolve from "prepare for the worst" to "prevent it entirely when you can." Detection is important, but it's not the only story. Relying too heavily on detection—even a beautifully defined one—misses the point when adversaries are hiding inside content itself. **CDR offers a way to proactively cleanse threats, reduce alert fatigue, and protect the downstream systems that detection depends on.**

I believe the future version of NIST CSF won't just ask organizations to *know* what's happening—it will ask them to rebuild what's coming in across every channel so they don't have to respond to what never should've been there in the first place.

ISO/IEC 27001

ISO/IEC 27001 is the gold standard for building and maintaining an information security management system (ISMS)—it's global, it's certifiable, and it's often the ticket to doing business in regulated industries and international markets.[2] Organizations that adopt ISO 27001 aren't just signaling technical maturity—they're making a public commitment to protecting data through structure, process, and accountability.

The strength of ISO lies in its auditability. It's all about showing your work, defining controls, applying them consistently, and proving they work under scrutiny. But despite this rigor, ISO still lags when it comes to one of the most critical file-based threats in today's ecosystem: embedded, evasive content.

In its current form, ISO/IEC 27001 references malware protection in controls like Annex A.12.2.1 (Controls Against Malware) and secure file sharing in Annex A.13.2 (Information Transfer Policies and Procedures). But it leaves file CDR out of the conversation. That's a gap. Here's how I believe ISO 27001 should evolve.

Future revisions will recognize that file-borne threats don't stop at detection. ISO will explicitly recommend CDR as a control that not only detects but neutralizes embedded threats before content reaches users, storage, or downstream tools. It will be treated as a preventive control, suitable for validation under audit.

In Annex A.12.2, CDR will serve as a complement to antivirus solutions, acknowledging that signatures and heuristics alone aren't enough. In Annex A.13.2, CDR will be recognized as a best practice for cleansing files during transfer whether they come from email, cloud, USB, or partner integrations. But to truly elevate CDR in the ISO ecosystem, we need more granularity:

- Files uploaded through web forms, APIs, or third-party connectors should be sanitized before being accepted into trusted systems.

- Files downloaded from shared folders or collaboration platforms should be rebuilt prior to local storage or processing.

- Content exchanged across borders or regulatory boundaries should be sanitized to remove metadata, embedded code, and revision history.

- Endpoint-level protections should include CDR as a layer that defends against offline or transient threats.

This is where ISO's strength—repeatability—can become CDR's biggest ally. CDR is not only effective, it's consistent. It can also create audit trails, produce logs, and be tuned by policy. These are the kinds of characteristics ISO thrives on.

---

2 "ISO/IEC 27001:2022," ISO, accessed July 9, 2025, https://www.iso.org/standard/27001

The future ISO 27001 should not only ask, "Did you scan it?" but "Did you rebuild it?" It should move organizations from policy-based intent to outcome-based integrity. When that happens, CDR will become a pillar of certification—not just a feature, but a control you can't pass an audit without.

NERC CIP

The North American Electric Reliability Corporation's Critical Infrastructure Protection (NERC CIP) standards are the cybersecurity backbone for bulk power systems in North America.[3] They mandate strict controls over critical cyber assets ranging from personnel authorization and training to physical protection, access logging, configuration change management, and electronic security perimeters. Few frameworks are as prescriptive or as essential to the day-to-day operation of a nation's critical infrastructure.

One particularly relevant domain is **CIP-010**, which governs Configuration Change Management and Vulnerability Assessments. It requires that regulated entities maintain strict file integrity through hashing, baselining, and audit logging.[4] The intent is clear: If a critical configuration file changes, you must know immediately and be able to verify the change. From a compliance perspective, hashes are sacred—they're the fingerprint of system integrity.

But here's the paradox: **Hashing ensures consistency, not safety**. A file with a matching hash may be the same but that doesn't mean it's clean. And this is where modern threats have outpaced traditional methods. A malicious macro, an embedded exploit, or a steganographic payload may be undetected by antivirus solutions and still pass hash checks because, structurally, the file hasn't changed in a way the hashing function can interpret as dangerous.

On the other side of the spectrum, **CDR breaks the hash**. Rebuilding a file to remove risky elements naturally alters the hash. This leads to compliance friction: Do you allow a hash mismatch if it means the content is cleaner and safer? Or do you trust the file because it "matches," even if what's inside could compromise your system?

This dilemma is not trivial, and we say this with humility. NERC compliance officers, auditors, and operational engineers aren't wrong to be cautious. In a world of tightly scoped regulatory obligations, deterministic hash integrity offers clear, reportable outcomes. And yet, as threats become more deeply embedded in content, we must wish for a broader, more nuanced understanding of integrity—one that separates **configuration control** from **content safety**.

---

3 "Standards," accessed July 17, 2025, https://www.nerc.com/pa/Stand/Pages/Default.aspx
4 "CIP-010," NERC, n.d., https://www.nerc.com/pa/Stand/Reliability%20Standards/CIP-010-1.pdf

How it will evolve: In time, I believe sanitization will be recognized not as a replacement for hashing, but as a critical **front-end filter** and pre-integrity gate. Before a file is hashed, stored, or deployed, it will be sanitized. This will ensure that **only clean, threat-free content can enter the integrity pipeline.** We expect future revisions of NERC CIP, especially CIP-010, to introduce clearer distinctions between configuration file integrity and transient file sanitization.

It may also include guidance around dual-hash pipelines: One for operational baseline verification, and another for pre-ingress validation, acknowledging that content can change for safety before it is stored for integrity. Such guidance would preserve audit clarity while elevating protection.

This is not about choosing between security and compliance—it's about finding the architecture where both reinforce each other and where CDR serves as the invisible-but-essential first step toward trusted operations. We hope to see that vision reflected in future NERC guidance—not just because it's technically correct, but because it reflects the reality we're seeing play out in the field every day.

I could go on—MITRE ATT&CK, Zero Trust, PCI DSS, SOC 2, HIPAA, GDPR—they all have room to grow. And if we keep applying this lens—of prevention over reaction, of rebuilding over guessing—they will move. Maybe not all at once, maybe not with the same urgency, but they will move.

I'm not making predictions from a whiteboard. We're seeing this in real-world deployments every single day in regulated industries, air-gapped environments, and in cloud-native architectures. The gap is real and the need is urgent.

The good news is that this evolution doesn't require tearing frameworks down. It just asks us to extend them—to fill in what's missing and to rebalance the scales between knowing something went wrong and making sure it never had the chance. Sanitization/CDR isn't a bonus feature—it's a mindset and a modern prerequisite for trust.

Ultimately, I believe, with humility and conviction, that in the not-so-distant future, we'll look back on this era of cybersecurity and ask ourselves one simple question: How did we ever build systems to trust files without rebuilding the files first?

United States of America

Presidential Executive Orders

2013	2017	2021
Executive Order 13636	**Executive Order 13800**	**Executive Order 14028**
Established the NIST Cybersecurity Framework, which quickly became a global model.[1]	Required federal agencies to modernize IT and adopt risk-based approaches.[2]	Issued in response to SolarWinds and Colonial Pipeline attacks, this EO mandated zero trust architecture, supply chain transparency, and improved software integrity.[3]

1   "Foreign Policy Cyber Security Executive Order 13636," The White House, accessed July 9, 2025, https://obamawhitehouse.archives.gov/node/298406
2   "Presidential Executive Order on Strengthening the Cybersecurity of Federal Networks and Critical Infrastructure – The White House."
3   "Improving the Nation's Cybersecurity," Federal Register, May 17, 2021, https://www.federalregister.gov/documents/2021/05/17/2021-10460/improving-the-nations-cybersecurity

The Role of Cybersecurity Executive Orders in Shaping National Defense

In the United States, cybersecurity isn't just a matter of corporate responsibility; it's a national security issue. And one of the most powerful tools available to the federal government for setting strategy and direction in this domain is the **Executive Order (EO)**.

What Is a Cybersecurity Executive Order?

An EO is an official directive from the President of the United States that manages operations of the federal government.[5] While it does not create law, it carries the force of law within the scope of federal authority. In the context of cybersecurity, an EO can be used to:

- Establish new security requirements across federal agencies

- Mandate changes in how government contractors handle digital assets

- Set minimum standards for software and cloud providers

- Accelerate modernization of government IT infrastructure

- Signal national priorities to the private sector and global partners

A cybersecurity EO is not just a policy document—it's a signal. Such orders tell agencies, regulators, technology providers, and industry leaders what matters most and where the country is going.

Why Executive Orders Matter in Cybersecurity

Cyber threats evolve faster than legislation. Waiting months for a bill to move through Congress isn't always feasible when ransomware groups can paralyze hospitals or foreign actors can compromise supply chains in a matter of days. EOs offer speed and clarity. And they can shape cybersecurity strategy far beyond federal networks. Let's look at a few examples on page 178:

These orders shaped real practices: SBOMs (Software Bills of Materials), endpoint detection, multi-factor authentication, and mandatory incident reporting have all seen acceleration because of executive direction.

How a Future Executive Order Could Drive Sanitization

In fact, we don't have to imagine too much, because the blueprint already exists. What follows is the full text of a proposed Executive Order I created.

5 "Presidential Executive Order on Strengthening the Cybersecurity of Federal Networks and Critical Infrastructure — The White House," accessed July 9, 2025, https://trumpwhitehouse.archives.gov/presidential-actions/presidential-executive-order-strengthening-cybersecurity-federal-networks-critical-infrastructure/

Executive Order on National Cybersecurity:

Mandating Content Disarm and Reconstruction (CDR) Across Critical Infrastructure

Section 1. Purpose

The United States faces rapidly advancing cybersecurity threats capable of undermining our critical infrastructure—systems that underpin national security, economic continuity, and public health. With modern attacks often delivered through malicious, evasive, or obfuscated file content, it is imperative to deploy advanced technologies capable of neutralizing threats before they reach trusted environments. This Executive Order mandates the use of sanitization technologies, also known as Content Disarm and Reconstruction (CDR), across all designated critical infrastructure sectors.

This order sets forth the policy of the United States to proactively disarm file-based threats across digital channels, strengthening the integrity and resilience of the nation's digital systems.

Section 2. Definitions

(a) "Critical Infrastructure" shall refer to sectors identified under Presidential Policy Directive 21 (PPD-21), including but not limited to Energy, Financial Services, Healthcare, Transportation, and IT.

(b) "Sanitization technology" refers to automated content-level security solutions that remove or neutralize potentially malicious elements from files and reconstruct safe, usable versions—without reliance on detection or signatures.

Section 3. Scope of Mandate

All federal departments, critical infrastructure operators, and government contractors are required to implement sanitization solutions developed or maintained by United States-based vendors.

Sanitization technologies shall be deployed across the following channels:

- Inbound and outbound email communications
- File uploads/downloads via web portals, mobile applications, APIs, and FTP servers
- Removable media such as USB drives and DVDs
- Internal document sharing platforms, cloud sync, and collaborative environments
- Machine-to-machine file transfers in industrial control systems, SCADA, and operational technology

Section 4. Sector-Specific Guidance

Each of the 16 U.S. Critical Infrastructure Sectors shall apply CDR based on their risk profile and operational context.[6]

- CDR must be enforced across all major data channels, including but not limited to:

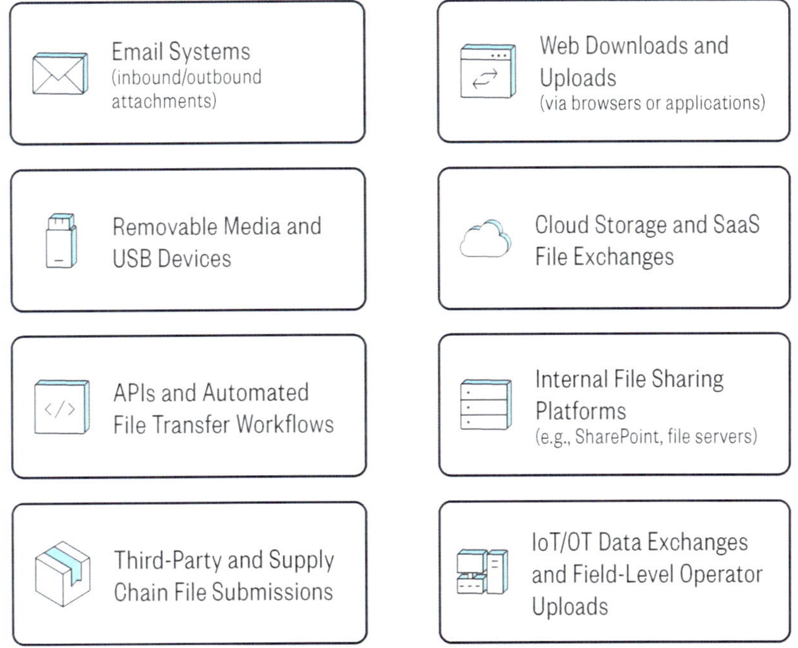

- All files entering any operational, administrative, or production environment shall be sanitized to eliminate embedded threats, malformed file structures, hidden scripts, and sensitive metadata leakage before use or storage.
- CDR policies must be tuned to the specific data usage patterns, threat exposure, and regulatory demands of each sector, while preserving workflow integrity and usability.

The Department of Homeland Security (DHS) and sector-specific agencies shall issue implementation guidance within 90 days of this order.

Section 5. Testing and Compliance

(a) CDR platforms must achieve at least 99.9-percent threat removal efficacy across supported formats in independent testing by at least two of the following: AV-Comparatives, AV-TEST, SE Labs.

---

6 "Critical Infrastructure Sectors | CISA," accessed July 17, 2025, https://www.cisa.gov/topics/critical-infrastructure-security-and-resilience/critical-infrastructure-sectors

(b) All CDR vendors must submit to third-party code audits by approved static analysis providers (e.g., Synopsys, Fortify, Checkmarx). Critical vulnerabilities must be resolved within five (5) business days.

(c) Compliance shall be audited annually by each agency's internal inspector general or equivalent cybersecurity compliance officer.

Section 6. Supported File Types

CDR solutions must support the following high-risk formats:

- **Microsoft Office:** .DOC/.DOCX, .XLS/.XLSX, .PPT/.PPTX, .RTF
- **PDF formats:** .PDF, .XFDF
- **Archives:** .ZIP, .RAR, .7Z, .TAR, .GZ
- **Images and multimedia:** .JPEG, .PNG, .BMP, .TIFF, .GIF, .MP4, .MOV
- **Web content:** .HTML, .HTM, .SVG, .JS, .CSS
- **Email and messaging:** .EML, .MSG, .ICS
- **Executable wrappers:** .EXE, .DLL (as attachments or containers)
- **CAD and engineering:** .DWG, .DXF, .SLDDRW, .STEP
- **Scientific formats:** .MAT, .HDF5, .NC (NetCDF)

Section 7. Enforcement

(a) DHS shall oversee the implementation of this order. (b) Non-compliance may result in funding delays, suspension of federal contracts, or additional oversight. (c) Annual reports detailing sanitization coverage and incident reduction shall be submitted to the Office of the National Cyber Director (ONCD).

Section 8. General Provisions

(a) Nothing in this order shall impair the authority of other agencies as defined in applicable law. (b) This order shall be implemented consistent with appropriations and law. (c) This order does not create enforceable rights for private parties.

X ____

THE WHITE HOUSE

DATE: ________________________________

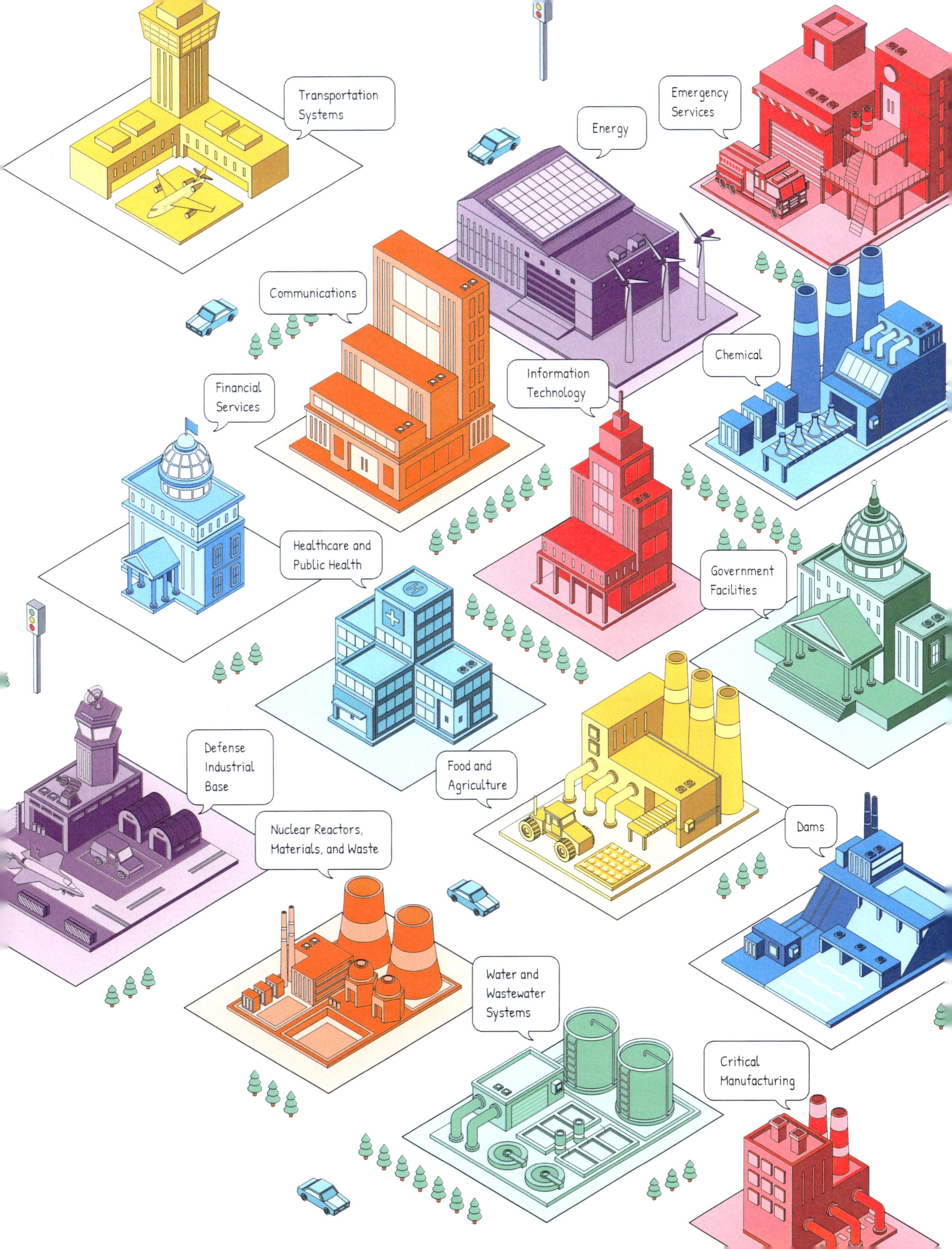

Transportation Systems
Emergency Services
Energy
Communications
Chemical
Financial Services
Information Technology
Healthcare and Public Health
Government Facilities
Defense Industrial Base
Food and Agriculture
Nuclear Reactors, Materials, and Waste
Dams
Water and Wastewater Systems
Critical Manufacturing

Use in AI Guardrails: CDR as a Safety Layer for LLMs

AI systems, especially large language models (LLMs), retrieval-augmented genera-tion (RAG) architectures, and copilots are changing how organizations work with data. But they come with a new kind of exposure. These systems don't just analyze files—they *ingest* them. PDFs, Word documents, spreadsheets, and structured and unstructured inputs flow directly into the model. And that's where things get risky.

Malformed files, obfuscated payloads, or embedded prompts can poison the system or skew the response. I've seen documents that looked benign trigger unintended model behavior, from hallucinations to prompt leakage. That's why I believe CDR will become a core part of every AI pipeline. Before a file is ever embedded or passed to a tokenizer, it will be rebuilt—cleaned of embedded scripts, macros, malformed metadata, and anything that might confuse the model or expose it to adversarial inputs. But it doesn't stop there. Outputs matter just as much.

AI-generated content reports, presentations, code, and even exported files will be sanitized *before* being shared or used downstream. Why? Because generative systems often synthesize content from mixed sources, and that synthesis can carry over unsafe fragments, broken links, or even copy hidden malware from original training data.

In this new environment, CDR becomes more than threat prevention—it's a trust enabler. It ensures that the data going *into* your AI is safe, and that the content coming *out* won't compromise the user, the endpoint, or the system itself.

We talk a lot about AI guardrails, ethical alignment, policy enforcement, and respon-sible use. But from a security perspective, CDR is a guardrail. It filters reality before the model sees it and protects everything the model generates afterward. And it's how we keep intelligence clean on both ends.

The Future of CDR Testing

In Chapter 3, I talked about independent antivirus testing organizations—groups like SE Labs, AV-TEST, and AV-Comparatives—and how they serve as trusted referees in the cybersecurity space. These organizations test what we build and they measure what's working. Most importantly, they give customers and governments a way to cut through the noise.

These labs were born out of necessity. Antivirus vendors needed third-party validation to prove effectiveness, buyers needed transparency, and the industry needed a way to separate marketing from measurements. Over the years, these labs have developed trusted methodologies to evaluate malware detection engines, behavioral analysis tools, mobile security platforms, and endpoint protection suites. Their influence on how we build, test, and adopt security solutions is massive—and deservedly so.

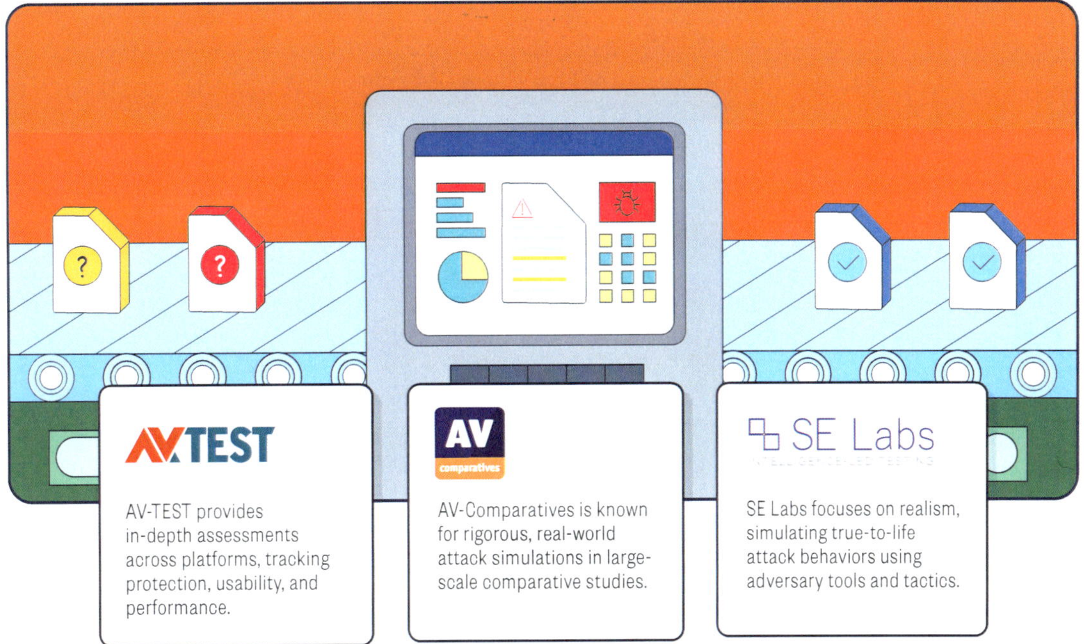

The Oversight in CDR Testing

Despite the progress these labs have made in standardizing security evaluations, **CDR has largely been left out.** Antivirus products are stress-tested with thousands of malware samples. Firewalls are assessed on their ability to filter or evade malicious traffic. But **CDR—by its nature—doesn't detect; it transforms.** It assumes a file is risky and rebuilds it to retain only the safe content.

Traditional testing methodologies weren't designed for this. And that's exactly where the gap lies.

We've done some meaningful work with **SE Labs** to begin validating our CDR engine. It's early, but promising. I'm grateful for the collaboration with Simon Edwards, CEO of SE Labs, who shares a vision that testing transformation requires its own rigor. He understands that CDR isn't antivirus—it's something new, something that deserves a distinct class of evaluation.

Other labs are beginning to take notice as well. I expect **AV-TEST, AV-Comparatives**, and even **Virus Bulletin** will begin considering standardized frameworks for CDR testing. Once they do, we'll see the same transparency and comparability that helped mature the antivirus market extended to this space, too.

Rethinking How We Test

CDR testing can't follow traditional malware-detection models; it needs a tailored methodology. Here are a few core areas that should define the future standard:

1. **Testing by File Type**
   CDR is only as effective as its file type coverage. Evaluations should include a wide spectrum: PDFs, DOCX, XLSX, PPTX, RTF, ZIP, PNG, and region-specific formats like .HWP or .JTD.

2. **Penetration Testing of Productivity Files**
   These aren't executables—they're real-world documents abused in attacks. Tests should simulate macro-embedded spreadsheets, malformed PDFs, steganographic images, and deeply nested ZIP archives.

3. **Evaluating the Security of the Engine**
   Attackers can and will target the CDR process itself. Testing must include file spoofing, parser fuzzing, overflow attempts, and efforts to compromise regeneration logic.

4. **Performance and Usability Metrics**
   Speed and fidelity matter. Tests should measure how quickly files are sanitized and whether the output retains usability, formatting, and readability across common document types.

5. **Auditability and Traceability**
   Every sanitized file should be traceable. Evaluations should confirm that engines log version information, policies used, hash comparisons, and structural validation, so organizations can investigate or audit any file in hindsight.

The Future Landscape

This collaboration with SE Labs is only the beginning. I see a future where **CDR test reports are as common as antivirus benchmark charts,** where vendors are asked, "How do you perform on steganographic JPEGs?" or "What's your sanitization fidelity score on embedded PowerPoint decks?"

Frameworks will evolve and procurement teams will demand real metrics. The industry will expect a proof-based model that measures prevention, not just detection.

That's the future I'm pushing toward. Let's build it—test by test, file by file.

By now, I hope it's clear that I'm not just advocating for another cybersecurity product. I'm advocating for a shift—a shift in mindset, a shift in trust, and a shift away from the assumption that content can be safely handled just because it passed a scan. We can confidently say this because we've seen how often scans miss infected files. And we've seen the cost of trusting in scanning alone.

What I've tried to lay out in this book is not only a story of how we created CDR technology—but a story of people, frameworks, infrastructure, and intent.

We built CDR because the tools we had weren't good enough. And when it worked, we didn't stop there. We tested it. We challenged it. We refined it. Then we pushed the industry to look again, to ask better questions, and to set a higher standard.

To my surprise—and delight—I'm not the only one pushing for this shift anymore. From industry labs to regulatory bodies to Ph.D. researchers and AI developers, we are starting to see a shift in how the world thinks about file-based threats. We're also discovering that CDR isn't just for email attachments or locked-down systems. It's a foundational layer for a future where clean content is the default, not the exception.

We have worked with SE Labs to develop some of the earliest independent evaluations of CDR. And we have seen frameworks, such as NIST and ISO, begin to open the door. What is even more exciting is the recognition we're receiving from the security community itself. OWASP (the Open Web Application Security Project) has already listed CDR as a required control in its "File Upload Cheat Sheet." This is a major signal. OWASP is community driven, and its guidance often becomes the blueprint that vendors, enterprises, cloud platforms, and even regulators follow.

When security leaders and practitioners identify a control as mandatory, it shows where the industry is headed long before any government regulation catches up. The community is moving faster than regulators, but the pattern is always the same. Government frameworks always lag behind by a few years, then adopt what the security community has already proven. That means this transformation to CDR is coming.

We are also seeing early adopters embed CDR deep into DevOps pipelines, cloud storage layers, and even AI model inputs. Students and educators are also experimenting with these ideas in academic research. The spark is there, but it is not enough to simply spark an idea. We need to fuel it and support the momentum the community has already created.

So here's what I believe: The future of cybersecurity won't be measured by how quickly we detect threats. It will be measured by how well we prevent them. It will also be measured by how seamlessly we rebuild trust into the tools we use every day—into the documents we open, the files we share, the pipelines we deploy, and the models we train.

CDR isn't the answer to every problem, but it answers a problem we've ignored for too long: *What do we do when detection is too late?*

The answer, of course, is that we rebuild. That's what this book is about. And that's what the next decade will be about, too—rebuilding not just our files, but our mindset. Because the most powerful thing we can do as an industry isn't to fear new threats, it's to make sure they never get a chance to be executed in the first place.

So let's build the future—quietly, practically, file by file—together.

ACKNOWLEDGMENTS

This book would not exist without the love, patience, and faith of those closest to me. First and foremost, to my incredible wife, Shira: You are my true partner in every sense. Not only have you helped build OPSWAT's offices and keep shaping hardware products, but you've also held me up emotionally and mentally, day in and day out. Your unwavering strength, your honesty, and your power is behind everything I do.

To our two amazing children, Talia and Eitan: You inspire me more than you know. Your curiosity, laughter, and resilience give me energy and perspective every single day. Thank you for reminding me of what matters most.

To my parents, Tziona and Israel, who taught me the value of discipline, curiosity, and kindness: You showed me what it means to work hard, pursue your passions, and treat people well no matter the circumstances. Those lessons guided this book as much as they have guided my life.

To Tom Mullen: Thank you for taking a leap of faith when I could barely pay myself a salary. You weren't just part of OPSWAT's first steps—you helped shape its foundation. And on a personal level, I genuinely believe that knowing you has made me a better person.

To every single employee at OPSWAT, past and present: You are the heartbeat of this mission. Day after day, you work with quiet intensity to protect the world's most critical infrastructure. Your work may not always make headlines, but it changes the world one sanitized file, one protected network, one solved problem at a time.

To Dan Woods: Thank you for coaching me, pushing me, and guiding me through the process of turning chapters into something coherent and compelling. You made me a better writer and, more importantly, a clearer thinker.

To Serge Seidlitz: My special thanks for bringing this book to life through your amazing illustrations. Your ability to combine elements of popular culture with diverse influences to create artwork that tells the story while bringing a smile to my face raises this work to a whole new level.

To Todd Smith: Your editing helped bring clarity and polish to these pages. Your precision turned messy thoughts into messages that count.

To Margaret Nussey and Rob Staeger: Thank you for your insight and input throughout this process. Your steady presence and support made a difference.

To the OPSWAT engineering team: Your brilliance, your obsession with getting it right, and your relentless pursuit of better security made many of the concepts in this book a reality. You don't just build—you build it right.

I also want to acknowledge the individuals whose contributions directly shaped Deep CDR: Nhut Ngo, Dung Ho, Phat Tram, Linh Ha, Trung Luu, Vi Le, Vu Ly, Linh Le, Thao Nguyen, Nhiem Tran, Huy Tran, Teddy Do, Lam Luu, Kim Le, Trang Trinh, Vincent Lin, Taeil Goh, and Phuc Luu.

Beyond engineering, Deep CDR was strengthened by my colleagues across OPSWAT who carried its message forward, brought it to market, and ensured its compliance and creative presence. First to Vinh Lam, who leads OPSWAT's CDR team, and Yiyi Miao, George Prichici, Stella Nguyen, Manya Oberoi, and Randy Abrams, whose valuable contributions made this book possible.

And to my creative and marketing team: Matt Keown, Anh Vuong, Dan Młynarski, Uyen Nguyen, Hien Le Nguyen, and Paul J. Bartolone—thank you for transforming technical achievements into design, visuals, and brand experiences that people can connect with. I am particularly grateful to VP, Brand and Creative, Berry Blanton for his steady hand in guiding this project from conception to publication. And my special thanks to VP of Corporate Marketing, Kat Lewis DeBree, for helping to promote the book digitally.

To Kimberly Howell and Tammy Conway: You've made the impossible possible. Thank you for helping coordinate dozens of moving parts to keep this book—and me—on track. Your behind-the-scenes work was crucial in pulling this together.

A special thanks to those friends who were kind enough to provide me with their feedback. Your insights were amazingly helpful: Dan Lanir, Senior Vice President of Customer Experience, OPSWAT; Aviram Jenik, General Partner, Rabbit VC; Yiyi Miao, Chief Product Officer, OPSWAT; George Prichici, VP Products, OPSWAT; Mike Gregoire, Founding Partner at Brighton Park Capital (BPC); Hamid Karimi, VP of Technology Alliances and Global OEM Sales, OPSWAT; and Steve Gorham, Chief Federal Officer, OPSWAT.

Finally, to everyone who believes in building a more secure digital future: This book is for you.

Benny Czarny

GLOSSARY

Adaptive Emulation: An emulation-based sandbox does not depend on a golden image or fixed-system snapshot. It uses a simulated operating environment that interprets instructions one by one. It specifically focuses on how the file behaves at the CPU and memory level, not on how it interacts with a specific predefined system setup. Since it emulates execution rather than running on a cloned OS image, it can expose malicious logic that tries to hide behind environmental checks or golden-image dependencies. This makes an emulation-base sandbox useful for catching malware that behaves differently when a full operating system is not present. And it's usually much faster.

API: Application Programming Interfaces

Attack surface: Any place where an attacker can access a system or network to steal data or do damage

BYOD: Bring Your Own Device

CDR: As defined by Gartner, Content Disarm and Reconstruction (CDR) is a proactive security approach that sanitizes files by breaking them down, removing potentially malicious elements, and rebuilding them into a safe, usable version. Unlike traditional detection methods that look for known threats, CDR assumes all active content is suspect and removes anything non-compliant with file type specifications to protect against zero-day and evasive threats.

CISO: Chief Information Security Officer

CLI: Command Line Interface

CNN: Conventional neutral network

CSF: Cybersecurity framework

CTO: Chief Technology Officer

CVE: Common vulnerabilities and exposures

Data Sanitization (CDR): Rebuilds files at the point of entry, removing active content and delivering safe, business-ready versions before they ever touch the endpoint

Deep CDR: An advanced version of CDR (Content Disarm and Reconstruction) that goes beyond traditional CDR solutions by recursively analyzing and sanitizing nested file structures, including those within archives and embedded objects

DLP: Data loss prevention

DOT: A dot directory (".") refers to the current directory name

Endpoint: Any device that connects to an organization's network, which serves as a potential entry point for cyber threats. These include user devices such as laptops, desktops, smartphones, and tablets, as well as servers and a growing variety of Internet of Things (IoT) devices, including printers and smart devices.

Executables: Programs that contain instructions that a computer runs directly. Once executed, these instructions can do almost anything: install software, change settings, steal data, or hold a system hostage.

Executable files: Files which contain code that a computer runs to perform specific actions

EO: Executive order

Firewall for Data: A solution that employs multiple file scanners working at the same time (multiscanning) with each file-scanning engine capturing a distinct set of malware

Fuzz testing: Also known as "fuzzing," a dynamic software testing technique used in data security to discover vulnerabilities and bugs within software applications. It involves feeding a program with large amounts of invalid, unexpected, or random data (often referred to as "fuzz") as input.

GDPR (General Data Protection Regulation): EU data privacy law that requires organizations to implement strict measures to protect individuals' personal data

Heuristic analysis: Looks at a file's characteristics and how it behaves to detect suspicious patterns

HIPAA (Health Insurance Portability and Accountability Act): U.S. federal law enacted in 1996 that sets national standards to protect patient privacy and safeguard Protected Health Information (PHI)

HTTP traffic: Data exchanged between web browsers and servers using the Hypertext Transfer Protocol (HTTP). As a core protocol of the internet, it facilitates web communication but can be susceptible to various attacks, making it a common focus of security monitoring and analysis.

ICAP: Internet Content Adaptation Protocol—an HTTP-based network protocol that allows proxy servers to offload content-related tasks, like virus scanning, content filtering, and ad insertion, to a separate, dedicated server. By offloading these functions, ICAP enables the main web servers to focus on high-throughput content delivery and improves performance and scalability.

IdP: Identity provider—a system for managing user identities and authentication

Internal file exchange: Refers to the secure, controlled transfer of digital files within an organization's network

IoT: Internet of Things

IR: Incident response

ISMS: Information security management system

JPEG: Joint Photographic Experts Group—a standard file format used for compressing photographic images so they can be more easily stored or sent via email

LLM (Large language model): The application of AI language models can be used for tasks like threat detection, malware analysis, and security automation. However, it also presents new vulnerabilities, like prompt injection and data leakage, that require specific LLM security measures to protect both the models and the systems they power.

Macros: Sequence of commands or instructions that can be stored and run as a single command, automating repetitive tasks by replacing multiple keystrokes or mouse clicks with one action

Malware: Malicious software—harmful software that's installed on a user's device without their knowledge. Common types include viruses, spyware, and ransomware.

Metadata: "Data about data" that provides descriptive, structural, and administrative information that makes data easier to organize, manage, find, understand, and reuse. It includes details like the author of a document, the format and size of a file, or the date and location a photo was taken.

MetaDefender: Layers an array of market-leading technologies to protect critical IT and OT environments, shrinking the overall attack surface by detecting and preventing sophisticated known and unknown file-borne threats like advanced evasive malware, zero-day attacks, APTs (advanced persistent threats), and more.

MetaDefender Cloud: Provides advanced threat detection and prevention for files and data by utilizing technologies like multiscanning with over 20 anti-malware engines, Deep CDR and adaptive sandboxing to neutralize known and unknown malware, including zero-day threats and ransomware.

Metascan: Advanced threat detection and prevention technology that runs multiple anti-malware engines concurrently to maximize the likelihood of catching known malware

MFA: Multi-factor authentication

MITRE ATT&CK: A globally-accessible knowledge base of adversary tactics and techniques based on real-world observations

NAC: Network Access Control

NERC CIP: North American Electric Reliability Corporation's Critical Infrastructure Protection

Nexperior: OPSWAT's next generation automated testing system that became the backbone of the company's quality-assurance process

NVD: National Vulnerability Database

OEM: Original Equipment Manufacturer

OESIS: OPSWAT Endpoint Security Integration SDK

OS: Operating System. This is a critical piece of software that serves as an intermediary between computer hardware and the user.

OPSEC: Operational Security Consulting

OPSWAT: Name originated by combining "OPS" (Operations) and "SWAT" (Special Weapons and Tactics) to connote the swift implementation and management of cybersecurity solutions

PCI DSS: Payment Card Industry Data Security Standard—a set of security guidelines for organizations that process, store, or transmit cardholder data, aiming to protect against fraud and data breaches

Peripheral devices: Storage drives, printers, and other hardware that can be connected to a system

Phishing: Type of cybersecurity crime where a bad actor impersonates a trusted entity to trick a victim into revealing sensitive information, such as passwords, credit card numbers, or personal data

Productivity files: Files containing information that people use to do their jobs, including documents, spreadsheets, images, presentations, and videos

Public file upload form: Allows anyone with access to the form's link to upload files

RAG: Retrieval-augmented generation

Sandbox: A secure, isolated environment used to run, test, or analyze untrusted code or software. It prevents potential threats from affecting the main system or network by containing all activity within a controlled space.

SBOM: Software bill of materials

SDK: Software Development Kit

SDP: Software Defined Perimeters

SIEM: Security Information and Event Management

Signature-based detection: Compares files against a database of known malware signatures (a unique string of bytes or a pattern that is characteristic of a specific piece of malware)

SLA: Service-level agreement

SOC: Security Operations Center

SOC 2: System and Organization Controls 2—an auditing framework developed by the AICPA that provides a standard for service organizations to manage customer data through a report that attests to their control environment based on the Trust Services Criteria (TSC) of security, availability, processing integrity, confidentiality, and privacy

Steganography: The art or practice of concealing a message, image, or file within another message, image, or file

Torrents: Method of sharing and distributing files using the BitTorrent protocol. This protocol allows files to be transferred in a decentralized manner by dividing them into smaller segments that are exchanged directly between users on a network, rather than relying on a single central server.

Trojan Horse (trojan): Type of malicious software that appears to be legitimate or harmless in order to deceive users into installing it. Once activated, a trojan can carry out harmful activities such as stealing data, disrupting system functions, or giving unauthorized users remote access to the infected device.

UI: User interface

VBA: Visual Basic for Applications

VPN: Virtual private network

Zero-Day: A cyberattack that exploits a newly discovered vulnerability in software before the software vendor is aware of it or has released a patch

Zero Trust: Cloud-native security model that eliminates implicit trust, requiring continuous verification for every user, device, and application before granting access to data, rather than relying on network location

ABOUT THE AUTHOR

When I started OPSWAT in 2002, I didn't have a blueprint or a checklist. I had a laptop, a big idea, and a growing conviction that something was broken in the way the world approached cybersecurity.

For too long, the industry has believed that if we detect threats fast enough, we can stop them. But I had seen too many breaches, too many missed alerts, and too many files that looked harmless until they detonated in the worst way possible.

I believed there had to be another way.

This book is the story of that belief and the journey it took me on. It is the story of how a simple conviction became a prevention-first philosophy, and how that philosophy grew into a global platform. The idea is straightforward but powerful: Don't just try to detect malware; remove the possibility of it altogether by regenerating every file before it has the chance to cause harm. That approach is now known as Data Sanitization, or Content Disarm and Reconstruction (CDR).

But this book is not just about a technology or a platform. It is about the path that led me there—from growing up in Israel to moving to San Francisco to long nights writing code, chasing customers, winning and losing deals, and slowly earning trust one step at a time.

It is about innovation: what it takes to create a completely new platform, how to embed that platform into existing systems to protect people, and how to ensure that platform holds under pressure.

Whether you are a CISO, an engineer, a policymaker, or simply someone who believes in a safer digital future, this book is for you. I didn't write it as a pitch. I wrote it as a perspective, because I believe it is time to stop playing defense against yesterday's threats.

It is time to flip the model. Cybersecurity doesn't need to be solely reactive. Malware prevention shouldn't depend on detection. It should begin with regeneration.

To make cybersecurity right side up, we first need to turn it upside down.